D0028227

A Carafe of Red

A Carafe of Red

Gerald Asher

UNIVERSITY OF CALIFORNIA PRESS

Berkeley   Los Angeles   London

University of California Press, one of the most distinguished
university presses in the United States, enriches lives around
the world by advancing scholarship in the humanities, social
sciences, and natural sciences. Its activities are supported by
the UC Press Foundation and by philanthropic contributions
from individuals and institutions. For more information, visit
www.ucpress.edu.

University of California Press
Berkeley and Los Angeles, California

University of California Press, Ltd.
London, England

© 2012 by Gerald Asher

Library of Congress Cataloging-in-Publication Data

Asher, Gerald.
   A carafe of red / Gerald Asher.
      p.   cm.
   Includes index.
   ISBN 978-0-520-27032-9 (cloth, alk. paper)
      1. Wine and wine making.   I. Title.
TP548.A787   2021
641.2'2—dc23   20110274210

Manufactured in the United States of America

21 20 19 18 17 16 15 14 13 12
10 9 8 7 6 5 4 3 2 1

In keeping with its commitment to support environmentally responsible and sustainable printing practices,
UC Press has printed this book on Natures Book, which
contains 30% post-consumer waste and meets the minimum requirements of ANSI/NISO Z 39.48–1992 (R 1997)
(Permanence of Paper).

In memory of Yvonne Chanrion Geoffray,
Chevalier du Mérite Agricole,
Officier des Compagnons du Beaujolais

CONTENTS

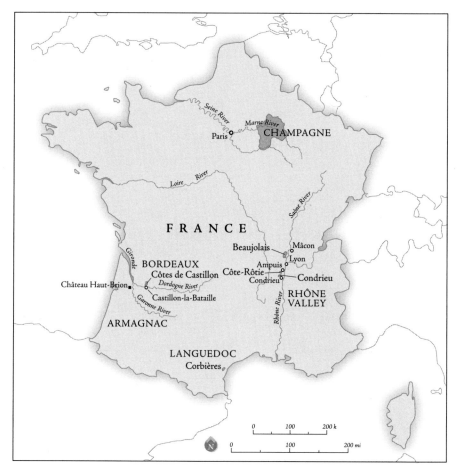

Map 1. Wine regions of France

Map 2. Wine regions of Europe

Map 3. Wine regions of Napa Valley

INTRODUCTION

Long ago, during my apprenticeship in the wine trade, I learned that wine is more than the sum of its parts, and more than an expression of its physical origin. The real significance of wine as the nexus of just about everything became clearer to me when I started writing about it. The more I read, the more I traveled, and the more questions I asked, the further I was pulled into the realms of history and economics, politics, literature, food, community, and all else that affects the way we live. Wine, I found, draws on everything and leads everywhere.

Those leads run through the chapters of this book. Each stands alone, yet each sheds light on an aspect of wine that will, I hope, add to your understanding of it. The very first—"A Carafe of Red," which gives its name to the collection—is a conversation that summarizes two thousand years of winemaking in France, from the first Roman colony to today's republic, explaining along the way how religion and politics, the Industrial Revolution, transportation (canals and railways), and the ravages of phylloxera helped shape the nature of French wine. "Malmsey" gives a glimpse of international trade and politics in the Middle Ages, while "Côtes de Castillon," a tale about the revival of a Bordeaux wine, looks behind the town's official name, Castillon-la-Bataille, to the battle fought there in 1453. Heavy artillery—giant cannons hidden on a hillside above the battlefield—was used for the first time to mow down knights in armor. While bringing an end to England's territorial aspirations in France, it also brought an end to the chivalry of the Middle Ages. Like a bookend to that historic moment, Castillon's winemakers have also been at the forefront of modern wine technology. They were among the first to adopt micro-oxygenation, a technique emblematic of their determination to improve the quality of their red wine, an effort so successful that Castillon wine leapt to the cover of *Le Point,* the French news magazine, where it was classified among the ten best wines of France. In "Jerez de la Frontera," I give you a glimpse of microbiology in action in the veil of *Saccharomyces* that plays a key role in the development of Fino Sherry, while "A Silent Revolution," about the meaning of "organic viticulture," looks at the role microbes play in keeping us fed. Small things often have large consequences: the spark of a weekend escape for a few writers and painters from nearby Tarragona, caught by a magazine article coinciding with the Barcelona Olympics, lit a passion that has brought back to life Priorato, a Catalan wine region on the verge of extinction, yet now producing one of the most sought after red wines of Spain. The chapter "Haut-Brion" shows how Bordeaux wine was transformed from tavern tipple into the yard-stick by which other wines are measured; in "Judgment of Paris" that yardstick has historic consequences for California. In "Missouri" I show how the German American culture of that state evolved alongside its early viticulture; and "Chardonnay," in recounting the origins of one variety's clones in California, illustrates, in effect, the significance of all clones of all wine-grape varieties everywhere. And in "A Memorable Wine," I reflect on the question often asked of me and others who have led a life professionally involved with wine: What is the best wine you can remember? The answer to any such question can only be subjective, of course. What is "best" for me, or anyone else, depends on personal preference, the context, and our mood at the time. But above all, it depends on the knowledge and the personal memories we bring to the wine in the glass. It's what we bring to it that can make even a suppos-edly simple carafe of red memorable. That's the purpose of this book.

Gerald Asher

San Francisco, August 2011

A CARAFE OF RED

We had stopped for a quick lunch at a pastry shop near the Place de la Madeleine. My friend sniffed approvingly at her glass of red wine. "This is good," she said. "What is it?"

It was from the Corbières, the block of wind-riven mountains between Carcassonne, Narbonne, and Perpignan on the French Mediterranean coast. While the world has been looking elsewhere, the growers of the Corbières have been busy recapturing for their wines a reputation that had always distinguished them from those grown elsewhere in the Languedoc. My friend was right: The wine was good.

And what did she think of the Bonington watercolors we'd seen that morning at the Petit Palais? She knows far more about pictures than I do, but she brushed Bonington aside. "Is that all you're going to tell me about the wine?" she asked.

How much did she want to know? The Corbières is the oldest wine region of France. Its story is virtually the story of French wine.

"Why don't you start at the beginning," she suggested. So I did.

The Romans planted their first vineyards in the Corbières soon after they built a harbor at Narbonne. In passing a decree establishing the colony in 118 B.C., the Roman senate had intended to secure for Rome the passage from the Mediterranean to the Atlantic by way of the Aude and Garonne river valleys. It was the route by which wine, much prized by the Celts, was bartered for Cornish tin. Rome, ever belligerent, needed tin to produce bronze for weapons and preferred to see her enemies (and victims) deprived of it.

The Seventh Legion was sent to protect the traffic (hence the region's ancient name of Septimania), and veteran soldiers, usually married to Celtic women, were encouraged to settle there when they retired from active service. It was probably veterans who planted those first vineyards. But they chose to trade their wine not to Cornwall but back to Italy in exchange for the small luxuries only Rome could provide. There, their wine was so highly prized that Rome's speculators rushed to extend the vineyards. Wine from Septimania was soon competing successfully with that grown on the Italian estates of Rome's most powerful families. Cicero reported the furious debates in which senators demanded that the vineyards and olive groves of Gaul not be allowed to render their own valueless. The emperor Domitian was prevailed upon in A.D. 92 to order half of them ripped out.

"Why had the wine been so good?" my friend wanted to know. All the usual reasons, I assured her: soil, climate, and the care taken by men whose survival—let alone their prosperity—depended on what they could produce from a patch of vines. Then as now, the Corbières farmer had little choice beyond vines, sheep, and goats.

Most of all, though, it was and is a unique combination of Mediterranean and Atlantic influences. Like the northern Rhône valley, the other wine region that flourished in that first century of Roman Gaul, the Corbières sit at a climatic crossroads. The *mistral,* the fierce wind that blows down the Rhône valley, has its equivalent in the *cers,* a powerful wind that blows through the Carcassone gap from the Atlantic to the Mediterranean. Atlantic weather patterns reach far into the Corbières, and the climate, less predictable than that of Italy, can run to extremes. The Romans were surprised that vines and olive trees native to Italy would grow there at all. Saserna, the leading agronomist of the time, took it as proof that the world was getting warmer.

"Global warming in the first century?" my friend murmured, half mockingly, as she refilled her glass. "Is nothing new?"

Bordeaux, at the other end of the Aude-Garonne connection, had to wait another century or two until the Romans stumbled onto grape varieties able to withstand the spring frosts and summer rains of its unabated Atlantic climate. But no matter how strange it might have seemed to Saserna, vines that did well elsewhere in the Mediterranean usually did well in the Corbières too. Growers had to choose among varieties available, of course. Some that were successful on the maritime plain could not be relied on to ripen their fruit at higher altitudes exposed to the *cers*.

The rugby-playing, garlic-fancying winegrowers who now live in the high valleys of the Corbières are descended from those Gallo-Roman farmers, many of whom had taken refuge there at some time during the Languedoc's turbulent past. The region's great sweep of mountains, gorges, and maritime plain fell prey to Visigoths, Arabs (who seized it after their conquest of Spain), and Francs under Charles Martel. In the early fifth century the Visigoths, fresh from sacking Rome, just walked into Narbonne. The inhabitants, perhaps under some illusion of the permanence of Pax Romana, had left the city gates open and the walls unguarded while they went to the vineyards to pick their grapes. An ancient illuminated manuscript recording the event, displayed in a Narbonne museum, expresses tersely the economic importance of wine to the region. "War can wait," it reads. "The vintage cannot."

But neither vineyards nor trade prospered in the uncertainties of the dark age that followed. This troubled time ended for the Corbières in 800 when Charlemagne, Charles Martel's grandson, approved the foundation there of Lagrasse Abbey. Among the objectives listed on the document of grant was the planting of a vineyard. Over the next two centuries fifty such abbeys were established in the area, and every one of them had extensive vineyards. They became, for hundreds of years, the sole repositories of viticultural knowledge and winemaking skills.

It is usual to say that an abbey's vines provided wine for celebrating mass. But more than that, they were a principal source of wealth. As

the abbeys' vineyards were expanded into formerly uncultivated wood-
land, the descendants of Rome's veterans were tied by contracts that
obliged them and their children to work land they would never own.
The arrangement brought order but provoked a resentment that still
colors the fiery politics of the region. My friend would not have needed
me to remind her of the great cruelty in the Corbières and in neighboring parts of the Languedoc in the thirteenth century. The Inquisition
was born right there and was used, in the name of religious orthodoxy,
to help consolidate the power of the Roman Catholic church and of
the French crown. The *vignerons* of the Languedoc have been chopping
trees, blocking roads, and raising hell for a long time since then.

~ ~ ~

The horrors can blind us, however, to two events that had enormous
impact on the region's wines. The first was the introduction of distilling. In the late thirteenth century, Arnau de Villanova, a Montpellier
physician, was the first in Europe to produce alcohol from wine heated
in an alembic. Distilling had been known to the Arabs since the tenth
century—both *alcohol* and *alembic* are Arabic words—and it is thought
that de Villanova had learned the process from his friend Raymon Llull,
a scholar of Arabic sciences at the University of Montpellier.

The second was the completion, in 1680, of a canal linking the Mediterranean and the Atlantic. Jean-Baptiste Colbert, Louis XIV's finance
minister, improved on what the Romans had started by using the Aude-
Garonne passage to cut what is now known as the Canal du Midi. He
hoped it would give the manufacturers and farmers of southern France
easier access to the markets of northern Europe. An extension of the
canal continued to the Rhône. Sète, the town founded by Colbert as the
canal's Mediterranean port, became a center of the international wine
trade.

Just as Colbert had intended, the canal gave impetus to other economic activity, including distilling. The Dutch, in particular, bought
huge quantities of Languedoc spirits. To keep the stills going, vineyards
were soon spreading from the hills onto the plain, where Aramon and

other common, high-yielding varieties (later to be the undoing of the Languedoc) were first introduced.

It needed only the winter of 1708–09 to divert these thin, coarse wines from the distilleries to the blending vats. From October 1708, until February 1709, temperatures in much of Europe rarely rose above freezing. To relieve the shortage of wine in Paris caused by the widespread destruction of vineyards normally supplying the capital, a royal decree of 1710 suppressed taxes on Languedoc wines shipped there. Languedoc vineyards had been barely affected by the winter's severity.

But once those cheap wines were used in this way, it became difficult to stop. Bordeaux's landowners were far from pleased and used every legislative trick to block the annual arrival and sale of Languedoc wines until their own crop had been sold. Disputes over shipment of Languedoc wines through the Canal du Midi continued until 1776 when Anne-Robert-Jacques Turgot, briefly Louis XVI's comptroller general of finance, abolished Bordeaux's privileges along with the special export taxes and myriad petty regulations imposed by the city to obstruct the free movement of Languedoc wines through its port. Turgot, some of whose ideas anticipated those of Adam Smith, was a similar curiosity: a modern economist at large in the eighteenth century. Had vested interests not succeeded in forcing him from office after only twenty months, it's possible—even likely—there would have been no French Revolution. One of his urgent projects had been an attempt to abolish the taxes that inhibited free trade of grain among the provinces—the principal cause of frequent, sometimes severe, local famines and therefore a major factor in the 1789 riots.

"Aren't we wandering from the point?" my friend said, drily.

Wine is a subject that leads everywhere, but it clearly wasn't the time to say so. Instead I explained how the effect of the Canal du Midi was as nothing once the railways arrived in the 1850s. Spawned by the Industrial Revolution—the first tracks in France were laid to move coal and ore, not people—the railways then fed it, literally, with calories garnered from Languedoc vineyards. French industrial workers of the nineteenth century, and much of the twentieth for that matter, relied on wine for the high-calorie diet their physical exertions demanded. Every liter provided seven or eight hundred additional bulk-free calories, and the cheapest of the wines arrived in the northern industrial cities by rail from the south. From the late 1850s until the mid-1870s money flowed into the Languedoc as fast as wine poured out. It was said at the time that a man could pay off the price of vineyard land there with the profits from his first two crops.

At the height of local euphoria, in 1867, a Languedoc grower reported to a meeting of the Central Agricultural Society in Paris a mysterious sickness affecting his vines. The problem was identified by the University of Montpellier as the insect *Phylloxera vastatrix*—the devastator—and the appropriateness of the name was soon made evident. In 1875 the wine harvest in France was larger than it had ever been or was ever to be again. One year later, in 1876, standing vines in the Languedoc's Gard *département* alone were reduced by more than one hundred thousand acres, to less than half of what had been thriving there before. Within thirty years, phylloxera had destroyed almost every vineyard in France.

The university was in favor of using resistant American rootstocks quite early in the course of the epidemic. Unfortunately, the American rootstocks available at that time could not tolerate the high chalk content of the best vineyards in the Languedoc hills; and on the plain (where the mass of cheap wine was grown) flooding the vineyards seemed to work just as well, cost a lot less, and was quicker. But flooding was the same thing as heavy irrigation. Yields rose fantastically and quality fell in just proportion. But no one cared: As the infested vineyards of other regions disappeared, demand for the wines of the Languedoc plain—whatever their quality—continued to grow. The wine sold in 1875 for sixteen francs a hectoliter had been of better quality than that sold for forty francs in 1880; but bouquet and finesse had become irrelevant. The industrial working masses simply needed the calories.

Once it became possible for the Corbières growers to replant, they found themselves unable to compete with the wines of the plain. There could be no question of flooding hillside vineyards, yet the merchants of Narbonne, Sète, and Béziers (now blending and shipping on a huge scale) refused to distinguish between the small production of quality wine of the Corbières and wine of the over-irrigated, high-yielding vines elsewhere.

In 1907 the Languedoc's uncontrolled production, aggravated by fraud, caused the French market in cheap bulk wines to collapse. Government troops fired on growers rioting in the streets of Narbonne, but in Béziers an artillery regiment mutinied rather than obey orders to do the same. The Corbières growers realized they had to protect their common interest by distinguishing their wines from those of the plain. It took them until 1923 to win a judicial decree by which they were defined as a region separate from the rest of the Languedoc. But even so, their wine was not officially recognized, even as a *vin délimité de qualité supérieure* (a very junior version of a controlled appellation), until 1951; and the Corbières was not raised to the distinct status of a full controlled appellation until 1985.

Until the 1960s Corbières wines sold at prices hardly different from those paid for the grossest of *gros rouge* of the Languedoc. To live, many growers found themselves obliged to adopt the high-yielding varieties of the plain—especially Carignan. Though never as productive in the hills, these varieties drew the growers into the same vicious circle of lowered quality and falling revenues from which the growers of the plain had been unable to extricate themselves.

～～～

But if this wine is anything to go by," my friend said, helping herself to the last of the carafe, "it looks as if they have somehow been able to do just that."

They had indeed. A turnabout began in 1967 when a small group of growers in the Val d'Orbieu between Narbonne and Lézignan came together and planned a coherent strategy to pull themselves up by their own vine-shoots. With seemingly quixotic pretension they defined what a Corbières wine should be, agreed on mutually binding standards of quality control, and invested together in equipment that each on his own might not have been able to afford.

As the growers' association grew, so it took shape. The original group drew into it some of the region's wine cooperatives along with the best of the independent growers. They kept standards high and objectives clear by admitting new members only after careful evaluation of vineyard, cellar, wine quality, and personal drive. A crucial step was to bring into the association a viticultural and enological research laboratory in Narbonne to which all members might turn for assistance at all stages of planting, caring for their vines, and winemaking.

With the support of the regional chamber of commerce the association established an experimental vineyard domain where they researched which varieties formerly planted in the Corbières should be brought back, which clones should be used, how vines should be trained, and how pruning should be done.

Aramon and a host of hybrid varieties have virtually disappeared from the Corbières. Those Carignan vines that remain are old: The variety offers worthwhile fruit only when the vines are over thirty and the yields are meager. New plantings are discouraged, and the regulations are periodically revised to reduce the permitted proportion of Carignan as old vines become uneconomic and must be replaced.

Increasingly the growers depend on Grenache, Syrah, Mourvèdre, and a little Cinsault—the grape varieties of Châteauneuf-du-Pape. Syrah and Mourvèdre, in particular, are referred to as "aromatic varieties" because of the flavor and character they bring to Grenache or Carignan. Growers in the mild maritime zone of the Corbières closest to the Mediterranean use Mourvèdre rather than Syrah: It gives depth of color and backbone. But farther inland, moving west toward the Atlantic (the coast of Mediterranean France runs north-south at this point as it drops down toward Barcelona), growers use Syrah for the same reason that their colleagues in the northern Rhône valley do. It resists wind, and, even in mountainous conditions at the limit of its tolerance—perhaps I should say *especially* in mountainous conditions at the limit of its tolerance—it gives grapes of particularly fine flavor where Mourvèdre would hardly ripen. Some growers have planted Merlot and Cabernet Sauvignon as a shortcut to market acceptance (the Val d'Orbieu's Réserve St. Martin Sélection Rouge, a blend of regional Cabernet Sauvignon and Merlot, is a very attractive bottle of wine selling at under five dollars), but sentiment in the Corbières is generally in favor of restoring a Mediterranean tradition and not borrowing from elsewhere.

Though Marsanne and Roussanne, known for the role they play in producing white wines in the northern Rhône valley, have also been reintroduced to the Corbières, most Corbières wine remains red, richly colored and sumptuous. But then the Languedoc is, after all, *daube* country, the region honored for that slowly braised beef dish of which Robert Courtine says in his *Hundred Glories of French Cooking,* "one finds oneself talking in terms of music, of poetry."

"That was a *tarte provençale* we were eating," my friend reminded me, just as I was ready to quote from the scene of Proust's *Remembrance of Things Past* in which Monsieur de Norpois becomes ecstatic over a cold *daube* "spiced with carrots ... couched ... upon enormous crystals of jelly."

~ ~ ~

Wouldn't it be more helpful to tell me if I will be able to find any of this wine when I get back home?" she asked. Not only could I assure her that she would, but I could give her the good news that most of it sells on the sunny side of ten dollars a bottle. Distribution of individual Corbières estate wines will always be patchy. Most of them are small, with limited production. But on a slightly larger scale, the cooperative cellar of Les Vignerons d'Octaviana are shipping three or four wines to several markets in the United States under the brand name Guy Chevalier. The Guy Chevalier Syrah, sold under the name of a vineyard with the curious name of Le Texas, is the most widely admired of them. Because the Corbières appellation does not provide for a 100 percent Syrah wine, it must be labeled Vin de Pays de l'Aude.

The group that started it all back in 1967 has recently set up a sales office of Val d'Orbieu Wines in Dallas to oversee the national distribution of their Réserve St. Martin and Resplandy brands. For the present, to conform to what they judge to be American expectations, Val d'Orbieu are concentrating their efforts on wines prepared from single varieties so that they can be labeled Syrah, Grenache, Marsanne, and so on. In this country we have been conditioned to pay more attention to a wine with a varietal identity and to place a higher value on it. Val d'Orbieu's Syrah is one of their finest wines—it is more intensely flavored but less fleshy than the Guy Chevalier Syrah. These Mediterranean varieties are usually at their best, however, when used to complement each other, as they do in most of the individual estate wines. Val d'Orbieu's Cuvée Mythique (a blend of Syrah, Mourvèdre, Grenache, Cabernet Sauvignon, and old Carignan) is based on this principle. The first vintage, 1990, has just been released.

If, in the Corbières, one can talk of an equivalent to California's Rutherford Bench or of the Medoc's *route des grands crus,* it would be a long, narrow, gravelly slope of perhaps eight hundred acres near the villages of Boutenac and Gasparets. Exposed to the southwest and protected from the *cers* by a thick grove of pines at its back, the area was the site of the first Roman commercial farm in Gaul. No one in Corbières would dispute that wines made from grapes grown there are always among the best and usually are the best of the Languedoc in any given vintage. The slope is divided among five estates, which, not surprisingly, led the Corbières' revival in the 1970s: Villemajou, Les Palais, Château La Voulte Gasparets, Fontsainte, and Les Olliex. All are producing excellent wines. Other Corbières estates to watch for include the Domaine Serres-Mazard, Château Saint-Auriol, Domaine du Trillol, and Château Beauregard.

Where Corbières growers have led, others have followed. Scattered all over—in the Minervois, in the hills north of Pézenas, and in secluded bays and valleys near Perpignan in Roussillon—there are other growers who have made tremendous efforts in recent years. Many of their wines, too, are available—spottily—in the United States. I am thinking of wines like the red Collioure of the Clos du Moulin and the Clos des Paulilles; the red (and white) Côtes du Roussillon from the Château de Jau; and the outstanding Saint-Chinian of Château Coujan and of the small cooperative at Berlou (their brand name is Berloup), the last and highest village in the Minervois where the vine will grow. The most impressive of them all, though, are the red Côteaux du Languedoc wines made by Olivier Jullien, a young man unique for these times, at his Mas Jullien. The little wine he makes is much in demand in Montpellier; in the United States it is available, as far as I know, only in New York City.

"Aren't there also Muscats and dessert wines produced in the Languedoc?" my friend wanted to know. "I am sure I read somewhere that a proprietor of Château d'Yquem in the eighteenth century went to the Languedoc to discover the secret of making sweet wines."

"Now, come on," I said. "It's past two o'clock and we were supposed to be out of here at half past one. When am I going to hear about Bonington?"

"How much do you want to hear?" she asked.

"Why don't you just start at the beginning," I suggested, and waved to a passing waiter to bring us another carafe of Corbières.

Originally published as "A Carafe of Red" in *Gourmet*, October 1992.

The special quality of the area around Boutenac has now been officially recognized with a distinct *appellation d'origine contrôlée*, Corbières-Boutenac. The name Réserve St. Martin is now used by Val d'Orbieu for a range of single varietal wines rather than for a blend. Their Cuvée Mythique is unchanged.

STORM IN A CHAMPAGNE FLUTE

A friend of a friend had taken a long lease on a house in West London in one of the few John Nash terraces—for all I know, the only John Nash terrace—outside Regent's Park. In Nash's hands, elegance had been more than an abstraction, and the house, built in the early years of the nineteenth century, had been carefully restored and handsomely decorated. Carpets had been laid and curtains hung. On the morning when a few of us were shown around the house, it stood empty but ready.

On the spur of the moment my friend's friend decided to throw a party. A black-tie party. The next night. Ten o'clock. We were all invited. And so, we later discovered, were at least a hundred others.

An exuberance of jazz musicians—I could hear them playing long before I reached the front door—had been hired. Someone had distributed folding chairs about the rooms. The catering was superbly confident and magnificently simple. On every floor, from basement to attic, were open crates of perfectly ripe, perfectly aromatic peaches brought straight from Covent Garden. The whole house smelled of peaches. And next to the crates were ice tubs filled with bottles of Veuve Clicquot Champagne. I was twenty-two, and life was in Technicolor. We talked, we danced, we ate peaches; we listened to the music, admired each other, and drank Champagne.

What is it about Champagne? Clearly not just the physical effect of the alcohol lurking behind the bubbles. In most circumstances even the sound of a cork popping lightens the mood and provokes an immediate sense of expectation. With a flute of Champagne in hand, the young feel wisely witty and the old feel young; everyone is better-looking. Robert Smith Surtees's character Jorrocks observed that Champagne "gives one werry gentlemanly ideas," which may or may not be so. I can only say that one glass of Champagne will raise the morale and two will fuse the most ill-assorted group into a dinner party.

~ ~ ~

Champagne began as a still, light red wine in the valley of the Marne, east of Paris. In the sixteenth century, thanks to a powerful sponsor, it captured the loyalty of the court of Henri IV. The king's own chancellor, Nicolas Brûlart, owned immense vineyards at Sillery-en-Champagne, north of the Marne, on what is now known as the Montagne de Reims. Brûlart knew the tastes of the court and taught his growers how to meet them. He commended them to pay special attention to delicacy, urging that the grapes be picked no later than ten o'clock in the morning to ensure their fresh and cool arrival at the press. The clear juice was separated from the black grape skins quickly to keep the wine as light as possible. Though it was elegance that interested Brûlart, not lightness of color for its own sake, Champagne destined for the court soon ceased to be red; by the late seventeenth century, it was no more than palest bronze-pink and was known as *vin gris*.

Shipped in barrel with traces of unfermented sugar remaining in the wine—at the time, both knowledge and equipment were spare—the wine inevitably resumed a slow fermentation as soon as spring temperatures set the yeast in motion. But by then the wine had been transferred into bottles and closed, the better to preserve its fresh qualities. Most wine in bottle in those days was protected by a film of olive oil or a loose cloth, to allow the gas of any continuing fermentation to escape. But in the tightly bunged bottles of Champagne, carbon dioxide generated by the renewal of fermentation was trapped in solution. As the wine was poured, it sparkled, captivating a court addicted to novelty and artifice. Just as Champagne's pale color had acquired importance without having been Brûlart's main objective, so its accidental sparkle became a mark of high fashion.

But the quality of the sparkle in a Champagne bottled at destination remained unpredictable. In 1724 the growers of Champagne appealed to the government for the right to ship their *vin gris* in bottles rather than barrels, the better to ensure and control the *mousse,* or foam. With permission given in 1728 and the development of the Saint-Gobain glassworks to provide the vast number of bottles that would be required, real sparkling Champagne, though still not quite as we know it, made its first appearance.

By the early nineteenth century, experience had taught Champagne producers to calculate the pressure of gas that would be generated by a given presence of sugar. They were then able to blend their wines and provoke a second fermentation by adding sugar and yeast before bottling instead of just hoping that the first fermentation would continue. Further improvements in the manufacture of glass bottles allowed a greater pressure of gas, and Champagne came closer to the wine we drink today.

The last step before its full commercial success was a process introduced by Madame Barbe Nicole Ponsardin Clicquot (the *veuve* of the eponymous Champagne), which removed the inconvenient debris of bottle fermentation without losing the wine's gas pressure. Her cellar master, Antoine de Muller, had the idea of inverting the bottles into holes in a steeply sloping tabletop. Repeatedly shaken and gradually turned during several weeks, the bottles were gradually brought from an oblique to an upright position as the debris in each was coaxed into a compact mass settled on the cork itself. Once the retaining wire was removed, the cork, with the debris adhering to it, flew from the bottle, propelled by the pressure of gas within before the operator's thumb stopped the flow. The slight loss of wine was made good and a new cork secured so swiftly that the sparkle was barely diminished.

French law recognizes the importance of the changes that occur during the time a bottle of Champagne is allowed to retain the yeasty lees of its second fermentation. That is why it imposes minimum aging for Champagnes with bottle lees intact. A vintage Champagne (one proclaiming the year in which the grapes were grown) must age with its lees for at least three years before being disgorged. Nonvintage Champagnes must spend one year, a minimum that might soon be raised and that, in any case, is already usually exceeded by quality-conscious producers.

Once disgorged, Champagne begins to lose freshness. Producers usually recommend that nonvintage blends, rarely assembled with the idea of long-term development, be consumed once released for sale. Vintage Champagnes continue to evolve in ways that depend on the style of the year. Some people do and some don't like their Champagne with this additional aging. The English were always notorious for liking theirs "old-landed"—aged, that is to say, in English cellars for several years after being disgorged. For most tastes, however, a vintage Champagne aged for three or four years with its lees and a further three or four without is amply ready to be consumed, even though there are exceptional wines that age superbly for fifty years or more. The best of them, especially if allowed to age on their lees for a late disgorging, acquire a bouquet of freshly baked biscuits or of toasted almonds.

Credit for "inventing" Champagne is often given to Dom Pérignon, the cellar master of the abbey at Hautvillers in the Marne Valley from 1668 to 1715. (His name is now used for a prestige *cuvée* produced by Moët & Chandon.) In fact, the evolution of Champagne as a sparkling wine had started long before his time and was to continue long after. Dom Pérignon is properly credited, however, with identifying the dominant characteristics of the wines from the various sites in the valley and on the hills north and south of it. He started the practice of blending grapes of disparate origin within the Champagne region to arrive at a balance of qualities superior to any that could be found naturally in one place. According to his contemporaries, he was so sensitive to the possibilities of each of the abbey's vineyards that he could say from tasting a single grape, where the basket had come from and decide, on the spot, to which vat it should be consigned.

Because the second fermentation, in Dom Pérignon's day, had really been no more than a resumption of the first, he had had to balance his blend from the start. Today's master blenders, thanks to their ability to control, stop, and provoke fermentation at will, can spend days tasting the year's new wines, the *vins clairs* as they are called, and can test-blend them before committing themselves. If wine of a particular vintage is deficient in some way, the blenders can restore the weak or missing quality with earlier vintages stored as still wines in tank, in cask, or in magnums. (Each firm has its preference.) A *cuvée* today, therefore, starts with hours of tasting and discussion. Dom Pérignon, poor fellow, only had a few seconds with a grape crushed against his tongue to make his decision.

～ ～ ～

Dom Pérignon probably worked with black grapes only, though his would have been a wider range of varieties than the Pinot Noir and its more rustic cousin, Pinot Meunier, used today exclusively. White grapes had earlier disappeared from Champagne, but in the eighteenth century Chardonnay began to appear among the Pinot Noir and Pinot Meunier vines in the Marne Valley. Chardonnay contributed to the delicacy of the wines, as one might expect, and was also found to improve their sparkle. It spread north onto the Montagne de Reims, and then entire vineyards of white varieties were planted south of the Marne, earning the hillsides there, formerly known as the Montagne de Vertus, the name by which they are still known: the Côte des Blancs. These three—the Montagne de Reims, the Marne Valley, and the Côte des Blancs—supported by vineyards still farther south in the Aube *département,* are the principal divisions within the Champagne region. Pinot Noir, Pinot Meunier, and Chardonnay are the three grape varieties grown there.

The individual *crus*—the village names once used to distinguish one Champagne from another—have largely disappeared from public notice in favor of the names of the Champagne houses. Early in the nineteenth century one would have chosen between, say, a Sillery or an Avize, just as, in Burgundy, we still choose between a Beaune and a Volnay. But the art of blending contributed so much to the commercial success of Champagne that by the century's end one chose not between *crus* but between a Mumm, say, and a Pol Roger. As a result, consumers are relatively unfamiliar now with the names of the villages and the specific characteristics of their wines, even though these *crus* play an important role.

All *crus* are graded by the Comité Interprofessionel du Vin de Champagne—the professional organization that represents both the Champagne houses and the grape growers—on a scale from 100 percent down to 80 percent. (The scale formerly went down to 50 percent.) Until 1989, when a thirty-year collective contract between the growers and the Champagne houses expired, the percent rating affected the price paid to each grower for his grapes. Here, roughly, is how it worked. If the price for the grapes of a particular year was agreed at, say, 28 francs a kilo, that is what the owner of a vineyard in a village at the top of the scale would get. The owner of a vineyard in a village rated 95 percent would get 95 percent of the agreed price per kilo, and so on down to those who received the minimum of 80 percent. The rating applied to the vineyards of a particular village as a whole, and one doesn't have to be a viticultural expert to recognize that a favored and well cared for vineyard in a village rated 95 percent could be giving better grapes than the least-favored vineyard in a village rated 100 percent. As a result, to secure the best grapes. Champagne houses occasionally offered premiums above the percentile of the negotiated price.

Those villages rated 100 percent—there are seventeen of them, and they account for 4,317 hectares of the 29,500 hectares of vineyard presently planted in Champagne—are known as *grands crus*. The forty-five villages rated from 90 percent to 99 percent—accounting for 5,249 hectares of vines—are known as *premiers crus*. Together, the *grands* and *premiers crus* of Champagne represent 32.4 percent of the total area under vines.

It is wines from these *crus* that earned for Champagne its reputation.

Used in combinations of villages, of the special sites within each village, or of Champagne's three grape varieties as affected by those special sites, they make possible the subtle variations that distinguish the style of one Champagne house from another. Chardonnay lightens a wine, Pinot Noir gives it weight, and Pinot Meunier brings a fresh quality useful in heavy years. But the wine of each village also has its particular characteristics, as Dom Pérignon well knew: Bouzy and Ambonnay give a blend body, for instance; Cramant, Ay, and Le Mesnil finesse; Mailly power; Verzenay flavor; and so on.

Henri Krug emphasizes the role of the *crus*. "People are always asking about the varietal composition of this or that Champagne," he said to me recently, "but one can discuss blends only in terms of varietals from *specific villages*. For example, we use Pinot Meunier only from certain places, like Leuvrigny.

"A *cuvée* can have fifty wines in it from half a dozen vintages. We have to think ahead. We must project what it will have become after bottle fermentation and six years in bottle with its lees. By that time each wine must have made its contribution to the overall effect, and the *cuvée* should have the harmony of a symphony where nothing jars but every note has its place."

According to André Lallier, head of Champagne Deutz, the work of assembling the *cuvée* should be no more than a last fine tuning. "The real decisions should have been made long before, when a producer chose to buy this rather than that vineyard or decided with which growers to sign long-term supply contracts."

But buying vineyards and signing grape contracts have both become extremely difficult in Champagne. A hectare (roughly 2.5 acres) of *grand cru* vineyard sold for ten thousand francs in 1960. By 1988 its value had risen to a million francs—when the land was available. A single hectare at Ay recently sold for five million francs. At today's rate of exchange that is four hundred thousand dollars an acre for agricultural land.

Other numbers help explain this. In 1945 Champagne sales amounted to 22 million bottles. In 1990 that figure had catapulted to 230 million bottles. Though sales have increased, Champagne's geographic appellation is finite, and production is just about as large as it can be. Producers who depend on bought grapes have a difficult time, especially as the supply has been further reduced by growers who prefer to add value to their crop by turning it into Champagne themselves (or making an arrangement with the local cooperative to do so on their behalf) and then selling it by mail order. The French market for Champagne is now dominated by just such private-producer sales.

The big Champagne producers, usually referred to as the *grandes marques,* have cannibalized each other simply to acquire vineyards. Some have established affiliated and similarly named wineries outside France to help deflect some of the worldwide demand for their brands. These sparkling wines, in California particularly, have done well and now frighten the Champenois, who are uneasy at the thought of having to compete with the very brand names that once carried the global reputation of Champagne. The situation has been brought to a head by a drop in sales coincidental with a sagging world economy, and, although Champagne has in the past always presented an elegant and unruffled façade to the world whatever its inner turmoil, this time we are being given a glimpse of problems usually dealt with behind Champagne's firmly closed doors.

In Britain, long Champagne's largest customer outside France itself, sales began to slide in 1990 after years of steady growth. Then in 1991 shipments fell 40 percent. Sales in France were also down, by 12 percent, and shipments declined to greater or lesser degrees in all other markets.

There have been similar setbacks before, most recently in the mid-1970s, but the anxiety is more widespread now because this time the quality houses are affected as much as the volume producers. Firms that would normally have three or four years' inventory maturing in their cellars are presently financing five or six. The call on their resources is further aggravated not only by the big harvests of 1990 and 1991 (contracts between the Champagne houses and their growers usually bind buyer and seller to the yield of so many acres, whatever that yield might be) but by the unprecedented prices paid for grapes when an industry-wide contract, already referred to, ran out.

A formula under that group contract had put limits on the quantities of grapes the larger houses could buy, a plan designed to prevent their offering premiums over the negotiated price, thus drawing grapes away from smaller rivals. When the contract's term ended, each house negotiated for itself; the limits were off. What the large producers wanted, in any case, was to offer prices that would encourage growers to sell their grapes rather than process them for direct-mail sales. Everything conspired to send up grape prices, which in turn put immediate pressure on current Champagne prices. The revenues to buy the grapes had to come from somewhere. As things turned out, it was an unfortunate time for prices to have been increased.

Earlier this year, at a sedate but unprecedented press conference, Christian Bizot, president and director-general of the venerable house of Bollinger, announced that Champagne was at a crossroads. He said what everyone knew: that problems created by falling sales were being compounded by high grape prices, excess inventories, and disappointment (expressed mostly in the British press) with the quality of much nonvintage brut. The region, he said, had lost its sense of direction.

Though critical of no one in particular, Bizot pointed out that a trade once dominated by family firms was now largely controlled by four groups (Louis Vuitton-Moët Hennessy; Remy-Martin; Seagram; and Marne et Champagne, a conglomerate of cooperatives). "I'm not saying that the change is for better or worse," he said, choosing his words carefully in French and translating them himself into impeccable English, "but change it certainly is."

Bizot said he saw Champagne's role eroding along with its distinction. He accepted, he said, the challenge of a rise in the quality of sparkling wines made elsewhere in the world, but he regretted the confusion sown by Champagne houses lending their names and, with their names, a credibility that belonged not to them but to the region of Champagne.

"California sparkling wines would not have the reputation they now have in the United States," he argued, "if French names had not been used to launch and support them.... Now more than ever," he said, "the producers of Champagne must demonstrate the distinction of their product."

Champagne Deutz's André Lallier, with whom I lunched the day after the Bizot press conference, agrees that California sparkling wines, including his own Maison Deutz in San Luis Obispo, were helped, when they started, by the credibility of the Champagne houses sponsoring them. "But the second bottle of any wine," he said, "is sold on the quality of the first. Our people in California are setting their own very high standards, and, yes, that is a challenge. But we don't think our development in California has worked against our interests in Champagne. Producing good wine in a country helps make it more accessible. That is as true for sparkling wine as it is for still wine. In France everyone has a cousin, an uncle, someone, who has a vineyard somewhere and makes wine. Champagne is a step up, but it is an easier step for people who are familiar with good sparkling wine. That must help Champagne. I would say that if there is a problem it is not in California but here in Champagne. We now have wines of a quality below the expected standard. Perhaps we need two classifications to make that clear.

"I am not anxious about our Champagne industry, however. On the contrary, I am very optimistic. I see the production of good sparkling wines around the world as a positive development that will stimulate and help Champagne."

Christian Bizot, presenting to the assembled press Bollinger's charter—a statement of the firm's own commitment to what it considers to be the basic ethical and qualitative tenets of a *grand vin de Champagne*—seemed also to suggest that it was time to restore distinctions within Champagne, between the *grands* and *premiers crus* and other Champagnes for a start.

"The *grands crus* of Bordeaux and Burgundy give credibility to those regions as a whole," he said. "Basically, the situation is the same in Champagne, but consumers don't know this because few people are familiar with the *crus*. The needs of blending, a fundamental part of Champagne, make it difficult to offer a wine that is assembled only from 100 percent *grand cru* grapes. But at Bollinger we think it is time to prepare a back label for blends from *grand cru* and *premier cru* wines only. Champagne must find a way to explain to the world what its distinctions are, how its quality is defined. The *grandes marques,* particularly, must define themselves and the role they play."

The difficulty is that many consumers are dazzled by well-publicized names, and others are deterred by Champagnes with real character when they have become used to rather bland wines produced on the same principles that give us flavorless food.

Antoine Gosset, head of the small, quality house of Champagne Gosset at Ay, gets quite heated on the subject. "Standardization is robbing Champagne of its character. Character costs money—money spent on quality grapes and aging. It is expensive to age a product that was expensive to produce in the first place.

"Those making fine wines find themselves at a disadvantage. This doesn't just affect wine, of course. Butter no longer tastes like butter; chicken doesn't have the taste of chicken. Losses of quality occur all in the name of producing these things more cheaply. But those who promote a product with the slogan 'It's cheaper' neglect to add 'And it's not as good.' Sometimes it's not even recognizable for what it is supposed to be. People are settling for shadows."

There is no need for that. Whatever the current brouhaha, there are plenty of superb Champagnes. For what it's worth in these confused times, here are those I hold in highest esteem and that give me most pleasure. The choice is subjective, of course, and is neither particularly unusual nor original.

Everyone agrees, for example, that Bollinger and Krug stand apart;

even the other producers are in agreement on this point. At both establishments fermentation in barrel plays an important part in establishing style, though Henri Krug maintains that what counts is not just the matter of fermentation in wood but of fermentation in small volume. I enjoy all Krug *cuvées,* and usually pick a Bollinger Vintage R.D.—the R.D. for *récemment dégorgé,* or late disgorged—for my own family celebrations.

I am never disappointed by Deutz. The current 1985 vintage of Cuvée William Deutz is surely the perfect example of all that Champagne should mean: elegance, harmony, refinement, length. I have great respect for Veuve Clicquot; the wines are always reliably delicious. Clicquot's Gold Label Brut Vintage can sometimes surpass the prestige *cuvées* of other houses, and I think that was the case with the Brut 1982.

I am also devoted to Roederer Cristal (who isn't?), to Taittinger's Comtes de Champagne (a prestige *cuvée* made of white grapes only, its delicacy and freshness more than Brûlart would have dared dream of), to Gosset's sumptuous style, and to Perrier-Jouet's Belle Epoque, known in the United States as Fleur de France. Fleur de France is packaged in such a charming bottle that it is easily (and often) dismissed by critics as a marketer's *cuvée.* I was all the more pleased when the French *Guide Hachette des Vins* gave the 1985 *cuvée* its prestigious Grappe d'Or for 1991. *Hachette*'s juries taste their way through thousands of wines presented "blind" each year to find the one recipient of that annual award.

I asked earlier, "What is it about Champagne?" yet didn't and can't answer my own question. But I remember many years ago watching a play in London's West End and hearing one character say to another: "Take a glass of Champagne with you while you dress for dinner, my boy. It'll give the right fillip to your tie."

And I bet it did.

Originally published as "Storm in a Champagne Flute" in *Gourmet,* December 1992.

From their low in 1991, Champagne sales worldwide have risen by 50 percent, from 214 million bottles to 320 million bottles. This soaring demand has led to a slight extension of the area qualified to produce Champagne and to a further increase in the value of vineyard land there. In 2010, the average value of a hectare of vineyard in Champagne was 852,000 euros, equivalent to 5.7 million former French francs or 1.1 million dollars.

CÔTE RÔTIE AND CONDRIEU

Drinking with Pliny and Columella

"On the banks of the Rhône, after its junction with the Saône, and in the adjacent territories, several precious wines are produced: but although the vineyards in these departments may be regarded as among the most ancient in France . . . it is only in recent times that the merits of their choicest produce have become fully known."

This could have been written yesterday, so new is our revived interest in wines of the northern Rhône, but I'm quoting from Alexander Henderson's *History of Ancient and Modern Wines,* published in 1824. Côte Rôtie—one of the wines Henderson is referring to—was then, with Hermitage, the rage of London, having already been the rage of first-century Rome. Rome had discovered Côte Rôtie when on business across the river at Vienne, a rich city then flourishing as the center of its empire's flax trade.

Pliny wrote that the wine of Vienne had a natural flavor of pitch, just as some might now refer to a tarry taste in a red wine. Plutarch said it was "pitched," suggesting that the taste was not natural at all. It was left to Columella to explain, in *On Agriculture and Trees,* that this special taste of the wine of Vienne, admired by his fellow Romans above all others, came from the bark of a local tree, dried and powdered and added to the wine as a preservative. Evidently even ancient Rome was captivated by the taste of oak in French red wine and was prepared to pay dearly, as many still are today, for an extra dose of tannin.

But Pliny, Plutarch, Columella, and even Alexander Henderson were far from my thoughts when I arrived at the Hôtel Beau Rivage in Condrieu in time for dinner: a fillet of John Dory with *sauce sabayon,* and Chapoutier's Deschants Saint-Joseph Blanc '91. The wine was rather subdued but had body enough for the unusual sauce.

Before *autoroutes* swept traffic from Paris to the south of France in hours, the Beau Rivage was for years a favorite stopover of mine, close enough to the Route Nationale 7 (known in those days, with good cause, as La Meurtrière, or The Murderess) to be convenient, but far enough away, across the river, to be tranquil—which it still is. What I now missed, I began thinking, was the Castaings, the former owners, but perhaps what I really missed more, in what were still family surroundings, was the style prevalent at small country hotels in France in the fifties and sixties. There was a simple warmth then, an absence of fuss, but a quick eye for the details that mattered. At any rate, dinner was good—excellent cheeses followed the John Dory—and was served by lamplight on the hotel's enlarged terrace overlooking the river. As darkness fell, the pretty bridge across the Rhône, a few hundred yards upstream, was softly floodlit, and its reflection shimmered in the water. Condrieu's dramatically steep vineyards were behind us.

Just north of Condrieu and extending to either side of the rather drab little town of Ampuis are the even more terraced vineyards of Côte Rôtie. (Lyon is at most only twenty miles farther on.) The Rhône here flows in a southwesterly direction, and so these slopes above its right bank face southeast and catch the morning sun. Recent research at the University of Bordeaux has revealed that vine leaves use the energy of sunlight more efficiently in the late morning than in the afternoon, which is perhaps the reason many of the great wine regions of France—in particular the Médoc, the Côte d'Or of Burgundy, and Alsace—have evolved where vineyards have an east or southeastern exposure. On the Côte Rôtie the vines, supported by high tripods of wood stakes rather than by wires, are planted very densely on narrow ledges held in place by walls of unmortared rock first constructed in the time of the Romans.

Gilles Barge, president of the association of Côte Rôtie growers, lives a short walk up the hill from the *place* in front of Ampuis's church. A youngish, articulate, and very friendly man, Barge had come in from his vines to talk to me and was in his work boots and shorts. I asked him about those ancient terraces.

"The terraces keep things here much as they've always been," he began. "Change would be difficult for the Côte Rôtie. When growers elsewhere began to take horses into their vineyards, we couldn't, any more than we can use tractors today. We must work our soil with our hands, as we've always done. The only novelty is that we can sometimes spray by helicopter.

"It's because the work here is largely done by hand that holdings are so small. One man can't cultivate more than two or three acres without help, and it's been difficult for us to find hired labor. Who wants to work with a hoe for eight hours a day?

"At the beginning of the century there were almost nine hundred acres of vines on the Côte Rôtie, but so many of the young men from these villages were lost in World War I that vineyards were abandoned. The situation was worse after 1945, when our wine sold for the same low price as the ordinary wine being grown down on the plain. It was discouraging. The fruit and vegetable farms by the river were doing well then. Industry was expanding south from Lyon toward Ampuis and offering young people good pay and security. By the beginning of the sixties there were no more than one hundred fifty acres of productive vines on the Côte Rôtie, and not more than a dozen growers."

In the general decline, as Barge went on to explain, even the mule tracks on the hillsides disappeared. Everything, including the harvest, was carried up and down on the backs of men. Alfred Gérin, the mayor of Ampuis at the time, thought the vineyards would disappear altogether. The world doesn't lack for wine, after all.

"But, when vineyards are two thousand years old," Barge continued, "and have been nurtured all that time to give a wine of unique charac-

ter, they have a spirit that must be preserved. We had a responsibility
to our children. So in 1963 Gérin built a road up the hillside to improve
access to the vineyards. It was a simple, narrow road and very steep in
places. But it made such an immediate difference to the growers that
Gérin built another, and now there's a network of little roads so that we
can get to the vineyards more easily with cars and small trucks.

"Gérin's move saved the *vignoble*. He saved the town. We are now back
to 450 acres of vineyard, and our association has 132 grower-members.
Forty of them produce enough wine to justify bottling it under their
own labels, and about twenty families live from their vineyards alone.

"But in the sixties we were still backward; even our standard of
winemaking had fallen. Côte Rôtie wines have always had power and
structure, but they had become rustic. We now have a new generation
of growers, the majority of them aged under forty and most of them
trained at the viticultural high school in Beaune. The resulting change
shows both in the vineyards and in the cellars.

"We stick to local tradition. We'd rather warm the must to get a slow
fermentation going with our own natural yeast than use a selected yeast
from a laboratory. Selected yeasts can make all wine taste the same. We
understand better today the why of what we do, and so we do it more
appropriately and more effectively."

~ ~ ~

Even those who know little else about the Côte Rôtie know that part
of it is called the Côte Blonde and part the Côte Brune. Wine books
recount legends of a land inheritance divided between two daughters
(one blond and one brunette, of course), but the difference between the
Côte Blonde and the Côte Brune is geological rather than legendary.
Such topsoil as there is on the Côte Rôtie is a sandy decomposition of
granite; but the formation of the quartzlike mica beneath differs from
the Blonde to the Brune, giving the vines on either side of the divide
different access to water and nutrients. (For the technically minded, it's
gneiss on the Blonde side and mica-schist on the Brune.) The difference
is made more emphatic by the presence on the Côte Brune of clay rich

in iron oxide. The iron not only darkens the soil of that part of the hill but also deepens the color and intensifies the tannin of its wine.

But there is more to the Côte Rôtie than the Côte Blonde and Côte Brune, which together account for only a hundred acres. Most growers have vines scattered along the entire slope, and so their wines, all reds, made from their assembled grapes, have traditionally been sold simply as Côte Rôtie. The fact is that the best-balanced wines usually are made from such combinations anyway. Nevertheless, small as the appellation is, the market, it is said, demands an even tighter specificity of origin. To satisfy (and perhaps feed?) this somewhat academic interest, Côte Rôtie's production is increasingly bottled with the names of various sections of its slopes on the labels. One has seen references to the Côte Blonde and Côte Brune, of course, for many years; but some producers now use names taken from old village survey maps that as yet have no legal standing. One official of the National Institute of Appellations of Origin in Paris told me recently, "The only officially recognized appellation in Côte Rôtie is Côte Rôtie, period."

"We're under pressure from the producers," Gilles Barge said, "to come up with distinctive names for every little part of the hill." He looked hard at me before adding, "The producers know that writers like something they can pick over."

I knew as well as he that dividing the steadily swelling production of Côte Rôtie into many small lots of individual wines, each carefully and separately promoted—with or without the connivance of wine writers, and with or without the support of appellation law—creates scarcities that usually lead in only one direction. It's an old marketing ploy. But I suppose the Côte Rôtie growers have to find the money to keep their terraces in repair and the hoes busy.

～ ～ ～

Armed with glasses, we went into the cellar where Barge keeps his wine in large and well-matured oak casks, each holding five hundred gallons or more. He seemed to have very few barrels, and with Columella in mind I asked him about the role of oak in making a Côte Rôtie wine.

"New oak barrels certainly add something," he began diplomatically, doubtless remembering his role as president of the association of *all* the growers of Côte Rôtie. Then he warmed to his subject. "But too often they are used to excess, and the finesse of our wines is lost. When oak dominates, the wine is no longer typical of this appellation. So often now one tastes only the oak—the toast, the vanillin—and not the character of this place. That's not in our interest. Anyone can buy new wood and sell the taste of it, even if the wine has no character at all. Obviously it's better to use new wood than old, spoiled barrels. But one must always use it with discretion."

Barge assembles his various lots to make one Côte Rôtie each year. He handed me a sample of the 1992, drawn from wood. It had the aroma and flavor of violets. The wine was full and velvety, yet firm.

In my experience, Côte Rôtie at its best is always more aromatic than Hermitage and more polished than Cornas, the two other major red wines of the northern Rhône. Cornas has more muscle and Hermitage more heart, but the refinement of Côte Rôtie has an almost intellectual appeal. Barge and I went on to the 1991: It was less sumptuous than the 1992 but equally aromatic and elegantly silky. Silkiness is a characteristic of Côte Rôtie when the use of the white grape Viognier is mingled with black Syrah, the grape that is normally dominant in the northern Rhône.

"The appellation law allows us to include up to 20 percent Viognier," Barge explained, "but nobody uses more than 5 percent; most of us prefer much less, and some none at all. Viognier is a very aromatic grape, and when picked fully ripe it adds a roundness and a slightly higher than normal alcohol to our blends, creating the "fat" that smoothes the edges of the Syrah. The little Viognier in my wine is important—it brings finesse and a certain grace."

Barge's 1990 had a rich color and concentrated flavor. It had been a dry year on the Côte Rôtie, and the vines suffered. Rain in late August helped, but the grapes dehydrated even as they ripened. Knowing this, I expected the wine to be tough. In fact, there was only a suggestion of hardness at the close, and I assumed that it was again a matter of the Viognier tempering any severity.

Although Viognier can now be found in some vineyards in the southern Rhône (and as far afield as California), it is associated with the adjoining appellations of Condrieu and Côte Rôtie more exclusively than any other variety is with any other place. While some believe Viognier to be descended from an indigenous wild vine, others think that it may have arrived in Condrieu from the Dalmatian coast of the Adriatic in the third century. At the time the emperor Probus had just lifted the edict, issued by Domitian two hundred years before, that limited the extent of vineyards outside Italy, and it's likely that there followed a big rush for cuttings from wherever one could get them. Why not from Dalmatia?

As the leading grower in Condrieu, Georges Vernay is, by definition, the world's leading Viognier grower. He said that in Condrieu, too, there had been long years of decline before the present revival. "As recently as 1980 only sixty acres of Viognier were left," he told me. "But there are two hundred now, and we hope eventually to more than triple that number, as the appellation allows.

"We do have a few patches of clay and chalk, where we could, if we wished, make a passable red wine," he went on, "but our sand is really better suited to white. The boundaries for the appellation extend up the hill from the village; that is, we go from 520 feet above sea level up to 975 feet, or 300 meters. Wine produced above that contour and on the plateau at the very top is simply *vin de pays*."

In addition to his 17.5 acres of Condrieu, Vernay has vines on the Côte Rôtie, within the Saint-Joseph appellation farther south near Tournon, and on some of the land entitled only to a *vin de pays* designation. With thirty-five acres in all, he has six men working full time with him and his son. "We do everything the old way," he told me. "We even do without herbicides; the grass comes in handy for mulch."

We tasted as we talked, and he got me started with a 1992 Viognier from vines outside the Condrieu appellation. A *vin de pays,* it had the flowery aromas I associate with Viognier, and an attractive but odd suggestion of hazelnuts. It was very good; but, tasting Vernay's 1991 Condrieu immediately afterward, I was reminded once more why certain vines are entitled to an appellation while others are not. The Condrieu was more concentrated, and its aroma much more intense, dominated by the smell of hawthorn blossom.

Vernay handed me next a glass of his 1991 Côteau de Veron, a Condrieu he makes with greater emphasis on oak (two thirds of the wine is fermented in barrel). The wood masks the essential aromas and flavor of Viognier. It was an interesting variant, carefully made to avoid exaggeration, but I did wonder what the advantage was when the other wine, to my taste, was so much more delectable. Vernay wouldn't make it if his customers didn't want it, yet I find this passion for the taste of wood for its own sake perplexing. I find that oak in wine is like garlic in cooking: If it is noticeable as a separate and distinct taste, then it's too strong. Someone should be marketing packets of Columella's oak powder so that those who want oak can add their own, to suit their own taste, and stir. But that would give the game away.

Finally we tasted Vernay's 1990 Condrieu. It was bigger than the 1991: The aroma and flavor were even more concentrated, and it had a fatter, richer texture with a much longer finish. Vernay also has about six acres of vines on the Côte Rôtie, most of which are more than fifty years old, and before I left he showed me the 1991 and 1990 wines made from them. The 1990 was especially remarkable—a sleek, aromatic wine with just a hint of bitter almond at the end. But what interested me particularly was a 1990 Côtes du Rhône bottled under his Saint-Agathe label, which we had tasted only in order to adjust our palates after the Condrieu. It was extraordinarily good—and more reasonably priced, of course, than any of the grander wines of the northern Rhône.

Before dinner, I decided to see for myself one of Gérin's roads, so I pointed my rented VW at the hill and went for it. Getting up was tricky: The engine stalled more than once approaching the awkward, unbelievably steep turns. But it was on the way down that the little car earned my respect. The descent was, shall I say, breathtaking, a real test of my steering (and nerves) and of the car's brakes.

Having collected myself, I slipped across the river to La Pyramide, in Vienne, a revered destination in the annals of French gastronomy, for it was here that Fernand Point reigned over what was, in his day, the finest kitchen in France. I had last lunched here a few years before, when the restaurant was being continued by Point's widow, and remembered a pleasant enough lunch served to me under a tree in the courtyard.

Since then the restaurant has been closed, sold and resold, turned into a cooking school, and finally purchased by Dominique Bouillon, a Paris businessman as well as a friend and client of Point's. He couldn't bear to see the repeated degradation of a place he felt should be recognized as the national monument it really is. Bouillon has taken as his partner Patrick Henriroux, a young chef who most recently worked at La Ferme de Mougins near Cannes and before that with Georges Blanc in Vonnas.

I had heard that a vast sum had been spent on restoring La Pyramide to its former splendor. When I arrived I found that, despite other changes, the old graveled courtyard, trees still in place, was much as I remembered it. It had merely been paved over to make a canvas-shaded, summer dining room. The atmosphere is both chic and relaxed, the service impeccable, and the food delicious.

The sommelier at La Pyramide is advertised on the wine list as having won all kinds of awards, including that of the Best Young Sommelier in France. I asked if he could find in the cellar just a half bottle of a Gilles Barge Côte Rôtie older than those I had tasted in Barge's cellar. He wasn't successful in finding the 1985 I was hoping for, but he did find a half bottle of the 1988. Though still young, of course, it opened up in a decanter, and with my veal chop and sauté of wild mushrooms it brought the day to a fine and fitting close.

The producers of Côte Rôtie and of Condrieu are so few and the volume of wine made by any one of them is so limited that these wines are not in broad distribution in the United States. Occasionally a retailer will have a Côte Rôtie or a Condrieu on display, but the allocation of any single wine is usually so small that it will be kept in the stock room for those customers who are seriously interested. Often a retailer will sell such wines prior to their arrival through a mailing to account customers or by placing a few telephone calls. Anyone interested in buying Côte Rôtie or Condrieu is well advised to ask to be included in any offering before a shipment arrives.

Originally published as "A Rhône Revival: Côte Rôtie and Condrieu" in *Gourmet,* December 1993.

The acreage of Viognier within the Condrieu appellation is now in excess of 330 acres. Patrick Henriroux and his wife, Pascale, are now sole proprietors of La Pyramide.

CÔTES DE CASTILLON

A Bordeaux Wine Reborn

Régis Moro, a wine-grower in the Côtes de Castillon, in Bordeaux, was astonished when his face made the cover of the French news-magazine *Le Point* last September. But neither he nor anyone else was surprised to find that the magazine had placed the Côtes de Castillon among the top ten wine regions of France. Some of the best of Bordeaux's most affordable wines are now being produced there, and they're cropping up in restaurants and on merchants' racks in the United States.

The area takes its name from Castillon-la-Bataille, a small town about six miles east of Saint-Emilion with a street market every Monday, a cycle race every August, and a bridge across the Dordogne. Of its historic past, there is little evidence—an ancient, creeper-strewn gate, vestiges of stone fortifications, and the site of the battle in 1453 that ended the Hundred Years' War. But the hills, the *côtes,* around the town are studded with castles, and the countryside is both pretty and green: Woods bordering the narrow, winding roads, and copses tucked among the vineyards shelter an abundance of game—especially doves and boar—and there are always *cèpes* in the fall.

The Côtes de Castillon appellation begins where Saint-Emilion's ends, but there's little to see that distinguishes one from the other: The limestone plateau and chalky clay slopes of Saint-Emilion simply become the limestone plateau and chalky clay slopes of the Côtes de Castillon. Some growers say that any change in the soil is negligible; it's the gradual shift in climate as one goes up the Dordogne valley that's responsible for any difference one can taste in the wine. The vines break bud, leaf out, and flower as much as two weeks later than they do in some parts of Saint-Emilion—without the tempering effect of the Atlantic, spring is delayed—and although warmer summers sometimes help the vines catch up, picking also often starts a week or two after Saint-Emilion. Others say it's the scattered pockets of Cabernet Sauvignon vines that give the wines their distinct character. Merlot and Cabernet Franc are traditional throughout this side of Bordeaux, but Cabernet Sauvignon, which is widely planted in the Côtes de Castillon, is rare in Saint-Emilion.

Over decades of replanting, the vineyards in the Castillon hills drifted down toward the plain (where cultivation is easier and cheaper). But in the 1970s, as the price of land in neighboring Saint-Emilion and Pomerol rose, any Castillon property that came onto the market was snapped up by someone from the more fashionable appellations next door. The vineyards again climbed to the slopes' higher reaches, where there is more sun and less clay (the limestone up there gives wine of greater finesse).

Local growers had already begun to plant higher, and to modify their wine-making to take advantage of the quality of the fruit, when they were galvanized by events at Château de Belcier, a Castillon estate with about 130 acres of vineyard that had been sold in 1986 to the Macif insurance company. "For years I'd made a light wine from the fruit here," Gilbert Dubois, Belcier's *maître de chais,* told me, "a simple wine ready for early drinking. But the new owners wanted a change. 'We want wine of a quality that justifies our investment,' they said.

"I was eager to go along with them. First, we trimmed the number of buds on each vine. That summer we thinned the leaves to let the light in. We thinned the crop, too, and checked it for ripeness, bunch by bunch, as it came to the crusher. I tried a new approach to fermentation and brought in new barrels—the first to be used anywhere in the Côtes de Castillon for quite some time. Cement tanks had become the norm. The changes cost money, and our customers were taken aback by our price. I thought I'd be looking for new clients, but they were all impressed by the wine and stayed with me."

Belcier's conspicuous success provoked a dramatic shift. By 1989 the market's perception of the Côtes de Castillon greatly improved, and the growers were ready to reclaim its name. For years its official appellation had been Bordeaux Supérieur, with the words *Côtes de Castillon* hyphenated to it almost as an afterthought. The trade liked it that way; the mention of "Bordeaux" in the appellation lowered the price ceiling and therefore allowed them to use the wine to improve their regional blends. In reforming the appellation, the growers dropped the Bordeaux Supérieur and tightened controls to raise quality further. For example, they placed on each grower an obligation to plant his or her vines more densely in the vineyard, increasing the minimum number of plants to five thousand to the hectare (about two thousand to the acre), roughly double the density of vines in many California vineyards. This meant that if the growers were to remain within the permitted yield limit, they would have to reduce the number of bunches ripening on each vine. The result has been consistently riper fruit with flavor more concentrated than ever, and a range of mature tannins that gives the wines a firm yet gentle backbone.

Confirmation by *Le Point* of the Côtes de Castillon's place in the front ranks of French wines just ten years after the growers imposed these and other changes on themselves has given great satisfaction. When I visited the area in late 1999, I found the growers' enthusiasm exhilarating and the quality of their wines convincing. "What has happened here," said Hélène Lapeyronie of Château Lapeyronie, "is that everyone recognizes more clearly that to make good wine you must have good fruit. There's a limit to what can be done in the cellar to remedy what should have been done in the vineyard. Our work has been transformed."

Lapeyronie and her husband, Jean-Frédéric, have roughly twenty-five acres of vineyard that border Saint-Emilion. Most of it—70 percent, anyway—is planted with Merlot, and the rest is divided between

Cabernet Franc and Cabernet Sauvignon. The latter arrived fairly recently. In the 1970s—a time when there was much replanting—it was the policy of the Institut National des Appellations d'Origine to encourage growers throughout Bordeaux to use Cabernet Sauvignon to improve the quality of the wines, regardless of the varieties they had been using before.

"The trouble with that policy," said Gilbert Dubois, "was that most growers put Cabernet Sauvignon in the low-lying corners of their vineyards, where there's the greatest chance of spring frosts. Because Cabernet Sauvignon breaks bud later than Merlot, they felt it would be at lower risk there. But low-lying sites are often on clay soils that are poorly exposed. Vines there don't get the sun they need to ripen properly. And if Cabernet Sauvignon is to make a contribution to a wine, it must be fully ripe."

Several growers told me of problems they have with Cabernet Sauvignon in all but the most propitious years, even though Hélène Lapeyronie insists that it ripens well in the Côtes de Castillon if it's planted in the right places. "It must be up on the limestone rather than down on clay," she said. "Limestone drains well and warms up quickly. The vines must be well exposed to the sun so that the tannin, the color, and the flavor are really ripe when the fruit is picked. Then Cabernet Sauvignon adds power to the wine and complexity to its bouquet."

To get that perfect ripeness in all three varieties, the Lapeyronies skirmish daily with nature, adjusting the crop loads on their vines as weather conditions change. "We rarely get as much as half the yield permitted for the appellation," she said, "but our fruit is always ripe." And their wines—regardless of vintage—are always densely colored, intensely fruity, and highly concentrated.

So are the wines of Robert Avargues of Château Robin. His were among several I tasted in which the flattering violet perfume of Cabernet Franc came through with unusual clarity. "That's because of picking at full ripeness," he told me. "We wait as long as we have to. And if it rains, too bad." Like most of the other growers, he sorts through his bunches as they move on a belt toward the crusher. Once they are crushed and destemmed, he lets the mass of skins and juice soak together for four or five days at low temperature. "That maceration helps bring out the fruit aromas and deepens the color in the wine," he said. "Fermentation starts naturally once I let the temperature rise. I don't use laboratory yeast. It gives greater security, but it standardizes the wine. I'm not organic or biodynamic or ecological, but I prefer to work with nature. I use organic fertilizer, for example, though it costs more, because I'm not prepared to put chemicals in my soil. When I take that kind of stand in the vineyard, it wouldn't make sense to do anything in the *chais* that smacks of industrial winemaking."

Ripe grapes give healthy lees (the residue that falls as the wine ages in the barrel, not the skins and pips that have been separated after fermentation) that help stabilize the wine. "Lees give the wine richness and nuance," said Patrick Erésué, winemaker at Château de Chainchon, his family's property, and formerly winemaker at Château Canon La Gaffelière, a *premier grand cru classé* of Saint-Emilion. "Richness and nuance, fruit and concentration—these are the qualities that give pleasure in a wine."

When Patrick Erésué talks about the lees of the wine, he parts company with most other Bordeaux growers. It has been a convention there for almost three centuries to draw a young red wine aging in barrel off its lees every three months and transfer it into another, as if the lees—mostly tartrates and spent yeast—were noxious and had to be eliminated. The transfer—known as racking—also allows the wine to pick up some oxygen. A few years ago, it occurred to Patrick Ducournau, a grower of Madiran, a red wine produced in the foothills of the Pyrenees, that the absorption of that small dose of oxygen rather than the elimination of the lees was the real benefit of racking red wine. Indeed, he wondered whether elimination of a red wine's lees was even a good thing. White wines, after all, gain in succulence and depth of flavor when held in barrel on their lees. They also benefit from the capacity of lees to attract any free oxygen, keeping the wine fresh. But red wines need oxygen to help bring color and tannin together in a way that deepens and fixes one while making the other more supple. Ducournau set up the kind of fine plastic oxygen-supply lines used in hospitals and gave minute, controlled doses to his red wines instead of racking them. The combined benefit of lees and oxygen was astonishing—the wines seemed more full and deeply colored. Côtes de Castillon growers were among the first to accept Ducournau's ideas and to follow his lead. Oxygen lines now trail through most of their cellars.

Régis Moro, the proprietor of Vieux Château Champ de Mars, and *Le Point*'s cover man, put it to me succinctly. "If I want the benefit of keeping my wine in contact with its lees, I can't rack it," he said. "If I don't rack my wine, it will lack the oxygen it needs for the stabilization of color. The lees will have taken it. So I inject micro-doses of oxygen to replace it. Eventually, as the wine develops, the lees are just absorbed into it. They disappear. All that's left are tartrate crystals."

~ ~ ~

Moro and others are installing new, open wooden fermenting vats—the kind that most Bordeaux growers threw out years ago in favor of stainless steel. It hadn't escaped Moro's notice that when Paul Pontallier took over the management of Château Margaux with an enviable budget to update the *chais,* he changed almost everything—except the wooden fermenting vats. Controlled experiments elsewhere in the Médoc a few years ago showed that although analysis reveals no measurable differences between them, two wines made from the same lot of grapes, one fermented in stainless steel and the other in wood, made a completely different impression on nose and palate. The wine fermented in wood was more aromatic and had a longer flavor.

I was amazed that the Côtes de Castillon, this small appellation on the margins of Bordeaux, should be at the cutting edge. But then I remembered that 1453 battle of Castillon, the one that changed European history. The French beat the English because they installed cannons with great explosive force on the slope over the water meadow where they expected to be attacked, then deliberately drew their enemy into the trap. For the fifteenth century it was an innovative ploy. Along with an end to the aspirations of the English crown in France, that day brought an end to knights in armor, chivalry, and that whole world we call the Middle Ages.

When you next drink a glass of Côtes de Castillon, picture that.

Originally published as "A Bordeaux Reborn" in *Gourmet,* June 2000.

LE BEAUJOLAIS NOUVEAU
EST ARRIVÉ!

Every year on the third Thursday of November, bars, cafés, and bistros all over Paris revel, with varying degrees of decorum, in the new harvest's Beaujolais. The cynical would say that the success of Beaujolais Nouveau—almost as great in Brussels, Amsterdam, Frankfurt, and New York as it is in Lyons—is a triumph of marketing and promotion. But commerce merely cashes in: The gaiety is spontaneous, and the joy a response to something beyond posters and bar streamers. A mouthful of wine that was grapes just weeks before, and earth, rain, and sunshine only weeks before that, is an exhilarating reminder of what really makes the world go round.

Well over half the annual production of Beaujolais and Beaujolais-Villages together is sold, shipped, and presumably paid for before Christmas. This is not an unhappy situation for the growers to find themselves in. Unfortunately, the intense but fleeting attention distorts our perception of the wine: It is more than a nine days' wonder. The phenomenon of Beaujolais Nouveau also means that wines of the ten Beaujolais *crus* are often considered stale news when released the following spring. (Brouilly, Côte de Brouilly, Chénas, Chiroubles, Fleurie, Juliénas, Morgon, Moulin-à-Vent, Saint-Amour, and Regnié may not be sold as *vin nouveau*.) They can hardly recreate the excitement generated the previous November, when the vintage made its debut. The result is that some of the region's best wines slip onto the market unannounced and unnoticed.

Once (and I mean centuries ago), when all wine was sold from the barrel and no one knew how to keep a part-empty container's contents from deteriorating, each new vintage was so eagerly awaited that it would be shipped off to market still seething its way through the final stages of fermentation. Most of those wines were boisterously rough; few could have been as delectable, drunk in their infancy, as wine made from the Gamay grape of the Beaujolais. Even without the help of controversial techniques to expand the wine's aromatic potential or boost its power, young Beaujolais, tender yet sprightly and, left to itself, redolent of peonies in full flower, is as seductive as any wine can be.

Growers were still shipping barrels of new (and probably fizzy) Beaujolais to Lyons as recently as the 1930s. The wine was set up on bistros' zinc counters and, once tapped, run off directly into the pitchers from which it was served. In Paris, too, there were bars known for the new Beaujolais that arrived each fall with much local fanfare. Such wine, with "beaded bubbles winking at the brim," brought to the shabbiest hole-in-the-wall a vision of distant countryside, of vines in sunlight, and, who knows, perhaps of Dionysus himself. Jubilant.

There was nothing either formal or official about the dispatch of these wines: no release date; no organized promotion; and, even when the machinery of controlled appellations had already been put in place, no trail of certificates. Eventually, however, bureaucracy stepped in to tidy things up. In 1938 the practice of selling a Beaujolais freely outside the bounds and documentation of the new appellation laws was curtailed, and then wartime measures that controlled the release of all wines broke the tradition altogether—at a time when it might have done most good.

The restrictions inaugurated under the Vichy administration (how fitting for that lot to have put paid to one of life's simple pleasures) were not revoked until 1951, when the authorities fixed December 15 as an annual date on which controlled appellation wines of the new vintage could be released for sale. Growers in regions that had traditionally sold some of their new wine earlier immediately lobbied for appropriate exceptions. On November 9, 1951, permission was given for Beaujolais growers, among others, to release certain wines for sale *en primeur*— which meant, specifically, one month earlier than the standard date.

That, then, was when Beaujolais Nouveau (or Beaujolais Primeur, as some people prefer to call it) was first given official recognition. In 1985 the *primeur* release date of November 15 was changed, as far as Beaujolais was concerned, to the third Thursday of November so that arrival of the new wine in far-flung places could be tied to a weekend during which everyone could enjoy it. Sales of Beaujolais Nouveau, which had grown to almost half a million cases by 1960, now exceed six million cases a year.

~ ~ ~

The Beaujolais region lies west of the Saône, just above Lyons. Though now perceived as an appendage to Burgundy (at the northern limit, Beaujolais vines fraternize with those of the Mâconnais), the Beaujolais and Burgundy have never been, historically, connected. In fact, rivalry between the Beaujolais and the Mâconnais was so extreme in pre-Revolutionary France that it erupted regularly in drawn-out legal actions and appeals to the courts and councils of the crown.

The Beaujolais growers, protected by Lyons's powerful archbishops, had been allowed to sell that city their wine free of taxes, an advantage denied their peers of the Mâconnais, regarded as denizens of the duke of Burgundy. This snub became all the more galling to Mâcon in the seventeenth century, when improvements to an ancient road west from Belleville, the small Beaujolais port on the Saône River, across the watershed to Pouilly-sur-Loire, gave Beaujolais producers easy access to Paris, a market the Mâcon growers had worked hard to open for themselves. On convoys of barges that passed through the newly constructed Briare canal, linking the Loire and the Seine rivers, Beaujolais made its appearance in the capital.

The town councillors of Mâcon relied on the archaic configuration of the revenue system under the *ancien régime,* in desperate attempts to crush Beaujolais with taxes. But in 1694, after years of squabbling, the

mayor of Villefranche (the Beaujolais's own "capital") and his supporters were granted a ruling in their wine's favor. They won their case on a
legal nicety but had suggested anyway that the crown's income would in
fact increase at a faster rate if no additional taxes were imposed. It's the
standard argument, of course, in such situations (*plus ça change,* and all
that), but the Beaujolais growers gave weight to it by predicting that, left
alone, they would be shipping to Paris at least 8,000 hectoliters of wine
a year by 1700. Their claim proved to be incredibly modest: A report
published in 1769 shows that Beaujolais growers were by then shipping
to the city 160,000 hectoliters a year—equivalent to 1.75 million cases of
wine. (This result eventually persuaded the growers of Mâcon to drop
Pinot Noir in favor of the Gamay they had sneered at in their litigation.)

This growth of sales caused a dramatic expansion of vineyards in
eighteenth-century Beaujolais and led to the spread of a system of
sharecropping already prevalent in the area. Groups of a dozen or more
small growers each held and tended ten to twenty acres of land—both
vineyard and arable—for an owner with whom they were obliged to
share their harvest. The system still exists on some large Beaujolais
estates; I sometimes see the great casks the French call *foudres* lined up,
each identified with the name of the grower whose crop is destined to
fill it. As for the Beaujolais's privileged relationship with Lyons, that
still exists, too, but in a different and curiously modern form: Anyone
driving down the *autoroute* from Paris to the Mediterranean discovers
that there is no toll for using the stretch of road between Villefranche
and Lyons.

~ ~ ~

The Beaujolais no longer has a political boundary. Partly in the administrative *département* of Saône-et-Loire and partly in the *département* of
the Rhône, it is defined viticulturally by the French appellation laws.
Villefranche is a convenient hub from which to explain the layout of the
various appellations that make up the Beaujolais. More confusing than
the article, which distinguishes "the" Beaujolais region from Beaujolais
wine, is the use of the word *Beaujolais* to refer broadly to the wines of

the entire region; they include Beaujolais-Villages and wines of the ten *crus* as well as plain Beaujolais itself. As a result one often hears wine from the basic Beaujolais appellation referred to (as above) as "plain" Beaujolais, "simple" Beaujolais, or "ordinary" Beaujolais when it may not be plain, simple, or ordinary at all.

The twenty-two thousand acres of vineyard southwest of Villefranche where "plain" Beaujolais is produced form both the largest and the most varied of the appellations. Beaujolais-Villages is produced northwest of the town in a region of wide, undulating hills. Its fifteen thousand acres of vines lie adjacent to, and sometimes surround, the vineyards of the ten *crus,* which vary in size from Chénas, with six hundred planted acres, to Brouilly, with three thousand. Together, the *crus* comprise some thirteen thousand acres of vineyard.

Those Beaujolais-Villages hills are the last outcroppings of the Massif Central, a granite formation far older than the Alps or the Pyrenees. Millennia of rain and wind, heat and ice, have reduced them to a coarse sand that now presents a deceptive softness of contour. Though never seeming so, the hills can be both high and steep. Their soils are less homogeneous than their common profile might suggest. Granitic sand predominates, but there are everywhere gradations and mixtures. In the Beaujolais-Villages, the sand, mostly gray-colored, is often mixed with clay. At Brouilly, Fleurie, and Regnié the sand, mostly pink, is fairly pure. On the Côte de Brouilly the vines are planted on a splintered blue-black rock (reputed to be among the hardest in France) that recurs, mixed with pink granite, at Juliénas. In Morgon, there's schist beneath the upper vineyards—notably its Côte de Py—and clay lower down, and Moulin-à-Vent has deposits of manganese so heavy that in the last century they were mined commercially. The relative toughness of Moulin-à-Vent wines is thought to be connected to this presence.

～ ～ ～

As might be expected, each *cru* has distinctive characteristics. One such might be no more than a particularity of aroma—Brouilly, it is said, is grapey, while Fleurie smells of violets, Saint-Amour of peach, and

Chénas of spices. These differences are harder to pin down, however, than the sharper divisions based on body and structure. It's far easier to see that, whereas Brouilly, Côte de Brouilly, Regnié, Fleurie, Saint-Amour, and Chénas have in common their elegance and fragrant delicacy, Juliénas, Morgon, and especially Moulin-à-Vent possess greater generosity, deeper flavor, and more lasting power. Chiroubles, of which there is very little anyway, stands apart from the others: Less aromatic than some, and without the fleshiness of others, it has a lacy texture and a sleek charm.

Markets usually show a marked preference for one *cru* over another. "Lyons traditionally prefers a Beaujolais with a firm edge," Paul Jambon of the Pavillon de Chavannes on the Côte de Brouilly told me. "The Lyonnais like structure, and they don't like the aroma to be too exuberant. Lyons drinks Morgon and Moulin-à-Vent. But Paris, which appreciates lighter red wines with fresh aromas, drinks Fleurie and Brouilly. The Swiss, too, have a passion for Fleurie, which is why it is now one of the most expensive of the *crus*."

Site—*terroir*—is important everywhere in establishing the personality of a wine, but Claude Geoffray of Château Thivin, also on the Côte de Brouilly, feels it to be especially so in the Beaujolais because Gamay itself is such a low-key varietal. A Gamay wine expresses the character of the vineyard or it expresses nothing. Which is why, Geoffray says, the yield of grapes from each vine must be severely restricted and winemaking as nonintrusive as possible. With roughly 4,000 vines planted to the acre, Geoffray expects to harvest no more than one and a half pounds of grapes from each. In comparison, most California vineyards carry 650 vines to the acre, from which they rarely harvest fewer than four tons of grapes. That's about twelve pounds of fruit from each vine.

Château Thivin's *cuverie*, built against a hillside, was planned to allow its wine-making to flow without pumps but by gravity from the tanks—where the whole bunches are allowed to ferment and macerate in a manner unique to the Beaujolais—to presses below and then farther down into the cellar. Fermentation is completed in old wooden *foudres,* each with a capacity of about one thousand gallons.

In a tradition imposed by the appellation regulations, the harvest must be brought to the *cuverie* in whole bunches. There these are dumped into reception tanks, preferably no higher than they are wide. The weight of the mass crushes the bottom bunches, which begin to ferment and release carbon dioxide. It fills the crevices between the rest of the bunches, stifles the yeast, and inhibits the spread of fermentation. But even in these conditions the warmth generated affects the uncrushed bunches in ways that extract color and flavor from the grapeskins without releasing tannin (not that the Gamay grape has much). Malic acid is also substantially reduced—a reason for the softness of new Beaujolais—and the grapes' sugars are freed for a more rapid and complete fermentation later, once the bunches have been removed from the vat and crushed. First, however, they spend from three to ten days in this state of anaerobic metabolism, a process basic to the universally appealing style of Beaujolais.

~ ~ ~

Each grower handles the maceration phase differently, of course, and distortions do occur. Usually they are the result of a grower's taking a shortcut, hoping to get quality results while boosting yields, or of his allowing the success of *primeurs* to influence the way he makes a *cru* wine. Or they are an exaggeration to attract star ratings from the more-is-more school of wine critics. One technique is to heat the grapes to 60° or 70° C, thereby increasing the extraction of color, before cooling them to a temperature at which a yeast culture can be introduced. Wines made this way are round and big but lack both vivacity and personality. Another technique is to push yields to the limit, despite the risk that the fruit will then not ripen fully. A heavy hand with chaptalization—adjustment of sugar levels from sacks held ready for the purpose—and the introduction of yeasts that generate powerful, if short-lived, aromas during fermentation mask the wine's inherent deficiencies. On the other hand there are many growers—young ones especially—whose approach to winemaking is practically in step with that of their grandfathers.

Olivier Ravier, of the Domaine de la Pierre Bleue and president of the Beaujolais growers' association, says that people accept clumsy wines made with exaggerated chaptalization and monster yeasts when they lose their ability to taste and appreciate subtlety.

"French children," he told me, "once went from water to water-and-wine, to wine-and-water, and, eventually, to wine. It was part of growing up, and they learned to appreciate the taste—and the use—of wine. Now our children drink heavily advertised sugary soft drinks with phony fruit flavors. One day they learn from their friends to add alcohol to it. And eventually they leave out the soft drink. This has led to both social and economic problems. We winegrowers have difficulty tempting such impaired palates back to wine. But it's the same with food. Too much of what we eat is processed and tastes of manufactured flavors. How can we expect anyone to understand and enjoy the infinite range of tastes and aromas that real wine and real food offer? These are things one must learn in childhood."

To get to the root of the problem, Ravier and other Beaujolais growers started a program—L'Univers du Goût—for Villefranche elementary schools, which teaches children how to taste. One of the most basic lessons for very small children involves each child's bringing to school a particular vegetable—a carrot, a leek, and so on—which the class tastes and then puts in a pot for making, with the help of the teacher, a soup that they all get to eat. Gradually the lessons go deeper. A discussion on varieties of pears, for instance, will include a simple history of the fruit, an explanation of how it is cultivated, the uses for each variety, and, of course, a chance to taste and compare them.

So far, forty-four of the town's schoolteachers have taken the voluntary training course for the program, which covers all fruits, vegetables, herbs, and spices. There is a Villefranche center for the program with its own reference library, but much of the teacher training is done in the well-equipped tasting room at Ravier's vineyard. There, each session ends with a wine tasting. Ravier just smiled when I asked if that might have contributed to the program's phenomenal success. The agricultural college of the next *département* has asked for his group's assistance in starting a similar program.

~ ~ ~

Food is important in the Beaujolais: The style of cooking has a solid, country quality. The serious reputation of the Auberge du Cep in Fleurie attracts a clientele from Paris as well as Lyons, whereas the Coq au Vin in Juliénas, with its slightly more flamboyant appeal, is presently popular with the local smart set. Other restaurants with excellent—and typical—food include Chez Christian Mabeau at Odenas, elegant and welcoming and with a large shaded terrace for lunching and dining in summer; Anne de Beaujeu, a small reasonably priced hotel and restaurant in an attractively appointed former private mansion in Beaujeu; and Le Morgon, a simple-looking restaurant, up a lane away from the village of Villié-Morgon, with a wide selection of Morgon wines listed by producer.

Visitors to the area may also enjoy a tour of George Duboeuf's Hameau du Beaujolais, a transformation of the former railway station at Romanèche-Thorins. Its hour-long mixed-media overview of the region includes exhibits (among them a slow-motion film of fermentation shot with an endoscopic camera, the kind surgeons use to take a look where the eye cannot go) on everything from geology to the history of making bottles. The show ends with a wine tasting accompanied by local bread and sausage.

The chalk-clay soil of the southern Beaujolais, rich in iron, has a golden color that has earned it the name of *terres dorées,* or golden lands. The terrain is precipitously abrupt and strewn with old castles, tawny Romanesque churches, and impossible legends. The clay and the iron, especially, lend the wines here—the plain Beaujolais—a natural rusticity. Good examples are the wines from Jean-Paul Brun's Domaine des Terres Dorées and Pierre-Marie Chermette's Domaine du Vissoux at Saint-Vérand.

On this area's back roads a succession of villages, each prettier than the last, has cafés and bistros offering a simple country lunch and a

carafe of wine from the vineyard outside the window. Those looking for more refined cooking will find that too, at restaurants like the
Vieux Moulin at Alix and Les Marroniers at Lozanne. Everyone hopes,
one day, to find a corner of France, true to itself, easily accessible, but
overlooked by tourism. Here it is. Just turn right off the autoroute at
Villefranche.

Originally published as "Le Beaujolais Nouveau Est Arrivé!" in *Gourmet*,
November 1995.

The sales of Beaujolais Nouveau have passed their peak and, at two
million cases a year in 2010, are now well below half of total Beaujolais
sales. Sadly, the program started in Villefranche schools, L'Univers du
Goût, has fizzled out, but has given rise to an annual Semaine du Goût
throughout France with events for the general public as well as schools,
all intended to encourage familiarity with the taste of good, natural
food and drink.

ARMAGNAC

The Spirit of D'Artagnan

Tucked away in southwestern France between the curve of the Garonne River and the pine forests of the Landes, the Armagnac region, though hardly more than an hour from Toulouse, is reassuringly bucolic in a way that farm country today rarely is. Bright red poppies line the roadsides in summer, and hedgerows strewn with wild roses divide scattered vineyards from wheat fields and patches of sunflowers. There are no vast tracts of anything. Corn and eggplant flourish alongside pumpkins and plum trees; herds of *blondes de Gascogne* cattle graze contentedly; and in the busy jumble of farmyards, geese and ducks and chickens keep up a lively banter.

The region's past is on display, too. Roman mosaics, somnolent abbeys, and once-impregnable castles dot the landscape between one thirteenth-century *bastide* and another. On weekly market days in these half-timbered village strongholds, farmers who come to sell their fruits and vegetables, butter and cheese, eggs and foie gras take a break to gossip over coffee or a glass of wine at tables set out under the medieval arcades. Doubtless wary after generations of protecting themselves from government tax collectors, they protest that they have no money. "Our wealth," they say, "is in our cellars and on our tables."

Visitors tend to agree once they've tried a lentil terrine studded with foie gras and confit of duck, a plain roast squab with *haricots verts*, sweetbreads *à l'ancienne*, sauté of suckling lamb with fresh-shelled beans, grilled *magret* with layered potato and leek, or a soufflé of *pruneaux d'Agen* in Armagnac—a specialty of the southwest. It isn't by chance that some of the most renowned chefs of France were born and learned to cook in this region.

And there are some delicious wines that locals are happy to keep mostly for themselves—Côtes de Gascogne, Pacherenc du Vic-Bilh, Gaillac, both dry and sweet Jurançon, and the red wines from Buzet, Cahors, Côtes du Frontonnais, Madiran, and Irouléguy. Best of all, in even the simplest restaurant, there's always a glass of old Armagnac to linger over after dinner.

Armagnac has the longest history of any brandy in France. The know-how of distilling came from the Arab world (at that time, just beyond the Pyrenees) early in the thirteenth century and was used at the University of Montpellier's school of medicine to extract essences from herbs and flowers. A medical treatise published around 1310 by Vital Dufour, an Armagnac man educated at Montpellier, reveals that less than a century later this new skill was already being used to produce *aygue ardent*—brandy—from wine. Dufour describes forty ways in which brandy helps maintain good health and inspires a sense of well-being. They include the relief of toothache, an end to mental anguish, the restoration of paralyzed limbs, and the gift of courage.

Produced on a very small scale, Armagnac continued to be used mostly as medicine ("Strengthens the memory, preserves youth," claims a document of 1441) until demand for it exploded dramatically in the seventeenth century. An important part of that demand originated in the Netherlands. The Dutch, masters of the largest merchant fleet of the time, sent three or four thousand ships to France every fall to buy the season's new wine. They themselves consumed about a third of what they brought back; the rest was blended, sweetened, and fortified before being shipped out the following spring to clients in other ports of the North and Baltic seas.

Unlike the wine growers of Bordeaux, Armagnac's growers did not have easy access to the Dutch ships; they would have had to haul barrels of their wine on ox-carts to the nearest navigable rivers and the cost would have been prohibitively high. Brandy was another matter. By distilling their wine, the growers reduced its volume and increased its value, making the cost of transport less of an issue. Their production of brandy increased, and so did its use. Large armies on the move during the seventeenth century's protracted wars discovered a need for it. No doubt D'Artagnan, a native of Armagnac, and his three musketeers took their share. And so did the swelling populations of the cities. The reason was simple. There were no cork-sealed bottles then, and as wine was drawn from steadily depleted barrels, what remained was soon spoiled. When dosed with brandy, the Dutch had discovered, wine kept better and longer. And then many came to realize that brandy just by itself could be a comfort and a pleasure.

~ ~ ~

As a young man I was told I'd find it easier to understand the essential difference between Cognac and Armagnac if I'd think of the former as fine, industrially produced worsted cloth and of the latter as home-spun, handwoven Harris tweed. The contrast intended—smooth Cognac against rugged Armagnac—is now less obvious than it once was. Both brandies have evolved over the years, but Armagnac is by its very nature both idiosyncratic and diverse. It finds its champions among those who prefer the unexpected and distinctive to the prosaic and conventional.

On the face of it, Armagnac owes its diversity to the common (but by no means universal) practice of bottling each batch—sometimes each barrel—unblended, to preserve the character that develops as it ages. But that character depends on the factors that make each batch, each barrel, different to begin with. First, there is the miscellany of Armagnac soils, ranging from black sand in the extreme west to sandy clay and, eventually, to chalky clay in the east.

A decree of 1909 attempted to define these differences by dividing the region into three segments: Bas-Armagnac in the west, Haut-Armagnac in the east, and Ténarèze between them. All three have since become official sub-appellations of Armagnac. Bas-Armagnac is credited with producing the most elegant and traditional Armagnac; Haut-Armagnac produces, in certain limited areas, small quantities that are highly aromatic and sometimes quite powerful; and Ténarèze holds the middle ground. Though the most productive of the three appellations, one rarely sees the name Ténarèze on a bottle because the umbrella appellation, Armagnac, is thought to be more acceptable commercially.

The second factor affecting diversity is the grape variety—or varieties—used for the wine from which the Armagnac is distilled. In the last century, Armagnac (and Cognac) was produced almost exclusively from Folle Blanche, a white grape found elsewhere in France under other names. It's a fragrant grape but risky to grow because it leafs early and is therefore particularly vulnerable to spring frost, a constant danger in a region that lies so close to mountains. But whether used alone or as the dominant element of a blend, Folle Blanche can be relied on to give a smooth, delicately perfumed brandy. Today it is used mostly to add grace to Ugni Blanc, the most widely planted variety in the region. Ugni Blanc brings structure to a blend, but it can be austere. For balance it needs the addition of either Colombard (a grape also used in the southwest for table wine) or Baco (an important hybrid that has Folle Blanche and native American vines among its antecedents). Baco was introduced into the region in the confusion that came with phylloxera at the end of the last century and has been the foundation of some of the most extraordinary brandies produced in the Bas-Armagnac in the last fifty years. Unfortunately, the wine regulators in Paris are determined to eliminate all hybrids from France, and Baco will be banned after the year 2010. Those who rely on it are unhappy (as we all should be) but are already experimenting with other varieties permitted by the appellation regulations but not presently cultivated in the area.

Armagnac growers turned massively to Baco rather than return to Folle Blanche when they replanted after phylloxera—for a time it was the principal variety planted there—while in Cognac, the growers preferred Ugni Blanc. The differences established by robust Baco and trim Ugni Blanc probably led to those worsted and tweed analogies of years ago.

But Armagnac's reputation for sturdy idiosyncrasy is based largely on the curious method of continuous single distillation—known as *chauffe simple*—developed in and for the region in the early nineteenth century. The words "continuous distillation" bring to mind the towering columns that keep the thousands-of-necks-per-hour bottling lines of the giant spirits industry running. In fact, the Armagnacais still is no larger than an ordinary pot still: It just works differently—its process retaining aromatics that a pot still discards. The mobile version of the continuous still, the *alambic ambulant*—an ungainly contraption wheeled into the barns of small farmers who produce too little to invest in one of their own—would make Rube Goldberg proud. It clanks, gurgles, and hisses day and night until the job is finished, while those who watch over it keep up their strength with food grilled in the embers of its wood-burning stove. (One of the jolliest lunches I've ever had in Armagnac was duck legs and potatoes cooked in the heat of the *alambic ambulant* and shared with the crew as they coaxed from the still the last of the new eau-de-vie, not to be Armagnac, by law, until aged in wood for a minimum of two years.)

Chauffe double—double distillation—was once standard practice in Armagnac, as it is to this day in Cognac. It was reintroduced into the Armagnac region in the 1970s after Cognac firms began to take an interest in the area and now accounts for about 10 percent of the region's production. The large merchant-blenders, especially, often use both double and single *chauffe,* but the estates generally stick to what is now, after almost two centuries, the traditional method of the continuous still.

Claude Posternak, for example, a small distiller at the Château de Neguebouc near Préchac, is one of the majority who rely on *chauffe simple.* A newcomer (having abandoned his work as head of an advertising firm in Paris nine years ago to bring his young family to a greener life), he bought a neighboring vineyard to get himself started while he replanted one that had long been abandoned on his own property. *Chauffe double* would make his brandies smoother faster and allow him to get his revenues flowing sooner, but he wants the aromatic power that, in the long term, only *chauffe simple* can give. So he sells about a fifth of his production as unaged white eau-de-vie from single varieties to get his income kick-started each year. Sitting in his sunny yellow kitchen early last summer I could easily distinguish in the three colorless liquids in front of me the intense fragrance of Folle Blanche, the elegant severity of Ugni Blanc, and the fat, rich, weighty flavor of Colombard.

"Armagnac distilled by the *chauffe simple* is usually more aromatic," says François Heron, production director of Janneau, a *négociant* where more than half the brandy is now produced from pot stills. "It can be rough when young, but it ages well; it develops for far longer and to greater effect."

He, too, showed me three single grape varieties, but these were from the 1988 vintage, had been double distilled, and, since then, had been aged in wood. The Ugni Blanc was still rather angular in a way that seemed to relate to the impression I'd had of this variety at Posternak's house. The Colombard was round and moderately full. Its aroma, less rich than that of Posternak's white eau-de-vie, was nonetheless subtly nuanced. The third sample was of Baco, and I could make no comparison except with the other two 1988s. Against those it was fatter and had a low-key, flowery delicacy.

Jean-Pierre Gimet, a small distiller at Cazeneuve in Ténarèze, also uses both double and single *chauffe*, but he thinks that the result of either depends largely on the distiller's experience and intent. "He has to have a sixth sense. Everything to do with a still, including the ambient atmospheric pressure, is shifting continually and must be monitored closely. It's crucial to catch any possible error before it happens because there's no way to correct it later. Well, one can distill out a fault, I suppose, but that means losing the character of the brandy as well."

At the Château de Laubade in the Bas-Armagnac, one of the largest estate distilleries in the region, they distill entirely by *chauffe simple.* "Our vineyard is half Ugni Blanc and a quarter Baco," says production director Michel Bachoc. "The rest is evenly divided between Colombard and Folle Blanche. We handle each variety separately, from picking to aging. We get the new wines to the still as quickly as possible because they're fragile, and in any case it is an appellation regulation that we distill the wines before the fine particles of fermentation have settled out. Those fine lees, suspended in the wine, make a significant contribution to the aroma of the eau-de-vie. And there you have the heart of the matter. Armagnac is, essentially, a rich and complex perfume.

"And that's why we use traditional single distillation only. The vaporization is very slow—contrary to what anyone might imagine from that word 'continuous.' It preserves the wine's more elusive esters. They give the young spirit a rougher cast, but they also ensure a long and worthwhile development in wood. Distillation by *chauffe double* eliminates many of them. That's why brandies distilled by the *chauffe double* can be used in blends after three years. You must wait a minimum of five before using brandy distilled by *chauffe simple.*" For many, that represents an important cost difference.

As I talked with Bachoc we tasted his VSOP blend, made from Ugni Blanc and Folle Blanche. It was supple and elegant. The XO was suavely delicate, too. Lastly, we tried a 1978 vintage Armagnac, every bit as smooth as the others, but richer—weightier—in aroma and flavor. I murmured my appreciation. "What you're tasting there is the effect of Baco in a well-aged *chauffe simple* from Bas-Armagnac," he said.

If Baco makes such an important contribution, it's easy to see why producers resent its banishment for reasons that seem ideological rather than practical. Yet it has no place on the Domaine Boingnères, the estate thought by many to represent the peak of Armagnac quality. In proportions at odds with most other growers, the Lafitte family have more than half of their fifty-three acres planted in Folle Blanche, the ancient mainstay of Armagnac now reduced elsewhere to a supporting role. On the rest of the property there is slightly more Ugni Blanc than Colombard.

Martine Lafitte, who has run the estate since her father died a few years ago, explains. "In 1997 frost took most of our Folle Blanche, but when we have it, it gives a good result. We pick early to get good acidity—that's what carries fruit to the spirit—and press the grapes as if we were making a delicate table wine. We ferment in stainless steel or cement tanks and make our *cuvée* of the different varieties just before distilling. That way the varieties marry as they age. We make one *cuvée* of pure Folle Blanche. That is Armagnac as it was before phylloxera."

Every barrel at Domaine Boingnères remains as it comes from the still, and although two or three of them are blended from time to time to make the domaine's five-year-old Armagnac, each is bottled separately, by hand, when it is needed. I tasted a 1995 pure Folle Blanche from the wood. Though young, it was like perfumed silk. Lafitte drew a sample of the *cuvée* of 1995 so that I could see the assertive, angular difference the other varieties make. We went on to taste the 1990 Folle Blanche, and then, the 1985; the first showing just hints of amber and the second already deepening in color. The 1990 was less suave than the 1995, but the 1985 was the most gentle. "For the first few years, the new spirit develops flavor and depth," she said. "Then it smoothes out and acquires finesse and delicacy."

Michel Bachoc had told me that as an Armagnac ages the wood plays an increasingly imposing role. "When an Armagnac is young—six years old, say—it owes perhaps 30 percent of its effect to the wine, 30 percent to the method of distillation, and 40 percent to the wood. By the time an Armagnac is twenty-five years old, the wood will have determined its style to an extent that overwhelms—though never entirely eliminates—the other two."

So I understood when Lafitte explained her insistence on using only the white oak from a nearby forest for her barrels—"the trees and the vines have grown together"—and why she is scrupulously careful in her choice of the staves from which they are made.

Marc Darroze, who now directs the business founded near Villeneuve-de-Marsan by his father, Francis, in 1973, also insists on aging his Armagnac in barrels made from the local white oak. Francis Darroze had already spent a lifetime buying from small producers in the Bas-Armagnac for his family's restaurant at Villeneuve-de-Marsan when he decided to set up as a trader in single vineyard, single vintage Armagnac of the finest quality. The stocks he acquired for aging, augmented by the continuing purchases of his son, now constitute an unequaled resource for top restaurants and retailers all over France.

The collection is a national treasure, boasting Armagnac from most years back to the 1940s, and some even older. There are often as many as a dozen vintages from the stills of small producers who have long since disappeared. Among them are many made purely or predominantly from Baco, including some of venerable age produced from vines planted in the early years of the century and torn out decades ago. Entire vineyards exist now only in the captivating and heady aroma of the Armagnac that was produced from them. With its suggestions of walnuts, dried fruits, and honey, and insistent reminder of sun on ripe figs, it's an aroma that is, near enough, a distillation of the region itself.

Originally published as "Armagnac: The Elixir of d'Artagnan" in *Gourmet,* December 1998.

Since this was written, the appellation law controlling Armagnac has been amended to allow the continued use of Baco vines in the production of Armagnac.

LES CHEVALIERS DU TASTEVIN

Of the ten thousand members of Burgundy's Confrérie des Chevaliers du Tastevin, two thousand live in North America. From Halifax to San Diego they are attached to groups known rather forbiddingly as *sous-commanderies,* the oldest and probably the largest of which was founded in New York in 1940.

No doubt more than a few Americans will be among the five or six hundred *chevaliers* and guests, black-tied and robed *du soir,* who will sit down on the evening of June 9 to dine at candlelit and flower-bedecked tables in the twelfth-century wine cellar of the Château du Clos de Vougeot. According to the calendar of the Confrérie, they will be gathered there for its annual *chapître* in honor of the flowering of the vine. In fact, Burgundy's vines, heeding no calendar, are sometimes disobligingly unpunctual, and so it is just possible that those assembled will be anticipating rather than celebrating the blossom in the vineyards. Either way, their enthusiasm, you can be sure, will be great.

A *tastevin* (the *s* is pronounced in English but is silent in French) is a Burgundian taster, a shallow silver dish perhaps three inches across with a thumb grip at the side to give it the misleading appearance of an ashtray. The slightly convex bottom and the traditional pattern of dimples and fluting on the sides are more than decorative: Their refraction of light through a few drops of wine reveals secrets of quality and style to the initiated. An old, family *tastevin* wrapped in cotton cloth is sure to be in the pocket of any Burgundian winegrower, merchant, or broker. It is for his or her professional use, of course, but it is also a sort of discreet talisman that the possessor would be unhappy to lose, or even to have left behind when leaving home.

The original intention of the founders of the Confrérie had been neither more nor less than to foster an occasional evening of good cheer to amuse their friends. Georges Faiveley, a wine merchant from Nuits-Saint-Georges, and Camille Rodier, then president of the local tourist office, had the idea in the early thirties. Times were difficult. Economic depression and the social upheaval of World War I had not helped Burgundy's wines. The benign art of the table that is based on good food and wine as enhancements of the company of others rather than as ends in themselves was in decline. "As our wines are not selling," they concluded, "let's ask our friends to come and drink them with us."

In the seventeenth and eighteenth centuries, drinking clubs and fraternities were as common in France as in England. In Burgundy the Ordre de la Boisson, with statutes written in verse, was founded in 1703. Its rule of punctuating gastronomic evenings with music and singing was carried over by a colonel of the 12th Hussars when, in 1812, he revived the order as the Confrérie des Francs Buveurs Bourguignons to enliven his retirement in Dijon. A manuscript on which he had recorded its procedures and formalities was unearthed by Faiveley and Rodier, who used them as a model for their new fraternity. Its first "chapter" took place in an old cellar in Nuits-Saint-Georges in 1934 and followed by and large the patterns retrieved from the Francs Buveurs, sparged with additional ceremony lifted from Molière's *Le Malade Imaginaire* and illuminated by a pageantry of scarlet and gold costumes loosely adapted from the robes and caps of the pre-Revolutionary French parliamentarians. It made quite a show.

Even in those early days the Confrérie had used the same sense of purpose and quality in picking its guests as its members used in picking their grapes for a good *cuvée*. Photographs of prewar *chapîtres* show leaders of the gastronomic world—André Simon, founder of the International

Wine and Food Society, for example, and Curnonsky, *"prince des gastronomes"*—breaking bread with key members of the French government, of the Académie Française, and of the Paris diplomatic corps. In 1937 the United States's ambassador to France, William Bullitt, was inducted into the Confrérie. (It was much later, at a *chapître* of the Confrérie in October 1951, that Curnonsky gave new life to Brillat-Savarin's rather lugubrious declaration that a meal without cheese was like a beautiful woman with only one eye.)

Over the years, *tastevin* in hand and possibly tongue in cheek, the Confrérie has succeeded in winning an ever-widening circle of influential friends, not just for Burgundy but for France itself. Those celebrated in government, business, science, and the arts have been delighted, and more than a little flattered, to be invited to a *chapître* of the Confrérie at Clos de Vougeot; to eat and drink sumptuously; to shout, clap, and wag fingers to the rhythm of the *ban bourguignon*. A guest at a past chapter might have been seated beside Alfred Hitchcock or Ingrid Bergman; Chancellor Helmut Kohl or the Comtesse de Paris, wife of the Pretender to the French throne; Mstislav Rostropovich or Sir Christopher Leaver, Lord Mayor of London; Peter Ustinov or Yehudi Menuhin; the president of Volkswagen or the chairman of Crédit Lyonnais; the Netherlands minister of finance or the British ambassador. Here might have been Mary McCarthy, there General Norstad; here a prince of Sweden, and there an American astronaut, a French Olympic equestrian, a German philosopher. So broad has been the reach of the Confrérie that, in not much more than half a century, it has become a French national institution.

～ ～ ～

The *chapîtres* continued to be held regularly in that old cellar beneath Nuits-Saint-Georges until the outbreak of World War II, but Etienne Camuzet, owner of the Château du Clos de Vougeot and from the first a supporter of the Confrérie, occasionally made the vast wine cellar there available for gala events, when the *caveau* in Nuits-Saint-Georges would have been impossibly small. The château had long been under separate ownership from the vineyards that surround it, and, after the liberation of France in 1944, Camuzet offered it to a group of the *chevaliers,* himself among them, with the specific intention of leasing it to the Confrérie. Classified as a *monument historique,* the château has long been what the French call an *haut-lieu,* not just of Burgundy but of France. For two hundred years now, all French troops passing the Clos de Vougeot are obliged by tradition to present arms. In terms both of its form—majestically solid, elegantly severe—and its history, it is symbolic of the two forces that have shaped Burgundy: the region's agricultural wealth and an intellectual brilliance that in the late Middle Ages radiated throughout all of Europe from the monasteries at Cîteaux and Cluny.

Clos de Vougeot's origin lies in a scrap of land—less than an acre—given to the monks of Cîteaux early in the twelfth century. (The Cistercians began as a community of extreme ascetics, devoting their time to prayer and rigorous field labor in reaction to what they saw as the soft monastic life practiced elsewhere at the time. They had settled in a desolate and swampy area a few miles from Nuits-Saint-Georges in 1098.) By the fourteenth century, as the order prospered, the Cistercians had expanded their holding to 125 acres of vines, the largest single vineyard in Burgundy. In 1336 they enclosed it within a wall—hence, *Clos* de Vougeot. Of the original buildings they erected there in 1150, the vat hall and the wine cellar—a stone barn rather than an underground chamber and now the dramatic setting for the Confrérie's dinners—are still standing. The better-known buildings visible from the road and more often seen in photographs and drawings were built in the mid-sixteenth century and judiciously restored around the turn of the nineteenth.

～ ～ ～

Each *chapître* dinner—there are seventeen of them every year—is timed with the precision of a rocket launching. I quote from Lucien Boitouzet's *Histoire de la Confrérie:*

8:10 P.M.   The first white wine is served

8:15 P.M.   Trumpets and hunting horns

8:20 P.M. The first speaker gives the Rabelaisian grace

8:30 P.M. The waiters enter with the first dish

8:40 P.M. Trumpets and the entrance of the Cadets de
Bourgogne ... and so on until ...

11:20 P.M. The Cadets de Bourgogne depart

11:25 P.M. Coffee, *marc,* and *prunelle* are served

11:30 P.M. Orchestra

11:40 P.M. Entrance of the Grand Conseil, and the ceremony
for the induction of new members begins

Attendance at a *chapître* of the Confrérie is, clearly, not to be undertaken
lightly.

To say that the Cadets de Bourgogne are a group of Burgundian
folk singers is like describing the Compagnons de la Chanson as a bar-
bershop quartet. Though they appear dressed in the black caps and
aprons of Burgundian cellarmen, the Cadets (a term to be understood
figuratively; many are grandfathers) are from numerous walks of life.
They jolly the evening along with ballads, old Burgundian drinking
choruses, and whatever else might seem appropriate. Not so long ago,
for a group of Houston astronauts, they donned ten-gallon white hats
to render "The Yellow Rose of Texas," and for Yehudi Menuhin they
sang a three-part chorale composed for the occasion by the director of
Dijon's music conservatory.

The group began, under their earlier name of Chanteurs Bourguignons, back in the 1920s, when a dozen or so men within the Cercle
Rameau, a Dijon choir, all of them as partial to wine as to music, would
meet over a bottle to sing. They were soon a part of every wine event
and celebration of the region and performed regularly at the Caveau
Bourguignon in Dijon. There they expanded their repertoire by introducing new songs, often Burgundian poetry set to music and harmo-
nized for them by the talented assistant director of the Cercle. Their
presence at the Confrérie's first *chapître* in 1934 was as inevitable as the

wine in the glasses, and so it has since remained as one generation of Cadets has replaced another.

But singing is thirsty work. When the Cadets break to moisten their throats, their Burgundian *confrères* take over and bring the assembly up to date with satirical news and stories of Burgundy and of the world beyond its borders. The pace is fast, the wit is sharp, nothing is sacred. The seemingly contradictory French qualities of measure and hilarity, charm and mockery, grace and ribaldry, pursue and complement each other. Both an urbane Molière and an earthy Rabelais would feel at home at a *chapître*. So would a worldly Talleyrand, the master statesman who lost neither time nor ground in adroitly managing his career from the reign of Louis XVI to the revolutionary government's and from Napoleon's to the restored Louis XVIII's. At the Congress of Vienna he is alleged to have said that the art of diplomacy is largely the successful deployment of a good cook and a battery of saucepans. Had he added "and a cellar of good Burgundy" he would have nailed the Confrérie's formula pretty well. Because it must be said that the delicious wine and the good-natured songs and the funny stories rest on the foundation of an impeccable kitchen.

The Confrérie originally relied on outside chefs, usually a local restaurateur, for its banquets. Lucien Boitouzet explains: "At the beginning there was a mobile kitchen, which was in itself a challenge. The food was cooked in the kitchens of the Croix-Blanche restaurant in Nuits-Saint-Georges and then transported in vans to the Château du Clos de Vougeot. An unexpected bump in the road could upset the sauces. Should the vans be late, the organizers had to improvise a speech to entertain the waiting guests . . . "

The château's medieval kitchen would have been perfect for roasting a whole ox but not for preparing more subtle dishes. A new kitchen was finally installed in 1953, however, and in 1956 Georges Garin, the new owner of the Croix-Blanche, raised the standard of Confrérie dinners immeasurably. (Garin left in 1960 to go to Paris. The restaurant he opened near Notre Dame, Chez Garin, quickly earned two rosettes from *Michelin* and for more than a decade, until he semiretired to the south of France, was one of the most distinguished, fashionable, and successful restaurants in Paris.)

Garin's successor at the Croix-Blanche, Jean Fargeau, accepted the challenge of maintaining the standard. When he left in 1968, the Confrérie hired a full-time chef of its own, with two *sous-chefs* and a kitchen staff of some twelve others to support him. Harry Yoxall in his book *The Wines of Burgundy* gives the menu of the dinner Fargeau prepared for the 1967 Chapître du Printemps, at which he was promoted to *commandeur* in the Confrérie. It is impossible to convey in translation the Rabelaisian flavor of the original French, but the list of wines and dishes alone suggests the style of a Chevaliers du Tastevin dinner:

> Cold suckling pigs in jelly and parsleyed ham served with strong Dijon mustard and Bourgogne Aligoté '64 from Magny-les-Villers
>
> Truffled soufflés of pike Nantua with Puligny-Montrachet, Les Combettes, '64
>
> A fricassee of young cockerels and morels, Beaune '64
>
> Baked gammon, Nuits Clos de la Maréchale '64
>
> Cheeses, Clos de la Roche '62
>
> Strawberries from Meuilly served *en Melba*

I had enjoyed several of Fargeau's dinners as a guest at various *chapîtres,* but by the time I was myself inducted as a *chevalier* of the Confrérie in 1981 his toque had passed to Hubert Hugot, the chef who now presides over the kitchens at Vougeot. The occasion was the Chapître de la Saint Hubert, always the first dinner of December, which is dedicated to the patron saint of hunters and is preceded by a mass at the old village church of Gilly-lès-Cîteaux. The note in my diary reads:

> Chapître de St. Hubert, began with mass at Gilly church, a hunting horn sextet, and a blessing of dogs. Priest said his church usually too big: The St.

Hubert mass was only day in the year he wished it bigger. We were six hundred, not including the dogs. Reassembled later in courtyard of Vougeot, decorated with huge fir trees that seemed to be growing there, transforming it into a forest glade. By torchlight, a stag (actually a skin filled with chunks of meat) was given to the dogs. Dogs obviously already too well fed and not much interested. Endless hunting calls on the horns. Bitterly cold, but cups of hot chicken broth handed round. Inside, brilliantly organized, vastly entertaining and superb dinner.

Would I be pushing it to quote the menu?

Roulade of foie gras with a Bourgogne Aligoté of the Hautes-Côtes de Nuits

Biscuit of salmon [a cream of salmon mounted like a soufflé and nothing to do with biscuits as we understand the term] with Meursault-Chevalières '78

Chicken Gaston-Gérard with Côtes de Nuits-Villages '77 [Gaston-Gérard was a minister of tourism, the first member of a French government to be made a *chevalier* of the Confrérie. I wish I could remember how he cooked his chicken, but I can't; I know the sauce was based on Dijon mustard, but the details are lost in a happy blur.]

Haunch of venison *grand veneur* with Chambolle-Musigny Premier Cru '74

Cheeses with Latricières-Chambertin '74

Pears poached in red wine, with petits fours

Wines served at *chapître* dinners are identified by no more than the label of the Confrérie, are selected twice a year, and are drawn mostly from wines already submitted blind for the approval of an independent jury now assembled twice a year at the Château du Clos de Vougeot to assign the right of *tastevinage*. The mix of the roughly two hundred jurors varies somewhat from session to session but includes wine professionals, restaurateurs, officials of government departments concerned with wine, and specialist writers, as well as connoisseurs at large. Never are officials or members of the Grand Conseil of the Confrérie included, and the work is divided so that the jurors taste in groups of five or six and no one has to judge more than fifteen to eighteen wines.

A wine that is approved—*tasteviné*—by a jury is allowed to carry the boldly decorative arms of the Chevaliers du Tastevin in association with the name of the grower or of the merchant who bottled it. As a support it is less important, perhaps, to growers and merchants with established international reputations. But the insignia gives the consumer the guarantee that the wine of a small or unknown grower is worthy of attention. It can even help a well-known merchant when he is offering a wine from an unfamiliar appellation. The insignia of the Confrérie encourages a consumer who might otherwise have hesitated to take a risk.

It should go without saying that any wine submitted must be from Burgundy, but it must also be of a specific appellation and of a single vintage. Jurors are expected to judge a wine by asking themselves whether it accurately corresponds to type for the appellation and vintage given. They must be confident that it will mature well—otherwise the Confrérie's label could be discredited. And they should be sufficiently impressed by the wine to feel they would be proud to serve it at their own tables. The tastings are not competitive, and no medals are awarded. Jurors are not expected to submit notes on the wines they approve, but they are required to give a specific reason when refusing a wine the privilege of the Confrérie's label.

This judging activity of the Chevaliers is the one most in the public eye. Bottles bearing the arms of the Confrérie can now be seen on wine lists all over the world. The growing value of such endorsement has led to a steady increase every year in the number of applications for *tastevinage*. In 1950, the year of the first jury, 133 wines were submitted and 103 accepted. In 1987 the number of wines submitted to the jury had increased more than tenfold to 1,429, and 773 were accepted.

Through the *tastevinage,* one might say, the Confrérie des Chevaliers du Tastevin has been able to extend its reach and its chances of making even more friends for Burgundy and for France. In a way, every bottle with the Confrérie's coat of arms carries the message of the Chevaliers du Tastevin. Of those who have been touched more directly, by being honored at Vougeot, none has responded more aptly than Maurice Chevalier when promoted from *chevalier* to *grand officier* at a *chapître* at the Château du Clos de Vougeot in October 1960. In thanking the Chevaliers du Tastevin and their guests assembled in that great wine cellar, he said, "My profession, ladies and gentlemen, has been since childhood to be a sort of commercial traveler for French friendship. In other words it was my job to make friends for my country wherever I went, rather like the wines of France." And rather like, he could have added, the Chevaliers du Tastevin.

Originally published as "Les Chevaliers du Tastevin" in *Gourmet*, June 1990.

JEREZ DE LA FRONTERA

Sherry and Tapas

Some years ago an opinion poll had uncovered the fact that though wine (presumably table wine) had now overtaken Sherry as the most popular drink in Britain, Sherry still appealed most to mature, "top" people, especially those who lived in the shires of the south and west of England and on the wide flat farms of East Anglia, a region where I spent my entire childhood without ever once feeling warm. (Copenhagen, the only windbreak between the Russian steppes and eastern England, is not very effective for the purpose.)

In England, Sherry is not just something that one consumes. At one level, I suppose, it carries an aura of petty gentility, but to balance that Sherry has associations of urbanity, of donnish civility, and, above all, of the well ordered, albeit old-fashioned, domestic life. In England Sherry is the symbol of hospitality at home. It is as right to offer a guest a glass of Sherry as it is wrong, somehow, to order one in a pub. "Will you have some Sherry?" is still a common, polite way to propose a casual drink even though it is understood that a guest is equally welcome to a gin and tonic or a glass of beer.

The name of the wine is a corruption of Jerez and was first recorded in English late in the seventeenth century. But as words, particularly then, often circulated for some time before they found their way into print, it is likely to have been in colloquial use long before. Sherry started, and starts, life as a white wine produced in an austere region of Andalusia in southwestern Spain close to the sea and confined between the Guadalquivir and Guadalete rivers. The three Sherry towns of Jerez de la Frontera, Puerto de Santa María, and Sanlúcar de Barrameda, about twelve miles from each other, form a triangle that encloses much of the best vineyard land.

I said *starts* as a white wine because Sherry is as much a result of the art of man as it is a consequence of nature. It is nearly thirty years since I was first sent to Jerez to learn about both. I had a small scholarship from the London Wine Trade Club and a modest inheritance from my grandmother to sustain me. Today's jets swoop down to the south of Spain in a couple of hours, but in the early fifties propeller planes had to stop for refueling in Bordeaux and Madrid. From Seville there was a long drive, and I eventually arrived after midnight to discover, to my northern amazement, groups of men still drinking and talking at tables in front of the bars and cafés of the Calle Larga as if they intended to remain all night, while streams of people, young and old, crowded the narrow sidewalk. Needless to say, I joined them, and six o'clock seemed to arrive as soon as my head touched the pillow. When do the Spanish sleep? Not in the afternoon, whatever the popular mythology. In Jerez they drank Sherry and nibbled on *tapas* until lunch at three. From five to eight there was often work to do, and from nine until eleven there was more Sherry and *tapas* before dinner. Theater and movies started at midnight.

The bitter coffee and sweet rolls of a Spanish breakfast revived and consoled me, and I reported for work at Mackenzie & Co., a small independent Sherry shipper now absorbed by Harvey's. Ramiro Fernandez-Gao, the managing director, was waiting for me in the tasting room, in front of him a line of tulip-shaped *copitas,* each with an ounce or two of liquid that ranged from almost colorless to a dark chocolate brown. Before we started to taste together he explained that when the juice of the Palomino grapes finished fermenting, each butt of wine—in Jerez referred to as *mosto* (grape juice) until a year old—began to acquire a character of its own. Identifying that character, encouraging its development, and successfully blending it to a constant style that could be shipped under a recognized label from year to year without variation was the role of the Sherry shipper.

The process starts when the foreman of the *bodega* checks every butt of new wine, drawing a sample with the aid of his *venencia,* a narrow silver cup at the end of a flexible wand of whalebone. Wines that are light, balanced, and clean are distinguished by a short stroke of chalk, a *raya.* Two *rayas* indicate a wine with less promise (between one and two there is a demi-grade, *raya y punto*), and three *rayas* mark wines that are harsh or inelegant, most often distilled for brandy.

The foreman looks for *flor,* the most important and distinctive influence in the making of Sherry. *Flor* is a yeast that grows on the surface of the wine in spring and autumn. Butts are left with generous air space above the wine to encourage it, but the spores are selective and develop most readily on wines with a light, elegant style. In those a veil spreads quickly and soon looks like a layer of lumpy cream. Pliny, almost two thousand years ago, recognized that this velvety growth was not to be confused with the vinegar microbe. On the contrary, *flor* protects the wine from any vinegar attack, diminishes volatile acidity, and greatly increases the nutlike esters and aldehydes that we recognize as the typical Sherry fragrance.

Once racked off their heavy lees into other casks, wines classified with one *raya* are again checked for their *flor* growth, essential to the satisfactory development of Fino-type Sherry. If the *flor* is strong and the wine delicate, the alcohol is marginally adjusted to the optimum level, between 14.5 and 15.5 percent by volume, the ideal strength to encourage further growth. If the *flor* is weak or the wine less delicate, the alcohol is adjusted beyond 15.5 percent to discourage further growth of *flor,* a move that will direct the wine toward the Oloroso type. The *raya* with *flor* is now further distinguished by a small stroke sprouting from the top of the larger one like a primitive palm tree, and the wine becomes known, in fact, as *palma.* Here, then, is the first parting of the ways: *palma* and *raya,* one with *flor,* the other without; the first destined for light Finos, the second, for more full-bodied Olorosos.

As Finos age they darken from straw to gold and take on a pungent, complex aroma. Olorosos acquire a deep amber color and aromatic flavor. Each, in its natural, unblended state, is quite dry. Sweetness, when required, is added to a blend at the last moment through judicious use of *vinos dulces,* special wines made from Moscatel or Pedro Ximénez grapes. Color, too, is adjusted through the use of minute quantities of wine made from grape juice concentrated in huge copper cauldrons, dark and spicy.

With this basic framework Ramiro Fernandez-Gao introduced me to the twenty or more samples on the tasting bench. They started with a young wine that had barely finished fermentation and could still develop in any direction: perhaps through a young *palma,* eventually becoming a mature Fino; or through a young *raya,* with the possibility of becoming an Oloroso of great age. Then came a series of Finos, ending with those that had rounded out with age and acquired the style known as Amontillado. Amontillado, unfortunately, is a name often abused. It should describe those Finos that have acquired, with age, something of the round, earthy style of the Montilla wines produced a hundred miles or so northeast of Jerez. But they acquire that quality along with others, notably a depth of flavor and viscosity that only full maturity can give—slowly. By its very nature a genuine Amontillado is costly to produce. Inexpensive blends, with color carefully adjusted and flavor judiciously balanced, might be satisfactory enough, but they can give no idea of what a true, aged Amontillado can be. To those who have never tasted one, it is a revelation.

As a bridge to the *rayas* and Olorosos, Ramiro had included a *palo cortado,* a rare changeling Sherry that combines the aroma of an Amontillado and the body and flavor of an Oloroso. As we tasted Olorosos of increasing age I could see how their flavor deepened with the years to a level that the palate could not accept, eventually reaching an intensity that seemed to burn. Such wines need the soothing presence of *vino dulce,* or must be used only in small amounts to give complexity to a blend. For the most part we worked with the nose alone, but, as the session was intended to teach, every wine was also tasted, often two or three times to get the differences clearly fixed in my mind. We finished by tasting unblended examples of *vinos dulces* and aged *vino de color.* It was an exhausting start.

~ ~ ~

There was to be a reward for my effort. The last big fight of the season was to take place that afternoon in the Seville bullring. Swept off along the dusty highway without discussion, I had no time to ask myself whether a bullfight was something to relish or not. We ate lunch in Seville at the Hotel Madrid. I have never been back, but I fantasize against all probability that it is still there unchanged. Built like a Moorish palace, its façade glittering with multicolored tiles on a narrow side street, and its cloistered interior a lush, tropical garden, the Madrid at that time was popular with the Spanish movie world. We sipped our Sherry under the shady arcade of the patio while actors with somber Byronic faces gestured melodramatically and actresses, softly rustling silk dresses in clouds of perfume, arched their heads gracefully, a posture neces-sary, perhaps, to support the weight of their extravagant eyelashes. I was young and impressionable, and they seemed to me to be infinitely exotic.

The *corrida* was an exhilarating spectacle, despite its uglier passages. Ramiro kindly explained the language and tradition of the ring, the sequence of moves, the ritual. For a moment, as the matador played the bull to show his complete control, the band struck up a *paso doble,* and the crowd threw an *olé* of encouragement and admiration at each turn of the cape, I felt myself part of an audience that had been sitting in that ring (or another) for several thousand years watching bulls, acrobats, and bravura.

We returned to Jerez to dine late at the Fernandez-Gao home, where I made the acquaintance of a typical Jerez *crema,* richer in color and taste than the usual *crème caramel* because the egg whites used for fining the wines leave huge quantities of yolks for cooking, and in Jerez they find their way into just about everything. I suppose cholesterol hadn't been invented.

At seven the next morning I was in the *bodega* and ready to learn about the *solera* system of blending Sherry. "The basis of the system," Ramiro explained, "is that a small quantity of suitable young wine, blended with a larger quantity of older wine, will in a short time be absorbed into the style of the older wine. It will be easier to understand," he said, "if you imagine ten butts of Sherry blended and aged to a certain required style. It would be very difficult, if not impossible, to replace those butts with wine from later vintages and expect that there would be no appreciable difference."

The problem is avoided by not selling off the ten butts, one at a time, but by selling a butt drawn in small quantities from each of the ten and filling the ullages with quantities drawn from a second rank of ten butts, slightly younger, ready for this very purpose. The second rank, in turn, is filled from ten other butts, and so on back to selected one-year-old wines chosen for their style to enter the "scales" of this particular system, *palma* or *raya,* as appropriate for Fino or Oloroso. The series of preparatory scales in the system is known collectively as a *criadera,* best translated as "nursery"; the final scale, the row of butts from which the wine is drawn for blending or bottling, is known as the *solera,* or "foundation." On a blackboard Ramiro drew a diagram with scales of butts stacked one upon another, pointing to them as he explained again how Sherry would be transferred, a little at a time, from one scale to another as the Sherry aged and as the *solera* of the system needed replenishment.

When I seemed to understand the theory, he explained that in practice the different scales of a *criadera* might be widely separated in different sections of the *bodega;* that a *solera* providing the basis for a popular brand of Sherry might have several hundred butts in each scale of its *criadera;* and that the final stage, the *solera* itself of a particular system, might be both a source of wine for a blend and the initiating source for the *criadera* of yet another *solera* system, aging some of the wine to an even higher level.

Finos, he told me, present special problems. By law no Sherry can be sold before it is three years old, but Finos, to retain their freshness during that period, must be moved constantly and rapidly through a *solera* system to keep the *flor* refreshed. Because the moves are frequent, the quantities each time need to be small so as not to change the style of wine in each butt. And because the process must continue over such a long time for the wine to conform truly to the required style of the *solera*, a Fino *criadera* needs many scales with many butts in each. There is much labor in producing a mature Fino.

The relationship between volume of sales and its demands on the *solera* systems in any *bodega* is crucial. Sudden, large shipments would deplete the *soleras* and *criaderas* too quickly, and, even if quality didn't decline, the styles of each *solera* could suddenly change. Recognizing that, the Spanish appellation law for Sherry, unlike any other, restricts a *bodega* to sell no more than 40 percent of its stock in any one year.

Wines drawn from a single *solera*, however, are rarely bottled and shipped without further blending. A *solera* might provide the basis of a particular blend, but added to it will be a proportion of wine from a second *solera*, perhaps, or some young wine not yet part of a *solera*. The formula for making each standard blend for shipment might require the addition of Pedro Ximénez wine to adjust sweetness or *vino de color* to reach a standard hue. My morning ended with some practical work in the tasting room, learning how to use the various *soleras* and other wines to match samples sent from England and Holland for price quotations.

~ ~ ~

Gradually my days took on a Spanish measure. In free time I explored the narrow streets between the Calle Larga and the Alcázar, the old Moorish citadel of Jerez. I roamed the undulating vineyards planted in the improbably white *albariza* soil of Jerez Superior. I walked in blazing sun to visit the town's remote Carthusian monastery. For a short time I was sent to work with another shipper in Puerto de Santa María in a *bodega* that specialized in Finos. (While there I lodged in an old hotel where at three every morning a servant arrived to light a small wood-burning stove in my bathroom so that I could have hot water at six. I offered to bathe at night to make life simpler for them, but they wouldn't hear of it.) Closer to the ocean, with cooler temperatures, Puerto de Santa María shippers emphasize their Fino and Amontillado Sherries, which do well there. But their difference from the Finos of Jerez is barely perceptible when both are compared to the Finos of Sanlúcar de Barrameda, the third of the Sherry towns, on the estuary of the Guadalquivir. There the wines have a light, brisk pungency that sets them apart. Manzanillas (as they are called) of Sanlúcar are made from Palomino grapes picked at least two weeks before the general harvest. Partly because of this premature picking and partly the result of cool sea air over the estuary, Manzanilla has unusual zest and fragrance. And then the alcohol of Manzanilla is slightly lower than that of other Fino Sherries, an aid, perhaps, to preserving delicacy and maintaining a penetrating aroma.

Manzanilla was at its best on Juan's jetty at Sanlúcar. Juan is now dead, alas, and the fishing boats unload a mile away. But in those days the fishermen landed their catch on the beach below, and it was understood that the best was reserved for him. While waiting at rickety wooden tables in the salty air, his lucky customers would watch the fish, still palpitating, on their way to the kitchen in his small house across the street. With a bowl of small green olives or a dish of prawns, a platter of fried octopus rings or morsels of swordfish to stave off hunger and a bottle of Manzanilla on ice to help generate patience, the time passed quickly.

Manzanilla—and other Finos, too—must stand alone. No matter how skilled the blender, he cannot add finesse or delicacy if either is missing. To me, it is the essence of Sherry, and the one that most reminds me of Spain.

Originally published as "Jerez de la Frontera: Sherry and Tapas" in *Gourmet,* November 1980.

MALMSEY

A Greek Classic

There had been violent storms on Crete all week. One morning at Rethymno the shopkeepers had had to flush out a muddy stream flooding their shops, and on another the tiny harbor had been a great bobbing mass of tables and chairs blown into the water from the quayside cafés. The rain on the day we drove from Agios Nikolaos to Sitia, near the eastern tip of the island, had been too much for the windshield wipers. Almost blindly we followed the water-slicked road through mountains that rose sheer from the seabed. The taped voice of Fleurie Dadonaki, one of the most gifted interpreters of Greek ballads and usually such a joy to hear, merely added to our sense of melancholy. Only those familiar with the Mediterranean in winter know how wet, how bone-chilling, and how sad it can be.

We were on our way to the wine cellar at Sitia's Union of Agricultural and Wine Producers Cooperative to taste the dry, slightly tannic Sitia wine—neither quite red, as it turned out, nor quite tawny—made from the local Liátiko grape. Sitia is one of Crete's four official wine appellations (the others are Peza, Archanes, and Dafnes, all in the mountainous center of the island), but most of the wine produced around the town is simple table wine. That is true of Crete generally. Though the island produces 20 percent of all Greek wine, the bulk of it, and especially the red, is blended from two or more of the island's long-established varieties and sold with neither appellation nor fuss. It appears under brand names—Minos Palace, Cavaliere, that sort of thing—likely to appeal to tourists who, in summer, crowd the *tavernas* of Chania and Elounda.

A different, and ancient, tradition of Cretan wine is only now fumbling its way toward a renaissance after being all but extinguished under the more than two centuries of Ottoman administration that came to a straggling close at the end of the last century. In the late Middle Ages, Sitia, like Rethymno and Heraklion, other ports on the island's north shore, had been famous for the production of Malmsey, a wine that had made Venice rich and England happy. It had probably resembled, at the very least, similar wines that had been produced on Crete from time immemorial. I had heard of attempts to revive it and had already tasted one produced on a limited scale at the Cooperative of Kastelli Kissamos, at the opposite end of the island. It was dark amber, with the smoky *rancio* of an old, dry Oloroso Sherry.

Yorgos Kounoulakis, the Sitia cooperative's oenologist, confirmed that he too was experimenting with such a wine, fermenting separately any batches of grapes with particularly high sugars and then adding unfermented grape juice and brandy to sweeten and fortify the result. The first quantity that he had produced in commercial volume was aging in 120-gallon puncheons in a cellar. At Kastelli Kissamos they had placed their puncheons of aging wine in a shed, deliberately exposing them to temperatures ranging from 40° F in winter to 140° F in summer. The Sitia wine was a rosy amber, much lighter in color than the wine I had tasted at Kastelli Kissamos. It had a mild and unobtrusive sweetness and an aroma and flavor that made me think of a confit of grapes. The wines were quite different, one from the other, and I could not know which, if either, came even close to the taste of medieval Malmsey.

But the question intrigued me. I found it hard to accept that a tradition of winemaking, having survived thousands of years, could, in two hundred, be lost even to folk memory—no matter how repressive the regime. Cretan wine had been distinguished for as long as we have records of its existence. Its reputation in imperial Rome was as great as it had been in classical Greece five centuries earlier. And at least a thousand years before that the Minoans had produced wine in the same central zones where the new appellations have recently been established.

Ancient myths suggest that the island had been a stepping-stone for the vine on its way from Asia to Europe. The story of Zeus carrying off to Crete the daughter of the king of Phoenicia, Europa, is usually illustrated, for example, with the god in the form of a bull and Europa, on his back, carrying a branch heavy with grapes. And then there is the legend of Dionysus, choosing as his bride Ariadne, daughter of King Minos of Crete. The huge wine crocks built into underground chambers at Knossos and Phaestos confirm the importance of wine implicit in the myths; one of the Minoan buildings excavated at Vathípetro, south of Archanes, revealed numerous wine jars and a press—clearly it had been a winery.

What had that ancient wine been like? Homer, entertainer (the successful screenwriter of his day) rather than historian, painted everything larger than life. Dare we take his descriptions of wine literally when they were almost always qualified by words and phrases suggesting honeyed sweetness? Was he writing of wine in general or only of wine at its most heroic? His descriptions of wines are at least consistent with his account of grapes left in the sun to dry before pressing. And that seemed still to have been the practice when we again become aware of Cretan wine at the start of the thirteenth century.

It was the time when, as her share of the spoils of Byzantium, Venice had grabbed Crete along with some smaller islands and a string of ports useful as trading stations and as naval bases. History, written as always by the victors, has drawn a discreet veil over the wickedness of Venice and her Crusader allies who, while gathered together ostensibly to protect Constantinople from the threatening Ottoman infidel, decided instead to plunder the city themselves and then to seize and share out a large part of her empire.

Venice exploited Crete by introducing to the island the cultivation of sugar, a new and profitable luxury for which European demand had been insatiable since the first Crusaders had brought it back from Syria, and by developing new markets for the island's wine. It was taken long distances by Venetian galleys after shipment through Monemvasia, one of the ports on the Peloponnese coast of Greece captured at the time of Byzantium's dismemberment. Monemvasia—as the wine was called—became Malvasia (Malvoisie to the French), a word soon further corrupted to Malmsey in English.

We can't be sure when the Venetians made their first shipment of the wine to England, but a cask of Malvoisie is listed among the provisions assembled for the celebration of the enthronement of Archbishop Robert of Winchelsea in 1295. By the 1330s Malmsey was arriving regularly, the merchants who delivered it taking raw wool in part payment. Shipped to Flanders, the wool was exchanged there for finished cloth and cloaks, which were then sold all over Europe. This triangular trade became so lucrative that in 1349 the senate of the Venetian republic decided to run it themselves as a state monopoly.

From this time there are references to the wine—sometimes as Cret, sometimes as Retimo (Rethymno), and sometimes as Candy (Candia being the Venetian name both for the island and for its chief city, Heraklion)—in various regulations as well as in records of wine sales and inventories in archives all over England. The wine was a raging success. Demand led to profiteering, however, and worse. A 1350 ordinance of Edward III attempted to control prices, but by January 1353, the exasperated mayor and sheriffs of the City of London had decided that fraud was a greater problem, and they banned tavernkeepers who sold Cretan wine from selling or keeping any other wine in the same establishment.

Meanwhile, the special duty imposed on what was called "sweet Levant wine" was double that collected on Rhine and Bordeaux wines, and half the revenue was reserved for the personal use of the monarch, who therefore had a direct interest in seeing the trade flourish. The City of London's restriction did not appeal to Edward III at all, especially as he was persuaded that merchants would not set up shop to sell

Cretan wine in London while it lasted. Within weeks he had issued the first of doubtless many injunctions to provide exceptions to the mayor's restrictive policy.

But by the late fifteenth century Malmsey had become so much a part of the fabric of English life—Chaucer's Shipman tells a tale of a monk, with an eye for a merchant's wife, making himself a welcome guest at the couple's house by bringing a gift of "a jubbe," almost four gallons, "of Malvesye"—that Venice thought it time to toughen its trading terms. First the senate insisted on payment entirely in cash rather than wool; then, having increased the price per butt, it reduced the size of the measure. In 1489 the Venetians went too far, however, by imposing a heavy and discriminatory tax on Malmsey exported from Crete on English ships, a move to protect the profitability of their own merchant marine. Henry VII of England responded by imposing an identical tax on Malmsey brought to England in Venetian galleys. The Venetians, fearing that a fight over shipping rights could kill their lucrative trade in Malmsey, eventually backed down and abolished their tax in 1499; but by then Henry, a king with the mind of an accountant and the scruples of a loan shark—he had been personally responsible for taking the royal treasury out of the red and into the black at the expense of his noble peers—had come to like the color of the money, and he declined to reciprocate.

~ ~ ~

The matter seems to have ended there, doubtless because Venice was already distracted by more serious problems provoked by yet another Henry. Prince Henry of Portugal—Henry the Navigator to most of us—had planted sugar on the recently discovered Atlantic island of Madeira. By the time Venice was involved in its squabble with Henry VII of England over who would control the shipment of Malmsey from Crete, Madeira's cane crop had reached such proportions that the price of sugar in Europe had fallen by half. Furthermore, Prince Henry had clearly taken Crete—by then a golden milch cow for Venice—as his model when colonizing Madeira. In addition to sugar, he had established on the island the grape still known there as Malvasia Candida, an allusion to its Cretan origin, with the intention of making Malmsey to compete with that of Crete. It is possible that Malmsey wine from Madeira was reaching England as early as the 1450s, even though William Younger, in *Gods, Men and Wine,* says the first butt of "Malvoisie from the Isle of Madeira" arrived in London in 1537, ominously the year the Ottomans took Monemvasia from the Venetians.

Regardless of this new competition, the production of Malmsey on Crete remained strong. Andrea Bacci, an Italian physician writing on wine in 1596, reported that the island was then exporting two hundred thousand butts of it a year to the Venetian mainland. The wine's continued popularity in England is clear from the frequent references to it in seventeenth-century plays ("We have no Greek wine in the house," exclaims a horrified Lord Bornwell in James Shirley's 1635 comedy *The Lady of Pleasure.* "Pray send one of our footmen to the merchant."). In addition, Gervase Markham's how-to book for the English housewife, first published in 1649, advises the reader to see to it that "her Malmseys be full wines, pleasant, well hewed and fine."

But it all came to an end in 1669, when Heraklion fell to the Ottomans after a siege that had lasted twenty-two years. They had already taken Chania and were in possession of the rest of Crete within a year.

~ ~ ~

Just from curiosity I asked Mr. Kounoulakis which wines the members of his cooperative drank. Did they, as do their counterparts in France and Italy, have the right to receive from the cooperative a quantity of wine for their household consumption?

"They always keep back some of their grapes. They know what they like and prefer to make their own wine for themselves," he said.

Oh?

"Would it be possible," I asked, "to visit one of the cooperative's members and ask him how he makes his wine? Perhaps even taste it?"

A telephone call before we went to lunch completed arrangements for us to stop, on the way back to Agios Nikolaos, at a village on the

Argilos, a high clay plateau where the best of Sitia's grapes are said to be grown. The grower we were to meet had a small café-bar at the village crossroad and would be waiting for us there.

The rain was coming down in sheets, but we found the café easily enough. Though we were well into November, great bunches of grapes still hung from an almost leafless vine stretched on rods over the small terrace outside, and the rain, collecting on them, dripped with noisy splashes into the puddles below. Inside, it was pretty basic: three or four tables on a concrete floor, beer crates stacked against the back wall, a refrigerator to the side, and a sink in the corner by a table covered in oil cloth and an assortment of tumblers. It was clearly a place where a farmer in work clothes and muddy boots would feel easy.

Three men sat at a plain wooden table, looking, in fact, as if they had been feeling easy for much of the afternoon. The owner, it soon appeared, was the one with the cloth cap. The other two, extravagantly mustached and wild-haired, had been keeping him company while he waited for us. Each held a glass of *rakí* and picked from time to time at a dish of small olives and a bowl of salted chick-peas. One of them had sliced a raw quince, which he offered to me as soon as we sat down.

They smiled a lot and spoke little until we began asking them what they did with the grapes they kept back from the cooperative for their own wine. Then they all spoke at once, very loudly, and with gesticulations that involved their entire bodies. As far as I could make out they kept back their best bunches and spread them on nets in the sun for three or four days. The concentrated juice, once pressed, would ferment until it stopped naturally, leaving a residue of unfermented sugar in the wine. When the concentration of sugar in the juice was not as high as they liked, they said, they added a little brandy to arrest the fermentation and allow a touch of natural sweetness to remain.

The bar owner's "cellar" was a small space behind the beer crates, and there he had two or three butts of wine surrounded by a litter of buckets, sacks of potatoes, baskets of walnuts, and a heap of pomegranates. The sample he drew was golden brown, and drier than I had expected.

It was quite nutty, almost like a Sherry. He drank it as an apéritif, he told me, and with his food.

I was glad we had stopped there, even though I felt none the wiser. We agreed to give the more exuberant of the two mustached men—he really could have been playing a rustic in one of Aristophanes' comedies—a ride to the other side of the village. As we pulled up to let him out, just near a roadside shrine, he asked if we would like to taste his wine, too. Why not? We slithered two or three hundred feet down a steep and very muddy hillside into the heart of an olive grove where a tethered donkey began braying, loudly and nervously, until the man calmed it. Below us was a stone hut built half into the slope, and he explained that he spread his grapes to dry on its flat rooftop—just as the ancients had spread theirs on their threshing floors.

We stumbled farther down and round to the front of the hut, where I was surprised to find his wife and a brother-in-law sitting under a wide projecting eave snugly toasting themselves at a roaring fire set into the hut's façade. They were eating warm potatoes roasted in the embers and regaling themselves with tiny black olives piled on an enameled dish.

We sat on the bench with them to dry ourselves a little, and they explained that the fire was heating an old alembic still, unobtrusively boiling away inside the hut to convert a bad batch of the brother-in-law's wine into good brandy. From time to time they roused themselves to feed the fire from a stack of old olive wood. Regardless of the rain, they were having a little fête together, protected from unexpected intruders by their watch-donkey.

We tasted the raw distillate—it was very rough—and then my new friend produced a glass of his fragrant five-year-old for me. A busybody rooster came to see what was up and had to be chased off a bright green patch of lettuce seedlings just starting to sprout under one of the olive trees. We were beginning to feel quite cozy when I remembered that I was supposed to be tasting his wine, not his *rakí*. So we went to the far side of the hut, where he kept his wine, squeezing first through a cramped anteroom full of more sacks of potatoes, baskets of quince, and boxes of apples.

There were no casks in his cellars; instead there were three big terra-cotta jars, just like the Minoan ones at Vathípetro, each holding, I would guess, about fifty gallons. He lifted a lid, dipped a small pitcher into the wine, and poured me a tumblerful. It was a rosy, golden brown, slightly sweet, with a marvelous flavor that just kept expanding in my mouth. Oxidation had obviously been part of the aging process, but it was not oxidized in the sense in which we use the term. This wine, he told me, had been made from grapes so rich in sugar that he had had no need to fortify it. He had pressed them; fermented the juice slowly, as usual, in the jar; and, as he needed wine, dipped into it. It was as simple as that, and the wine was delicious.

"It's my 1988," he said.

Give or take a few thousand years, he may have been right.

Originally published as "Malmsey: A Greek Classic" in *Gourmet,* June 1992.

BARBARESCO

A Glimpse of Paradise

I've never been much interested in the latest food fad. Nouvelle, Cajun, Southwestern, Thai, high this and low that have all swept past me. I prefer familiar dishes; they talk to me. I'm happiest with lentil soup, good risotto, a roasted bird, lamb cooked almost any way, beans, grilled peppers, a wild mushroom sauté, and *stracotto*—that slowly cooked Italian beef stew that gives a glimpse of paradise. And though I enjoy wine of all kinds—how could I not?—when I eat one of those comfortable, comforting old favorites the wine I most enjoy is a Barbaresco, preferably one with a little bottle age and an aroma that reminds me of dried apricots, damp earth, and old leather.

Barbaresco, like Barolo, is made from Nebbiolo grapes grown in the Langhe hills near Alba, southeast of Turin in Piedmont. Alba is the chief market for the surrounding white-truffle country as well as a center of red-wine production, a dual role that places it at the hub of a regional cooking so delicious and so bountiful that only Gargantua could really do justice to it. Mind you, in November, at the peak of the truffle season, hungry Swiss and Germans swarm through the Alpine passes and do their best. For a month they fill every hotel, inn, and restaurant within fifty miles of Alba. And there they feast. And feast.

In most other parts of the world the four or five antipasti served without ceremony at such Albese restaurants as La Contea di Neive, Belvedere, La Fioraia, Guido, and the new San Marco in Canelli would alone constitute a banquet of major proportions. There might be veal *carpaccio* with slithers of truffle; some rabbit-liver pâté, perhaps; then, just a small fillet of sea trout; a tiny soufflé aromatic with herbs; some tender cardoon in a cheese *fonduta....* And surely one couldn't refuse a slice of homemade sausage on creamy puréed potatoes? The tempting little dishes, so simple, so chaste, follow each other in a seemingly never-ending succession from the kitchen. But then how can one manage the risotto *al Barolo* or the *agnolotti*—stuffed crescent-shaped pasta envelopes—in meat sauce, the braised shoulder of lamb, and all the rest of the real business of dinner? Somehow, one can and does.

Both Barbaresco and Barolo rank among the greatest of Italy's classic reds. We are inclined to believe that any "classic" wine must have been around forever, but neither of these two even existed—at least, as we know them today—until the middle of the last century, a mere snap of the fingers against the four thousand years that vines have been cultivated on the Italian peninsula. When Thomas Jefferson visited Piedmont in 1787—a journey during which he jotted down everything he saw that might be of use to the newly independent United States, from how to prepare *mascarpone* to the best way of constructing a pontoon bridge across a swiftly flowing river—he wrote that he found Nebbiolo wine to be "about as sweet as the silky Madeira, as astringent on the palate as Bordeaux, and as brisk as Champagne."

Paris wine merchant André Jullien's 1816 book, *Topographie de Tous les Vignobles Connus,* an account of all the world's vineyards as they existed in his day, was the primary source for almost all other books on wine written in the nineteenth century. In it he described Piedmont's Nebbiolo wine in terms similar to Jefferson's, referring to its "sweet taste... accompanied by an agreeable sharpness." At that time Nebbiolo wines tasted sweet and sharp simultaneously because the grapes were partly dried on mats or racks to concentrate both their sugar and acid. Hence the astringency Jefferson noted, too, given the greater proportion of skins to juice. Much the same happens now in Valpolicella in the making of *recioto.* The "briskness" that Jefferson charitably compared with Champagne's sparkle was probably the result of poorly managed fermentation. Jullien, either less tactful or less kindly than Jefferson, simply castigates the wine as defective. Contemporary opinions of Piedmont winemaking were nowhere very high, I have to say. My 1810 edition of the *Encyclopaedia Britannica* describes Piedmont wines as *brusco*—a word Italians usually reserve for bad weather and disagreeable manners—and dismisses them, without further explanation, as "very wholesome for fat people."

Matters changed only in the 1840s, when Victorine Colbert, the French wife of a nobleman in Barolo, hired a compatriot, Louis Oudart, to take charge of winemaking on her husband's estate. Burton Anderson, in his *Wine Atlas of Italy,* says that Oudart's "conversion of previously sweet Nebbiolo into a dry wine aged in barrels was such a revelation that Piedmont's Prime Minister Cavour hired him to do the same" at his property nearby. Oudart's work for Cavour (later the architect of Italy's unification) was followed by a spell at the Castello di Neive, near Barbaresco; here the lever-screw presses Oudart used for the then-owner, Conte Castelborgo, still stand in a corner of the castle's cellar, just as Oudart must have left them.

Oudart's ideas were more quickly adopted in Barolo than in Barbaresco, some twenty miles distant, giving Barolo a lead in the market that developed for this new style of Nebbiolo wine. Barolo's place on the best tables was assured, in any case, once Victor Emmanuel II installed his special friend, a Barolo girl known to all as La Bella Rosìn, in a royal hunting lodge nearby. There was more than a little nudge, nudge, wink, wink behind the promotion of Barolo as the "wine of kings," but then the court was still a novelty in late-nineteenth-century Italy even if mistresses weren't, so the association—of the king with Barolo, that is—was too great an asset to be wasted.

The winemaking changes Oudart initiated were consolidated in the 1880s by Domizio Cavazza, founder of both Alba's wine school (still one of Italy's best) and, in 1894, of a wine cooperative in Barbaresco that helped complete the transformation there. Barbaresco remained for some time, nevertheless, a sort of junior partner to Barolo. Not only had it entered the market later but it also had only half the acreage of vines.

Cavazza's cooperative was compulsorily disbanded during Italy's fascist era, but its revival was instigated in 1958 by parish priest Don Fiorino to encourage young men, drifting away to the booming Fiat factory in Turin, to stay at home. The cooperative's new building—erected in 1961—takes up one side of the tiny piazza by the church at the top of Barbaresco's only street. With fifty-seven members, the association of Produttori del Barbaresco now incorporates half the growers and half the vineyards of the village (but not of the Barbaresco appellation, which also covers the neighboring communities of Treiso and Neive). Its members contribute grapes grown on some of Barbaresco's most favored sites, but the quality of even the finest grapes would be squandered without the strict controls imposed by the cooperative's president, Celestino Vacca. Members are required, for example, to bring their grapes to the winery in small baskets rather than by the truckload so that an appropriate selection, almost to the bunch, can be made before any fruit passes to the crusher.

It is standard practice for cooperatives to insist that every member deliver his entire crop of grapes to the winery. A cooperative doesn't want to be just a useful dump for imperfect grapes growers prefer not to keep for themselves. The Barbaresco cooperative goes further. It requires its members to deliver their best grapes but reserves the right to refuse any of them it considers substandard. Members are encouraged by a system that rewards especially fine lots. As a result the cooperative's wines, impeccably made and appealingly plump, have a ripe, concentrated style. Were André Jullien to return to Piedmont now and taste them he would have to drink his words.

～ ～ ～

The cooperative's wines also point up the differences among Barbaresco's discrete vineyard sites because it receives grapes from just about every one of them and processes each batch separately. In good years it bottles them separately too, labeling each wine with the name of the vineyard location—the *cru*, as they say, using a French word for which there is no Italian equivalent—where it was grown. (Dialect words like *sorì*, for "sunny place," and *bricco*, meaning "hilltop," are now commonly used in Piedmont to designate a site with a distinguishing microclimate.)

Cavazza had drawn up a map of Barbaresco's vineyards a hundred years ago, basing it on exposures and microclimates. Aldo Vacca, Celestino's son and the cooperative's vineyard adviser, talked to me about the differences among the sites and slopes when I visited Barbaresco last November. "Alba's wine producers and bottlers have always taken such distinctions into account when buying grapes," he said. "They buy grapes from one section for body, look somewhere else for structure. They get aroma from here, strength from there."

In the 1960s Prunotto and Vietti, two particularly respected regional producers who have longstanding relationships with Barbaresco growers, started to give their wines *cru* designations. Allowing the consumer to become familiar with the vineyard names stimulated interest and demand. The producers didn't seem to mind that it gave more power, more control to the growers. The greater prestige and added value of the wines were what counted most.

By and large Barbaresco wines are assumed to be softer than Barolo, more fragrant and more delicately finished. But the choices we now have among *cru* wines allow us to see that Barbaresco varies from one vineyard to another almost as much as Barolo does. Nebbiolo ripens late, when autumn days are already shortening and mist drifts through the valleys, so the more southerly a vineyard's exposure the better the fruit will be. That's why it has always been the rule in Piedmont to plant prime vines where winter snow melts first. But, because even south-facing slopes have shoulders exposed to the east or southeast, west or southwest, variations of style are inevitable.

A wine from vines grown on Barbaresco's Montestefano, for instance, is indistinguishable from the firmest Barolo; it is closed, even austere, when young, and a serious mouthful only when mature. "But there are many contrasts," Aldo Vacca told me. "Though Montestefano wines are difficult at first, Pora wines, which age just as well, are forward and easier to enjoy from the beginning. Those from Ovello are much the same. Wines from Moccagatto, which faces southeast, have less power but are more flowery; they have finesse rather than body.

"The best, and best known, of the sites here in Barbaresco, however, are probably Rabajà and Asili. They are really two halves of a single slope, with Martinenga, owned entirely by Marchesi di Gresy, nestled between and below them. Rabajà wines can be as aromatic and graceful as those of Moccagatto, but with more substance. Asili wines have the best of everything: Austerely tannic when young, just as are Montestefano wines, they soften with time and develop a wonderfully intense perfume. Montefico and Rio Sordo have the same exposure as Montestefano, and they too need age before they mellow. But, unlike Montestefano, they never lose a certain rustic quality."

The wines of Barbaresco's Pajè (sometimes found in books as Pagliere) can be rustic, too, even angular. But thanks to good acidity they remain fresh over the years even as they develop the typical Barbaresco aroma of the forest, of mushrooms and game. Among those growers with vines on the Pajè slope, the best is Alfredo Roagna. Roagna's wines have a hand-hewn quality typical of Pajè; but one of them, bottled as Crichët (a dialect word) rather than Barbaresco and aged entirely in new French oak barrels, is so rich and unctuous, so atypical of a Barbaresco Pajè, that the official tasting commission won't allow Roagna to sell it with the Barbaresco appellation on the label. Not that he minds. "My customers are willing to pay more for Crichët than they pay for my Barbaresco," he told me.

Barbaresco wines produced on the hills of Treiso and Neive have characteristics of their own. Treiso's vineyards are higher than those of Barbaresco (1,400 feet as opposed to 800), with cooler temperatures and thinner soil. But what a Treiso-grown Barbaresco might lack in body it makes up for in aroma. Neive wines, on the other hand, are particularly muscular, even to the extent of seeming clumsy if the fruit isn't handled well.

~ ~ ~

Through their good example the Produttori del Barbaresco have helped raise the standard of all wines in Barbaresco. But it is Angelo Gaja, a grower with skill, enthusiasm, boundless energy, and a flair for promotion, who has pulled Barbaresco into the international limelight. If, as many think, Barbaresco has now taken the starring role from Barolo, it can only have been thanks to him. His superbly crafted wines reflect an intense, lively, and focused personality as much as they do a contemporary style of winemaking—a style that owes much to Gaja himself and to the ideas he has brought back from extensive study in France and California.

A couple of years ago, when I spent a day with Gaja discussing his aims, he told me that he had begun to develop his philosophy in the early seventies. Gaja speaks rapidly, passionately, and without pause, switching from Italian to French to English without seeming to notice. "The quality of any wine comes from the vineyard, obviously," he said. "Making sure the quality is in the fruit in the first place is exhausting work. We can't control the weather, so we must constantly adapt to it.

"The key problem, however, is to transfer that quality from the grapes to the wine. To make that happen, yet leave behind any hard, green tannins, is easier to talk about than to do. For a start, the winery must be suitably equipped. We decided to do away with wood and concrete fermenting tanks and replace them with stainless steel. Stainless-steel tanks with water-cooled jackets allow control of the temperature at which our wines ferment. That means we can monitor the speed of fermentation and therefore the time the juice spends on the grape skins. Because grape skins are the most important source of tannins, this was a first step toward their better management.

"Still, even though we switched to fermenting in stainless steel, we continue to age our wines in wood. Wood aging helps stabilize the color of a red wine, for one thing, and, curious though it seems, the tannin in wood helps soften the wine's own tannins once they combine. We give a new wine six months in small barrels made of French oak and then transfer it to larger, wooden casks for another year or two before bottling. The size of the container—a sixty-gallon barrel against a sixteen-hundred–gallon cask—makes a difference because in the barrel the ratio of wood to wine is higher."

Eager to experiment, to test his latest idea, to meet the newest challenge, Gaja has sought constantly to align his wines with the best the world offers. In his search for perfection no detail escapes him. When I visited him in Barbaresco a few months ago, for example, I saw stacked in the open behind his winery thousands of barrel staves waiting to be assembled in his own cooperage. Buying staves from France, holding them in Barbaresco, and then making the barrels himself was the only way that Gaja could be sure the wood would be adequately air-dried.

As the demand for barrels has forced up the price of oak along with the cost of holding inventories of drying staves, coopers in France have found themselves under pressure to move their stocks a little faster. But the benefits of long air-drying are real—two or three years is considered the minimum for rain, sunlight, and bacterial action to leach out bitter components—and it's just the kind of thing Gaja would not leave to chance. His wines reflect his obsession with detail, with polish, with technical control. Their flavors are pure, their structure is elegantly logical, and their refinement is absolute.

Bruno Giacosa, a Neive producer whom some think of as tradition personified, does not use barrels. I visited him, too, when I was in Piedmont last November. "We tried putting our Barbera in barrels a few years ago, and we weren't satisfied," he told me with a certain calm finality.

Gaja and Giacosa are a study in contrasts. Whereas Gaja—an affable man usually dressed in a chic Missoni sweater—receives his visitors in a sophisticated, artfully lit, high-tech setting, Giacosa's office, with bare white walls and a barred window, opens off a bottle-packing floor in a drab concrete blockhouse on a busy main road. He is retiring in manner, and in appearance is indistinguishable from the other middle-aged, plainly dressed men—brokers, merchants, growers—who discuss prices and make deals over lunch at Neive's busy Trattoria Ferroveria, on the Piazza Garibaldi. Where Gaja is voluble, Giacosa is laconic. Where Gaja is highly visible on the fashionable wine circuit, Giacosa is almost reclusive, sending his daughter Bruna in his place to visit distributors around the world. And where Gaja is ready to discuss the whys and wherefores of his numerous wine-making theories, Giacosa shrinks from being too precise about anything. "Wine-making involves a great many small decisions," he says, "each affecting the next. One can only hope to get them all right, to capture what there was in the grapes to begin with."

Giacosa, who buys all his grapes from growers with whom he has had long-standing relations, ferments his wine, as does Gaja, in stainless-steel tanks. But then he transfers it directly into huge wooden casks—no barrels—to be aged for three or four years. The wines for which he is best known, Gallina and Santo Stefano, are made from grapes grown in namesake vineyards on the extensive domain of Castello di Neive. In good years Giacosa's Gallina is as violet-scented as textbooks say a good Barbaresco should be. And year after year his Santo Stefano is a wine against which all other Barbarescos can be judged.

Both Gallina and Santo Stefano have the structure and the elegance of the best of Gaja's wines, and the robust fleshiness of the best of the cooperative's. And like every wine Giacosa produces—even his Dolcetto and Barbera—they have a rich harmony of aroma and flavor that is his alone. Castello di Neive makes a Santo Stefano of its own with the same grapes, and remarkably good it is, too. But it doesn't have the resonance of Giacosa's wine. I would compare Giacosa's Santo Stefano with a Beethoven symphony if I thought I could get away with it.

The wines from Marchesi di Gresy's estate are different again. Alberto di Gresy's grandfather bought the present family property essentially as a hunting retreat, leaving the cultivation of the vineyards to his tenant farmers. When Alberto assumed management of the part of the estate he and his siblings had inherited through their father, he soon concluded that merely selling grapes meant he would always be growing a crop for a buyers' market. "It would have been difficult to keep the place going for the family on the income," he told me. "There's a payroll to meet, social-security payments, taxes. I had to increase the value of what we produced. Do you know that by transforming my crop from grapes to wine my revenues increased as much as tenfold? Even allowing for the necessary additional investment and the cost of labor, bottles, corks, and so on, the change from selling grapes to making wine made it possible for the family to keep the property." Di Gresy, need I add, trained as an economist.

"But I wanted to make wine anyway," he went on. "I had spent all my summers here as a boy, close to the farmers, and I knew how good our Martinenga grapes were. It upset me to sell them to producers who just mixed them in with others. We started to make wine ourselves in 1973. I had no preconceived ideas except that wine, first and foremost, is a pleasure. It exists to be enjoyed. I wanted each of our wines to be agreeable, elegant, harmonious. But—pride of ownership, I suppose—I also wanted each wine to reflect the personality of the vineyard. So, although our chief concern is to produce wines that make people happy, we never force their styles in ways that would divorce them from the vineyards themselves."

Di Gresy succeeds in imbuing his wines with his own engaging charm while preserving the distinctive, spicy personality of the Martinenga vineyard. His wines' grace and discretion, furthermore, mask a structure every bit as firm as Gaja's.

The Produttori del Barbaresco, Gaja, Giacosa, and di Gresy are the Big Four of Barbaresco. But there are forty or fifty other producers. Some, like Alfredo Roagna, are small growers in Barbaresco, each with a few acres of vines. Three of the best have vineyards adjacent to each other on Rabajà, just above di Gresy's Martinenga: Romano Marengo; Giuseppe Cortese, an inveterate winner of gold medals; and Bruno Rocca, who, with his wife and mother, goes through his vines three or more times at each harvest so that every bunch is picked when it is perfect. ("I don't do it to impress people," he says. "I just want my wine to give joy.") Some, like Castello di Neive, are large growers but small producers, preferring to sell outright a large part, if not most, of their grapes. And others are producers elsewhere, particularly in Alba and in the Barolo area, who either buy Barbaresco grapes or own vineyards there. Among them, the finest Barbarescos are produced by Prunotto, Pio Cesare, Vietti, and Fontanafredda.

I had gone to Barbaresco to compare the 1988, 1989, and 1990 vintages and found myself liking all three. Each year was better than the one before. As in Bordeaux, the 1988 wines were classically elegant, the 1989s more exuberant, and the 1990s the biggest, richest, and fleshiest of them all. Among the several dozen wines I tasted, there were few I wouldn't be happy to drink, in the fullness of time of course, with a garlic- and rosemary-scented loin of lamb or pheasant braised with cabbage. Or perhaps a *stracotto*. With a wine like one of these, that would be as good as glimpsing paradise twice over.

Originally published as "Barbaresco" in *Gourmet*, May 1993.

PRIORATO

A Heady Success Story

The first storm of winter had done its worst just days before I arrived in Priorato last November. In four hours, more rain than is usual during an entire year had washed out dirt roads, hillside terracing, and young vines. But local winegrowers were in high spirits, buoyed by their first impression of the year's new wine. The rain had marked the end of a summer so dry it had taken the vines to the limit of their endurance, and it was already obvious that the resulting wines would be concentrated and aromatic. The essence, one might say, of Priorato.

Tucked away in wild and precipitous hill country west of Tarragona, Priorato, easily Catalonia's poorest region, was for long the butt of local politicians' jokes. So when Joan Clos, the mayor of Barcelona, having announced that he wanted to establish, within the city's limits, a municipal vineyard "like the one in Montmartre," then went on to say, "except that I want ours to produce a great wine. a wine this city can be proud of, a wine like Priorato's Cims de Porrera"—it made an impression.

For Sara Perez, who makes that wine as well as the wine at her family's Clos Martinet, the recognition was gratifying. For Priorato, it was something of a miracle. Though it's not the first time that God's finger has strayed there. In the twelfth century, a local man claimed to have seen a congregation of angels working together on a hillside, each one carrying grapes up and down a great staircase to heaven. An account of the incident so affected Alfonso II of Aragón that he established on that very spot Spain's first Carthusian monastery—called, appropriately,

Scala Dei, Stairway of God. Monks began planting vines there in 1163, the first in the region since the Romans had packed up and left, centuries before.

~ ~ ~

Priorato's secret is its schist—a crumbly gray-green slate that forces the Grenache and Carignan vines traditionally grown there to send roots forty feet or more in search of water. The nutrients and minerals they draw from that depth contribute to the intensity of the wine, giving it a strength that throws into relief the rich fruit and ripe, velvety tannins that are Priorato's hallmark.

A mix of Grenache and Carignan is common all around the Mediterranean coasts of Spain and France because these two varieties complement each other. You can see it just by looking at the vines. The Grenache is open, and its oval grapes hang in loose bunches. Its wine, though perfumed and soft, is equally unstructured, despite its considerable alcoholic power, and tends to fade quickly. A Carignan vine, on the other hand, is tight and knotty; there are deep indentations in its leaves, and its thick-skinned grapes hang in compact, cylindrical bunches. Though flavor and balance improve as the vine matures, a wine made from young Carignan vines seems edgy and raw. Used together, Grenache and Carignan complete each other, the gentle finish of one braced by the structure of the other.

Over a dinner of tender roast kid, an *escalivada* of grilled peppers and eggplant, and a glass of Cims de Porrera '98, I talked with Salus Alvarez, the mayor of Porrera, one of the twelve scattered villages that produce Priorato wine. He told me that because of its rich texture and heady mountain flavour, the local wine had been in demand as far back as the sixteenth century. Curious about local history, Alvarez likes to browse through old letters and accounts stowed away in his neighbors' attic trunks. "I learn a lot," he said. "For example, recently, among orders and inventories, I found a seventeenth-century sheet of instructions for blending our wine to the taste of the Spanish colonies in South America. Another, prepared a hundred years later, proposed a rule that would restrict Priorato wines to shipment in bottle, to protect its reputation."

"It used to give me a strange feeling," he added, ruefully, "to be holding evidence of centuries of past prosperity while watching the decline of our village. Our vines were being abandoned, and our people were disappearing with them. A hundred years ago Porrera had a population of more than two thousand. Today it has fewer than three hundred. It has been the same everywhere in Priorato."

Phylloxera ruined Priorato, as it did many other marginal wine regions with labor-intensive hillside vineyards. They all had difficulty getting started again, and some never did. Priorato's growers made things easier on themselves by replanting their vines on flatter land wherever they could find it and, more significantly, by changing their varietal emphasis. They planted more Carignan and less Grenache. They knew that Carignan on its own gives a terse wine that can be coarse when the vines are young, but its fruit sets more reliably than Grenache, and even in the particular conditions of Priorato will usually yield twice as much. The growers sold land to finance the replanting, and to supplement what they could afford to pay them in cash, they gave small vineyard plots to their workers. It was the beginning of a long disintegration. By the 1950s, there were hundreds of tiny holdings—mostly planted in Carignan—and control of local wine production shifted from the former estates to the cooperative cellars that sprang up in most of the villages.

The cooperatives were there to make wine, not to market it. But when sold in bulk for others to blend, even Priorato fetches only a commodity price. The growers tried to cover their expenses by boosting yields. Quality fell and revenues fell further. The financial return to member-growers was eventually so low that particularly steep vineyards (where quality was likely to have been highest, but cultivation costs most onerous) were abandoned, the grapes left to hang. Men and women of all ages left Priorato at an accelerating rate to find jobs in the hotels on the coast or in shops and offices in Tarragona and Barcelona.

It was rare for a young couple to set up house there. In the outlying villages the elementary schools closed; and as one depressed decade followed another there was an increasingly eerie feeling of desertion.

～ ～ ～

But the fundamentals of Priorato's past success remained: schist, exposure to a Mediterranean sun, and an altitude for the most part above twelve hundred feet (ensuring lively acidity no matter how rich and heady the wine). Once Spain entered the European Union and began a sustained campaign to upgrade all its wines, it seemed certain that change would come to Priorato, too. It needed only a spark to set things in motion. In fact there were two. José-Luis Perez, Sara Perez's father, and René Barbier. Perez, a wiry biologist now in his sixties, arrived in Falset, the regional hub, in 1981 as director of the local school of agriculture. He fought for viticulture programs, hoping they would give the young an incentive to stay and a chance to succeed. Barbier—grandson of a *négociant* who had moved to Tarragona from the Rhône valley at the end of the nineteenth century—bought, in 1979, an abandoned property in the Priorato village of Gratallops as a weekend retreat for his family. The steeply pitched vineyard came with the ruin of a house, a magical place he named Clos Mogador.

Though trained in Bordeaux, where he also worked with the Moueix family—of Pétrus fame—Barbier had spent time with his cousins in the Rhône valley before taking a job with Bodegas Palacios Remondo in Rioja. But he understood Priorato's potential well. When still a child, he had accompanied his father on buying trips there. Friends from Tarragona—writers and painters mostly—spent time with him at Grattalops, helping him salvage old vines and nurse them back into production. Carles and Mariona Pastrana, now owners of Priorato's Clos de L'Obac, next door, were among them. Others, romantics perhaps, but also excited by the possibilities they saw in these old vines, bought vineyards. At about one hundred dollars an acre at the time, the land was cheap enough. They restored, replanted, and extended the vineyards, turning to each other for help and support and to José-Luis Perez for advice. Catching their enthusiasm, Perez, too, bought land and, in 1986, planted the vines that would eventually produce his Clos Martinet.

Some, having made a start, got cold feet and pulled back, selling their vines to each other or to newcomers. That's how Alvaro Palacios—son of the Rioja producer with whom Barbier had worked and by then a close friend—came to acquire Finca Dofi in 1989. Strapped for cash, they all thought of themselves as pioneers. (Palacios, too, was on his own. His father, having tried to discourage him from what he saw as a risky venture, refused to finance it. For several years, Palacios travelled five days a week as a barrel salesman so that he could support himself and devote his weekends to his vineyard.)

The group shared resources. In fact, their sense of camaraderie was so strong in those days that it seemed perfectly natural that their 1989 vintage—their first—should be made in common as a single *cuvée* in a winery they had jointly set up in a former sheep-shed. Each took his or her share of the finished wine and labelled it accordingly, though the wine was really all the same. They continued to share the sheep-shed winery until 1992, but after that first 1989 *cuvée*, each made his or her own wine independently. Or they had René Barbier make it for them. As they labored together in those early years for what had become a common, passionately pursued cause, they did everything themselves. To outsiders, they must have looked like an incarnation of that twelfth-century vision.

In fact, given how few of them there were and the limitations of their annual production—at that time, it was only in the hundreds of cases—it might have taken years for outsiders even to notice them. But in April 1992, to prepare its readers for the Barcelona Olympic Games, *Gault Millau* published a guide to Catalonia that included a thumbnail sketch of René Barbier and an account of the revolution he had insti-gated in Priorato. In giving the 1989 vintages of his Clos Mogador and the Pastrana's Clos de l'Obac appropriately identical ratings of 18/20, the reviewer described their seductively explosive fruit and rich tex-ture. He also warned his readers that the wines, difficult to find, were sold, when available, almost drop by drop. The response was predictable—everyone felt that he or she had to taste it. The new Priorato was launched.

Barbier and his friends had sought out and bought old plantings of Grenache, regardless of their condition, and, in an effort to restore the varietal balance lost decades earlier, they planted yet more of it. Of the 1,000 hectares (2,400 acres) of productive vines in Priorato, well over 300 are now Grenache, more than twice as many as in 1980. There is still plenty of Carignan, but the vines are mature because little of this variety has been planted. There has been a preference to look to three classic French varieties—Cabernet Sauvignon, Syrah, and Merlot—for the structure Grenache lacks, with an initial enthusiasm for Cabernet Sauvignon gradually shifting to Syrah because of its less imposing varietal character. Clos Mogador, Clos de L'Obac, Finca Dofí, L'Ermita, and Erasmus—estates prominent in the initial revival—all use, to stunning effect, one or the other (or all three) of these French varieties rather than Carignan. When the proportions are right and the Carignan fruit is from really mature vines, however, traditional combinations of Grenache and Carignan can be equally impressive. In fact, the elegant and distinctive 1998 Cims de Porrera I enjoyed so much on the first evening of my visit (quite possibly the very wine that inspired Joan Clos) was predominantly Carignan with only one third Grenache and no more than a dash of Cabernet Sauvignon for seasoning. Tempranillo, the red variety used for Rioja, has been around in Priorato for some time. It's used sparingly, but gives a grace note to Miserere, for example, the second estate wine of Carles and Mariona Pastrana.

～　～　～

Success breeds success. Torres, the leading wine producer in neighboring Penedès, has recently bought land in Priorato, and Codorniu has taken a stake in Scala Dei, one of the region's older (and larger) estates. But the most heartening effect has been on small growers, with an economic impact on the region. As recently as five years ago most of the Priorato cooperatives were distributing to their grower-members forty pesetas (twenty cents) a kilo for grapes they had delivered two or three years earlier. Today, depending on the quality of their fruit, most growers in Priorato can expect to receive from three hundred to six hundred pesetas—usually paid three months after the vintage. The growing notoriety of Priorato wine has seen the start of a tourist industry based on simple country restaurants in villages that for years had seen few visitors. It's difficult to unravel an exact sequence of events that were only tenuously related to each other anyway. But the wider effect almost certainly began in 1990, when Alvaro Palacios of Finca Dofi started buying small lots of grapes from the owners of old vines to make Les Terrasses, a *cuvée* distinct from his own estate wines. He wanted to augment his production to justify building for himself a modern winery. Until then, each of the group had made his or her wine—ostensibly, at least—only from grapes grown in their own vineyards. The price Palacios was willing to pay for high quality grapes (Carignan as well as Grenache) put pressure on the cooperatives to rethink their strategies if they didn't want to see their best fruit simply slip away from them.

In 1991 five small cooperatives joined together to form Vinicola del Priorat, with a new and well equipped central winery at Gratallops. Although they had a difficult start—old habits are hard to break—a new management team has, since 1995, introduced a system of paying members for quality rather than volume. "We still sell in bulk any wine that doesn't satisfy us," Jordi Miró, the sales director told me. "But that's no more than 5 percent of our annual production now." Most of the twenty-five thousand cases Vinicola sells each year are Onix, a robust and lively blend based on the fruit of its members' old Grenache and Carignan vines.

Other cooperatives, too small to hire winemakers and sales directors with the skills required to upgrade and launch their wines, have formed alliances with successful producers in other regions to get the technical and marketing skills they need. Through just such an arrangement, the village cooperative in Poboleda now has the help of Joan Maria Riera, a talented and experienced young winemaker who worked for a time at

Saintsbury in California's Carneros. Its new partners have upgraded the equipment in the cooperative's modest quarters, and although members still have the right to deliver all their grapes there—that was part of the deal—there is a rigorous selection on arrival and about a quarter of the wine is sold off in bulk. "We give the growers all the help we can," Riera told me. "And by way of encouragement we routinely pay five hundred pesetas a kilo for impeccable fruit." Riera imposes strict organic cultivation standards on all the cooperative's members. "All our wine is made from fruit grown organically," he said, "and the Swiss and German authorities send inspectors here for certification regularly. Both countries are important markets for us." *All* the red wines are traditional blends of Grenache and Carignan, but the best of them, bottled as Mas Igneus, usually contain small proportions of Merlot, Cabernet Sauvignon, or Syrah.

Best known of the cooperative partnerships is Cims de Porrera. The Perez family, with their partner Luis Llach, rents the village cooperative's winery, where the huge underground cement tanks in which the wine used to be made have been turned into vaults housing French oak barrels. The fifty-two member-growers, who sell their grapes to the winery, cultivate a total of 54 hectares (130 acres) of vines spread over 150 different plots. "They're all at different altitudes, with different exposures, and often with the Grenache and the Carignan mixed together," Sara Perez told me. "We do our best to pick the two varieties separately anyway," she said, "because they don't ripen at the same time. We judge ripeness by the taste of the skins. When the fruit is ripe, the aroma tells you so. It was nature's way of attracting animals to eat the fruit when the seeds were ready. We follow the same rule, and it seems to work for us, too."

Originally published as "Priorato" in *Gourmet,* April 2001.

Increasingly, Priorato is now referred to by its Catalan name: Priorat.

SCHOOL DAYS ON THE RHINE

"Good morning!" said Dr. Otto Currle, counselor to the regional chamber of agriculture. "I hope you ate a good breakfast!" Thirty-six of us, some rumpled from the bus, some from lingering too late the night before in a local vintner's parlor, were on the brink of our fourth day of lectures, tastings, and visits in a week-long course on German wines. We had been disgorged into the morning mist of Alzey, near Mainz in the Rheinhessen, and stood at the door of the official testing station where local wines, once they are approved for sale, are certified with their batch number.

"We shall show you how we do it," promised Dr. Currle. "We shall show you the problems. We shall teach you. We shall also test your ability to taste. I hope you ate a good breakfast!"

We had indeed eaten a good breakfast. We had learned by then that a copious breakfast, a solid lunch, and an ample dinner were essential bulwarks against the course's four or five daily tasting sessions. A wholesomeness altogether appropriate to scholastic endeavor seemed to be the guiding principle in the choice of food served. When one's days started with a foundation of ham, cheese, sausage, and eggs, one was later able to sustain boiled beef with onion sauce, roast pork tenderloin, braised beef with red cabbage, stewed chicken with *Spätzle*, or boiled salt pork with mashed potatoes. No one picked at the food, and no one had need to send desperate messages home for care packages.

Every year the German Wine Academy conducts seven courses in

English. Most run from Sunday evening to Saturday morning, but one is expanded to eleven days to allow a more leisurely pace and some sightseeing, and another has been designed as a special follow-up week for previous participants. All except the expanded course are based at Winkel, a pretty wine village on the Rhine west of Wiesbaden where each group is housed in the comfortable seventeenth-century beamed and gabled Hotel Schwan. (Some students might find themselves lodged in the more utilitarian annex next door.)

The lectures and tastings are given in locations as diverse as the Baroque refectory of Kloster Eberbach, a former Cistercian monastery; the old stables of the Deinhard estate at Deidesheim; cellars probably first burrowed into the Moselle hillsides by retired Roman veterans; and around barrelheads among the vines of the Liebfrauenstift-Kirchenstück at Worms, the vineyard that lent its name to Liebfraumilch. By bus and river steamer, the course meanders from Winkel to Worms, from Bernkastel to Bad Kreuznach, and from Rüdesheim to Heidelberg.

The arrangements run like clockwork, of course. The bus is always waiting, speakers have their notes prepared, glasses are in place, wines are chilled and listed on a tasting sheet, and, in every inn or restaurant along the way, meals are ready to be served the moment the group arrives.

On the first evening we gathered at the Schwan for dinner and found, over a glass or two of sparkling wine, that though English was to be our common language we were in fact from Sweden, the Netherlands, Canada, Denmark, the United States, Norway, Britain, and New Zealand. Professionally we ranged from sommeliers and wine distributors to bank managers, engineers, civil servants, accountants, teachers, physicians, journalists, secretaries, and designers. Two young women from a Norwegian hotel school had won scholarships to be with us. You could say we were a mixed bunch. Helmut Jung, director of the academy, welcomed us officially with an exhortation to be punctual.

We soon understood why. Every day was crammed with visits to cellars, vineyards, and research stations. There were lectures, tastings, and instruction in everything from current trends in grape breeding by Helmut Becker, head of Germany's renowned State Research Institute of Viticulture and Oenology at Geisenheim and one of the wine world's major figures, to an illuminating tasting of faulty wines conducted by Dr. Currle, who made sure we would never again confuse mishap for character.

Though no two days were the same, the first gives the flavor of them all. We set off for Kloster Eberbach, the academy's headquarters, at 8:30 *sharp*, with the far bank of the Rhine still lost in early morning fog. Kloster Eberbach is also the administrative center of the Hessian state vineyards. Originally ecclesiastical property, it was ceded to the dukes of Nassau when the estate was secularized in 1803 and was then transferred to the Prussian royal domain. The buildings, impressive for their scale and severity rather than their ornament, are enfolded in a wooded valley so unspoiled that they were used for scenes in the movie *The Name of the Rose,* a story of fourteenth-century monastical mayhem. On long oak tables in the splendidly paneled refectory, a fat binder of information was waiting for each of us. It was packed with answers to questions we hadn't even known to ask, from production statistics, distribution flow charts, and extracts from German wine-labeling law to schedules of the annual value of German wine exports worldwide and drawings that showed us how to prune a vine.

In an introductory session, Helmut Jung, assisted by Dr. Hans Ambrosi, director of the state vineyards, painted in broad strokes the background of German viticulture and its place in Europe and the world at large. From the many numbers we were given, two struck me as particularly significant: one hundred thousand hectares of vines and one hundred thousand growers. The average vineyard holding in Germany is no more than a hectare—two and a half acres. German viticulture is highly fragmented and therefore essentially an artisan's occupation.

Jung explained how Germany's northern climate influences the styles of wine produced there. He discussed the grape varieties grown in Germany and explained where and how they were used and what to expect from their wines. All we had been told was then illustrated by a tasting of wines carefully selected to point up the differences among the German wine regions, grape varieties, degrees of dryness, and degrees of grape ripeness when picked. After a brief tour through Kloster Eberbach, we returned to the refectory to find that the staff had removed our glasses and replaced them with the same series of wines, but this time unmarked and jumbled. We retasted them "blind" and enjoyed that first rush of confidence in finding that we could recognize for ourselves what we had earlier been taught to identify.

After lunch at the Kloster's own tavern-in-the-trees, and just as soon as the last of the group could be retrieved from the medieval labyrinth of cellars and dormitories where they had managed to lose themselves, we were off to Schloss Johannisberg.

~ ~ ~

It is said that Charlemagne himself first ordered vines to be planted on the steep hill now dedicated to Saint John the Baptist. From the palace at Ingelheim across the Rhine, Charlemagne had seen that this was where the snow melted first every spring. By the eighteenth century the hillside estate belonged to the prince-abbots of Fulda, who replaced the monastery on the site with an elaborate priory. In restoring the vineyards, damaged and neglected during the Thirty Years' War and its aftermath, the current prince-abbot ordered the best of them to be planted exclusively in Riesling vines, the first time vineyards anywhere had been planted solely with this variety. Riesling in California is referred to still as Johannisberg Riesling because of this association with Schloss Johannisberg.

Records have been kept of every harvest at Schloss Johannisberg since 1716. Those detailed accounts support the story of the 1775 incident that led to the discovery of the benefits of late-harvested grapes. That year the courier, returning from Fulda with the prince-abbot's permission to begin picking, was delayed. The grapes were already overripe and shriveled; by the time the harvest was under way, they showed signs

of the rot we now know to be *Botrytis cinerea*. The result was an astonishing success. In the two hundred years since then, wines made from
deliberately late-picked grapes—*Spätlese, Auslese,* and *Beerenauslese*—have
made the reputation of this section of the Rheingau.

At the beginning of the nineteenth century, Schloss Johannisberg
passed in rapid succession from the prince-abbots to the Prince of
Orange, to Marshal Kellermann as a gift from a victorious Napoleon,
and finally, on Napoleon's defeat, to the Emperor of Austria, who presented it in perpetuity to his chancellor, Prince Metternich. Metternich's
great-grandson still holds the estate: all eighty-six acres of it now planted
exclusively with Riesling.

After we had admired a statue of the tardy courier, the view from
the terrace, the fiftieth parallel marker (the fiftieth parallel is considered the northern limit of tolerance for *Vitis vinifera*), and the handsome
buildings of the Schloss, largely reconstructed because of heavy damage in an air raid during World War II, we trooped down a long, stone
stairway into a vast, ancient cellar, a remnant of the original monastery.

German wines travel perfectly. If handled correctly, they will taste
the same in Kansas City as in Koblenz. But any wine tasted in the cellar
where it was made, within yards of the vines that bore it, has an extra
dimension, a magic that has nothing to do with balance or flavor or critics' approval. We knew we should not expect any Schloss Johannisberg
wine we might meet elsewhere to taste quite the same as the three we
sampled that afternoon. On the other hand, did any of us realize that
it would be impossible from then on to take even a sip of a Schloss
Johannisberg wine, anywhere in the world, and not be reminded of how
it had been, standing in pools of candlelight among shadows a thousand
years old?

We took a short break in Rüdesheim before continuing to Schloss
Vollrads in Oestrich. Those who wanted went in search of coffee or
tea. (I looked in vain for the pastry shop where thirty-five years ago,
as a wine trainee, I used to stuff myself on Sundays with fruit tarts
and whipped cream.) Others shopped for postcards, souvenirs, and fam-

ily gifts or went to gawp at the Drosselgasse, a noisy Rüdesheim alley crowded at all hours of day and night with wine pubs, sausage stalls, oompah bands, and flush-faced polka dancers.

The Schloss Vollrads property has been in the Greiffenclau family for at least eight hundred years. Sales of wine by the knights of Greiffenclau from their vineyards at Oestrich are documented as far back as 1211, and the family is known to have been in possession of part of the property for at least a century before that. Such a long tradition imposes its own responsibilities on the present Count Erwein Matuschka-Greiffenclau, who lives at Schloss Vollrads and devotes himself to managing its affairs.

In an elegant gilt- and brocade-paneled salon there, we tasted in sequence a dry 1986 Schloss Vollrads, a semidry '85, a 1985 *Kabinett,* and a 1975 Hallgartener Schönhell *Spätlese* from the Fürst Löwenstein estate, a neighboring property acquired by the family in 1979. Count Erwein talked to us about the wines, the estate, and, a subject close to his heart, the common misconceptions about German wines with food.

It is best to choose wine, he said, to suit the intensity of flavor or the texture of the food or its sauce. These are more important considerations than whether the meat is light or dark. He accepted that there were occasions when a red wine was needed to achieve balance but thought such a limited choice occurred less often than we were led to believe. We knew how well medium-dry German wines went with pâtés, mousses, and terrines, but not all of us understood how easily the fruity acidity and barely perceptible sweetness of these wines harmonize with the slight acidity and similarly moderate sweetness of many vegetables and sauces.

The wines Count Erwein had chosen for us to taste were delicious and established high criteria for the last tasting of the day—a comprehensive selection of about a dozen Rheingau wines waiting for us a few miles away at Schloss Reinhartshausen, formerly the estate of Prince Friedrich of Prussia and still the property of his sons, the great-grandchildren of Kaiser Wilhelm II. The tasting was introduced and conducted by Dr. Karl Heinz Zerbe, managing director of the Schloss Reinhartshausen estate. He gave such a comprehensive account of the Rheingau that I could barely take notes fast enough.

All the tasting sheets handed to us during the week gave details of the alcohol level, acidity, and residual sugar of each wine presented. At first I had thought it a pity to distract us from the wine with numbers, but I soon realized how subtly we were being taught that a number, out of context, meant very little. We came to see for ourselves that residual sugar and acidity had to be read together to be understood, one always modifying the other; and even so, intensity of flavor could shift their effect considerably. At the Schloss Reinhartshausen tasting, for example, a 1986 Geisenheimer Mönchspfad Riesling *Kabinett* from the Weingut Schumann-Nägler, rich with almost 3.2 percent residual sugar and only .75 percent acidity, had such deep, intense flavor that it seemed in perfect, lively balance. But another grower's 1986 Lorcher Schlossberg, with less residual sugar (2.4 percent) and a higher level of acidity (.89 percent), lacked flavor, and, despite the crisper definition promised by the numbers, it tasted flat and zestless.

There were many remarkable wines given to us to taste that evening, but I shall mention only two more, both from Schloss Reinhartshausen's own vineyards: a superbly ripe 1976 Erbacher Schlossberg Riesling *Auslese* and a rare and curious Erbacher Rheinhell '87 made from a combination of Chardonnay and Pinot Blanc vines planted on an island in the Rhine. Under German wine law Chardonnay may be planted in Rheingau vineyards only by special permission and for controlled experiment. The wine had an austere, pebbly style, not unlike a Chablis, and was a great curiosity among so many floral and fruity Rhine wines.

We drove back to Johannisberg to eat dinner at a small restaurant perched in the vineyards above the village. There should have been a romantic view of the vines and the river by moonlight, but the rain that had been threatening all day came down in torrents. At last, tired after a very full day, we climbed into the darkened bus, ready for our sleepy ride back to Winkel. The engine started, the door swung closed, and suddenly from speakers overhead came the unmistakable twang of Willie Nelson: "On the road ageeeeehn . . . "

Originally published as "School Days on the Rhine" in *Gourmet,* June 1989.

The German Wine Institute has discontinued the German Wine Academy and has no immediate plans to reinstate it.

FRANCONIA

Going for Baroque

A year ago, at the end of May, I was in the German city of Würzburg for the final night of the annual Baroque music festival. While dusk gathered over the rose garden of the Residenz, the sumptuous eighteenth-century palace of the former prince-bishops, its scented arbors and pathways illuminated by flickering torches, three hundred of us, decorously black-tied or discreetly bejeweled, sat under the vast Tiepolo ceiling of the Imperial Hall, listening to soloists of the Leipziger Gewandhaus Bach Orchestra play, as a prelude to dinner, music by Corelli, Handel, Bach, and Vivaldi.

It was a brilliant performance, and as we moved to our candlelit tables in the adjoining White Hall (the room's every surface encrusted, by Antonio Bossi—who later went mad—with the world's most extravagant display of Rococo plaster-work), I wondered what wine on earth, let alone what dish, could possibly make an impression against the competition of all this splendor. I need not have been concerned. Dinner began with a succulent terrine of smoked trout, from streams on the Spessart mountains to the west of Würzburg, accompanied by a memorably stylish Franconian wine, a Würzburg Stein Sylvaner '91, grown just a few hundred yards from where we sat and made in the palace cellars beneath our feet. After a pigeon consommé and a pause for a glass of prize-winning Eschendorfer Lump Sylvaner Spätlese '89, we went on to enjoy a 1990 Bürgstadter Centgrafenberg Spätburgunder *Kabinett*, one of Germany's rarest red wines, with a fillet of young venison, cranberry sauce, and sesame-strewn potatoes.

～～～

Mention Würzburg or its region, Franconia, and most Americans (other than members of the United States 3rd Infantry Division stationed there) draw a blank. Yet Franconia—the storybook Germany of forests and vineyards, venerable castles and comfortable old inns, Baroque palaces and Rococo churches—is little more than an hour's drive east of Frankfurt's steel-and-glass metropolis. Those who go there find gingerbread houses and cobblestone streets within the walls and turrets of medieval villages; delicious food garnered from local farms, rivers, and woods; and of course Franconian wine, to enjoy in a grower's snug parlor or in a wisteria-draped courtyard.

Franconia's art treasures and architectural riches are a legacy of the time when packhorses and mule trains carting the world's luxuries—silks, dyes, pepper, saffron—wound their way from the Alpine passes and the upper reaches of the Danube to the valleys of the Main and the Rhine and to the headwaters of the Weser and the Elbe. From Genoa to Lübeck, from Constantinople to Antwerp, and from Venice to Hamburg, all roads passed through Franconia. (Wagner, which means wagoner or teamster, is one of the region's most common family names.)

Great trading and banking dynasties were founded there. To get goods from one watershed to the other, bills of exchange and letters of credit were as essential as horses. Taxes, dues for right of passage, commissions, and profits on reworked commodities enriched Franconia's merchant families and paid for the adornment of their cities. These were people who lived well and drank well. The religious institutions they supported established the area's vineyards, first mentioned in seventh-century documents, on the sites best calculated to provide them with the finest wine.

In 1802, when Napoleon deposed the ruling prince-bishop of Würzburg in the course of bringing the map of Germany's principalities closer to his own taste in political geography, Franconia was annexed to Bavaria, a German state distinguished for beer rather than wine. But Franconia has remained faithful to the vines that line the valley of the Main River as it meanders from the hills of the Steigerwald in the east to a gap south of the heavily forested Spessart in the west. (The Main then flows past Frankfurt to join the Rhine.)

The Spessart's mountainous mass protects the vineyards from the rain of the prevailing westerlies, but it cuts them off from maritime influence, too, leaving the Main valley exposed to an extreme continental climate. Summers are hotter, winters colder (the Main freezes over regularly), and both spring and fall are shorter than they are on the Rhine. Late spring frosts are common and can damage a potential crop severely—as happened in 1985. Ideally, Franconia needs grape varieties that bud late and ripen early, to reduce the risk of damage by spring frosts and to make the most of the short span of an intense Franconian summer.

But the Main valley, compressed and convoluted between the Spessart and the Steigerwald, encompasses a series of subtly changing weather patterns as it twists repeatedly to and fro, ensuring, in its turns, the benefit of many sheltered and south-facing slopes. The valley's soils are varied as well. In the west, a reddish sandstone (which reappears on isolated sites farther east) gives full white wines and, from Pinot Noir, Germany's most reputed reds. Closer to Würzburg, in the middle section of the valley—known as the Triangle *(Dreieck)* because the river there follows the form of a giant V—a particularly active limestone formed from seashell fossils promotes in the wines a characteristically sturdy finesse and the delicate but intense fragrance most associated with the best of Franconian wines. Farther east, the vineyards on the gypsum and heavy clay of the Steigerwald give firm wines of greater substance that, though slower to disclose themselves, age well.

Mature Franconian wines have always been keenly sought out, jealously hoarded, and highly prized. In his book *Vintage: The Story of Wine,* Hugh Johnson tells of being one of a privileged few who tasted, in London in

1961, a wine grown on the Stein vineyard at Würzburg in 1540, a hot, dry year in which, records show, there was no rain from April to October. Under those conditions, the wine was probably as difficult as it was concentrated. At any rate, it spent more than a hundred years in a regularly replenished cask in the cellar of the prince-bishops before being bottled in the late seventeenth century. In the nineteenth century, following Franconia's complete absorption into Bavaria, the bottles were transferred to the royal cellars. From there they were eventually sold off at auction, along with much else, during Germany's republican era after World War I. Even though four hundred years old, the wine, Johnson tells us, was still lively, reflecting, as it were, "the sun of that distant summer."

The vigorous elegance of Franconian wines has been their chief attraction. They were favorites of Goethe (whose last recorded words, in 1832, came in the form of a question about the Franconian wine being offered him: "You haven't put sugar in it?" he is said to have asked). André Jullien, in his reliable *Topographie de Tous les Vignobles Connus,* first published in Paris in 1816, described the wine of Würzburg as "a dry wine with spirit, perfumed and very agreeable" and, making much of the high prices it fetched, ranked it with the most esteemed of Germany. Henry Vizetelly, in his 1875 report on the wines of the world presented at the International Exposition of 1873 in Vienna, said much the same, praising its "flavour, fullness, and delicacy" as well as its "singular vigour and fire." He, too, ranked Franconian wines among the greatest.

High praise of Franconian wine continued into this century: Morton Shand, in his *Book of Other Wines—Than French* published in 1929, was as enthusiastic as Goethe, Jullien, and Vizetelly. Usually a carefully observant writer, hardly given to purple prose, Shand got carried away when writing of Franconian wine. (He mentions *Steinwein,* incidentally, using as a generic term a name that should have been—and now is—legally restricted to wines from the Stein vineyard in Würzburg.) While telling of German writers who compare Franconian wine to madrigals, Shand out-does them with an embarrassingly fey comparison to "a dewy posy of wild flowers, fresh picked by fairy fingers" but settles down to describe, more matter-of-factly, the wines' "subtle delicacy of flavour and . . . rare, if almost evanescent, bouquet."

～ ～ ～

The world virtually lost sight of Franconian wines after Shand's book. For years they were all but unobtainable in Germany and quite impossible to find elsewhere. There are many reasons why the area under vines had shrunk severely by the early twentieth century, chief among them the cost of replanting Franconia's steep hillsides after phylloxera struck in the 1870s. Vestiges of the Napoleonic inheritance law that divides vineyards—and divides them again with each succeeding generation—had already imposed an awkward and expensive pattern of cultivation as families struggled to deal with their many minute and widely scattered parcels of vines acquired through past marriages. The problem exacerbated the already high risk of growing grapes in a region where a year's crop could be lost in a single spring night's frost.

By the 1960s the production of Franconian wine did not meet local demand. A vintner had only to provide a few tables and benches in his leafy garden in summer or a cozy wine room with candles and checkered tablecloths in winter for customers to arrive to spend a pleasant hour with a *Schoppen* (traditionally a quarter liter of young wine) and a snack of bread and sausage. Inevitably, a case or two of wine would leave the house with each visit. Even when the vintage had been abundant, the cellars were soon empty.

Changes in Germany's wine laws in 1971 and a program that helped consolidate Franconia's vineyards into workable holdings through an officially sponsored exchange among growers of widely separated small plots revived interest in viticulture. In the last twenty years the area under vines in Franconia has increased from barely five thousand acres to fifteen.

The steadily rising production has been further swollen recently by a series of exceptionally abundant harvests. For the first time since anyone can remember there is presently not only enough wine for Franconians but wine to spare. This statement is all the more significant if one bears in mind that a fear of running out of wine is of such long standing in Franconia that there were times in the eighteenth century when growers were forbidden by decree of the prince-bishop of Würzburg from selling any wine at all outside his territory.

Almost 90 percent of all Franconian wine is still consumed within Bavaria, but a number of growers are now making small shipments to other parts of Germany and even to the United States. In recent months I have seen the distinctive *Bocksbeutel* (the flattened, round-bellied flagon in which Franconian wines are sold) on merchants' shelves as far apart as Santa Monica, California, and Amagansett, New York.

In Franconia, the wines are generally drier than elsewhere in Germany, though their labels sport the same classifications—*Kabinett, Spätlese, Auslese*, and *Beerenauslese*—to denote the maturity of the grapes, or at least their level of natural sugar when picked. Franconia's hot summers reduce acidity, making residual sugar less important to the wines' overall balance; that's why the growers there can allow a drier fermentation, imposing on themselves a stricter parameter of dryness for wines labeled *trocken* (dry) and *halbtrocken* (semidry) than Germany's national law requires of them.

Though almost half the vines planted in Franconia are Müller-Thurgau—since World War II the most widely planted variety in Germany because of its large yields and low-risk cultivation—the classic grape of the region is Sylvaner. The new plantings show a steady return to it. "Consumers here have had a fling with all the new varieties," Jochen Freihold, director of the Franconian Winegrowers' Association, told me recently, "and it's interesting to see that those who really appreciate their wine eventually return to Sylvaner."

Sylvaner has a long history in Franconia. In fact, the variety made its German debut there in 1659 in the vineyards of Schloss Castell in the Steigerwald. It is thought to have found its way into Franconia by way of the Danube, just like the silks and spices that preceded it. The earliest Sylvaner wines must have made an impression because the variety spread rapidly.

Riesling is grown on only the most favored sites in Franconia. (It covers just 3 percent of the region's vineyard acreage.) The structure imposed on Franconian wine by climate and soil—a structure that gives Franconian Sylvaner its uncommon elegance without affecting its natural tenderness—can be too severe for the inherently steely Riesling. That's why Riesling is planted only on vineyard sites—such as the Würzburger Stein, the Würzburger Abtsleite, and the Randersackerer Teufelkeller—where summer starts earlier and finishes later. When a Franconian Riesling succeeds, however, whether thanks to site or summer or both, it succeeds with rare magnificence.

Other traditional German grape varieties are grown in Franconia, but the area became known, in the first years of its revival, for its considerable acreage of new crossings, many of them specially developed in response to the region's short, hot summer. Each of them has its supporters, but mostly their wines have the quick and easy appeal of pop music—and pall as rapidly. Some say it's simply that the newly crossed vine varieties are highly prolific, and that their wines would have a more classic style if the yields were more strictly controlled. But small yields—and therefore smaller revenues—raise other issues in a place such as Franconia where production costs are high. Rieslaner, a cross between Riesling and Sylvaner as its name suggests, is one new variety that works well there, especially when used for rich *Auslese* and *Beerenauslese* wines. Its intense bouquet, almost like fresh apricot, and deep, lasting flavor become particularly attractive when supported by luscious sweetness.

～ ～ ～

Even after the consolidation of land holdings the average vineyard in Franconia remains small: The fifteen thousand acres of vines are divided among 7,735 registered growers. Those figures must be carefully interpreted, however, because a few large estates reduce yet further the average for others. A third of the growers, usually those with less than an acre or so of vines, take their grapes to a growers' cooperative, where the quality of wine will depend on the vineyards of its members and on their diligence. The cooperative at Thüngersheim, just north of Würzburg, shows how well the system can work if local vintners so will it. A selection of wines from Thüngersheim, the best being from the Johannisberg vineyard, a great block of red sandstone thrusting through the limestone of the Triangle, is now being distributed in the United States.

Of the large estates, the most significant are those of Würzburg's Bürgerspital, founded in 1319, and Juliusspital, established in 1576. Both are charitable foundations supporting—with the revenues of their vineyards, farms, and timberland—homes for the elderly, mental institutions, and hospitals. The holdings of the Juliusspital make it the second largest wine estate in Germany. And the vineyards bequeathed to both the Bürgerspital and the Juliusspital by their original founders and by later benefactors are the finest in Franconia. The Bürgerspital's highly privileged sites have allowed it to specialize in Riesling (the variety makes up roughly 30 percent of its production), and a Riesling style—tight, austere—is the hallmark of its wines.

The Staatlicher Hofkeller, formerly the private domain of Würzburg's all-powerful prince-bishop, is now the property of the state of Bavaria. (Some of its vineyards are used for research and teaching.) I have never seen a more spectacular cellar than that beneath the Würzburg Residenz. The long, vaulted aisles, wide and high enough to accommodate a bus, are lined on both sides with enormous and beautifully carved oak casks. Lit by candles, as they are for special occasions, they make an unforgettable sight.

Two of Germany's noble families also have extensive vineyards in Franconia, in the Steigerwald. Schloss Hallburg is the property of Count von Schönborn, and the domain of Schloss Castell has belonged to the family of Prince (and eminent banker) zu Castell-Castell for almost a thousand years. In addition to fine dry wines, weightier and more intense than those of the Triangle, the Castell domain produces exceptional dessert wines—*Spätlesen, Auslesen,* and *Trockenbeerenauslesen*—from Rieslaner and Scheurebe grapes grown on its Casteller Kugelspiel vineyard. A 1979 Casteller Kugelspiel Trockenbeerenauslese the color of dark amber, offered to me at the close of a lunch at Schloss Castell, smelled and tasted of praline and rose petals, apricots and honey. Count zu Castell-Castell, the prince's nephew and estate manager, told me that 1992 had produced the best wines in Franconia since that spectacular 1979 vintage.

What's extraordinary is that all these great estates make a score or more wines every year (the Juliusspital makes sixty) by separating grapes according to variety, provenance, and quality—and each one is worthy of representing that estate as if it were the only wine it produced.

~ ~ ~

There are smaller estates making superb wines too. For example, though I'm not enthusiastic about German red wines, I acknowledge that if the best in Germany are from Franconia, then the best in Franconia are from the Weingut Fürst in Bürgstadt. Paul Fürst makes Germany's most distinguished Pinot Noir—in German, *Spätburgunder*—but I prefer his superb Pinot Noir *Weissherbst* (the word used for white wine made from black grapes). Light gold in color, subtly flavored, and remarkably full-bodied, Fürst's *Weissherbst* is a favorite in Germany's top restaurants.

Outstanding producers in the Triangle include Artur Steinmann and Ernst Gebhardt, both of Sommerhausen, a community of artists and writers a few miles upriver from Würzburg. There, in a tiny but perfect theater above the village gatehouse, are regular performances of plays, concerts, and late-night political cabaret (a German tradition). The local inn offers such delicacies as lilac-blossom, rosebud, and fir-tip ice creams from a sort of homeopathic dessert trolley.

Steinmann lives nonchalantly with his family in the house where Francis Daniel Pastorius was born in 1651. Pastorius, as German Americans know, brought thirteen families to Pennsylvania in 1683, the first Germans to settle in what was to become the United States. On summer weekend afternoons Steinmann plays his accordion for the visitors who sit at tables on the grass in front of his house or has local writers and musicians give poetry readings and recitals. The most popular entertainment, though, is the occasional concert by the band of the U.S. 3rd Infantry—in homage to Pastorius, one could say.

Iphofen, in the Steigerwald about twenty miles southeast of Würzburg, is one of the most charming of the wine towns, with a Renaissance council house, pretty squares, tree-lined streets, and fine Baroque doorways. Two of the region's leading growers are based there: Hans Wirsching and Johann Ruck. Wirsching has made a specialty of Pinot Gris *(Grauburgunder)* from his holdings on the town's Julius-Echter-Berg—where the Main valley's red sandstone appears amid the Steigerwald's deep clay—but is best known for his powerful Riesling and Sylvaner wines. Ruck prides himself on his old vines and the backbone they give his wines. "They have a deeper root system," he says, "and are more consistent in yield and quality." He, too, makes Riesling and Sylvaner—enticingly spicy—from his vines on the Julius-Echter-Berg and on the Kronsberg vineyard. (An Iphöfer Kronsberg from the Juliusspital was one of the wines served to Queen Elizabeth at her coronation banquet in London in 1953.)

Iphofen is a center of good cooking as well as fine wine, with two outstanding restaurants. The reputation of Kammer, a tiny restaurant on the marketplace, draws customers from as far as Frankfurt and Nuremberg. The Zehntkeller, an old tithe barn divided into intimate rooms with no more than three or four tables in each, specializes in typical hearty Franconian dishes, including a local style of *pot-au-feu* made with kid and young vegetables and a venison soup served with mushroom dumplings.

But then one eats well almost everywhere in Franconia. The Juliusspital, the Bürgerspital, and the Hofkeller at the Würzburg Residenz all have restaurants where their wines are available with a choice of simple but well-prepared dishes. Zur Stadt Mainz, also in Würzburg, has a family atmosphere and a Franconian kitchen—wild boar and red cabbage, oxtail in red wine, and some kind of meat dumplings with onions are usually on call. Zum Stachel, Würzburg's oldest wine tavern (it opened in 1413), has an astonishing list of Franconian wines and is so popular in summer that guests happily share tables with strangers just to have a place in its magically beautiful courtyard. And at the Bären, in the town of Ochsenfurt, braised veal and potatoes becomes a dish fit for a king.

Those who go to Würzburg for the Baroque music festival at the end of May or for the Mozart festival a week later—or both—arrive in the middle of asparagus season. (For the Mozart festival the Würzburg City Philharmonic plays on the terrace of the Residenz for an audience that can choose between folding chairs on the gravel or bring-your-own-blanket on the grass.)

From around early May until late June, German restaurants vie with each other to see which can offer the most tender, the most creamy-white, and the thickest asparagus stalks. Special menus offer dishes that are simply excuses to serve each customer a full pound of white asparagus, usually with a bowl of steamed, freshly dug new potatoes on one side and a bowl of melted butter or hollandaise on the other. The season starts whenever the first asparagus is ready to be cut, but no matter when that might be, whether late or early, it ends punctually on June 24, the Feast of Saint John. The day always comes too soon; but if the season has been satisfactorily long and the asparagus particularly good, one can hear, on June 24, all the way from the Spessart to the Steigerwald, a great sigh of contentment as each and every person swallows the last bite of his or her last pound of asparagus for the year. Any regrets are then drowned in a glass of Franconian Sylvaner.

Originally published as "Going for Baroque: The Pleasures of Franconia" in *Gourmet*, April 1994.

CALIFORNIA CABERNET SAUVIGNON

Cabernet Sauvignon was introduced to California in or before the 1880s together with other varieties from southwestern France, including those traditionally associated with Cabernet Sauvignon in the vineyards of Bordeaux and some, such as Tannat, used for less opulent wines grown in the Béarnais region closer to the Pyrenees. As in France, these varieties were seen as means to an end—the production of claretlike red wine—not as ends in themselves. No more than in France did California growers at that time seem to be seeking to make a "Cabernet Sauvignon," and, with rare exceptions, it was only after Prohibition, when attempts were made to break with European place names applied generically to California wines, that Cabernet Sauvignon became the name of a *wine* as well as of a grape variety, thereby confounding end and means in a way that is still not resolved. Most of us can only guess at the style and quality of those pre-Prohibition wines made from Cabernet Sauvignon grown in California, though a half bottle of the 1936 vintage from E. H. Rixford's legendary La Questa vineyard at Woodside, tasted recently, gave me some idea of how they might have been. La Questa's reputation ("the most expensive Cabernet listed . . . on most . . . California wine lists of the early 1900s," according to Frank Schoonmaker in *American Wines*), was based on "red Bordeaux varieties planted," says Charles L. Sullivan in *Like Modern Edens,* "in the precise proportion as they were then grown at Château Margaux."

A half bottle almost fifty years old cannot be relied on, and when I broke the blob of wax that sealed the cork and poured wine directly, without decanting, I was expecting little more than a ghostly curiosity. To my surprise, the wine was deep red, almost opaque, merely tinged with terra cotta at the glass edge; there was that immediate and extraordinary bouquet with hints of chocolate, charcoal, and cassis we associate with distinguished classed growths of the Médoc; on the palate the wine was lively, intense, impeccably balanced. It was, in fact, among the best wines of the Cabernet Sauvignon genre that I have tasted.

A more recent, and therefore more practically influential, legacy of California Cabernet Sauvignon has been handed down by Louis M. Martini, Charles Krug, Inglenook, and Beaulieu Vineyard, Napa wineries that alone from the end of Prohibition until the renaissance of the sixties and seventies ensured a continuum of fine winemaking in the state. During that time, they invested their skill and greatest effort in Cabernet Sauvignon wines. Remarkably, we can still see, within the scope of the disparate styles they chose, the seeds of all options available to winemakers today. They composed a theme that has since been taken up in ever widening fugue and variation. At Charles Krug, for example, Cabernet Sauvignon was unblended, and aged in well-seasoned vats and barrels; at Inglenook proportions of Cabernet Franc and, in later years, Merlot were introduced in quantities carefully judged to give subtlety without changing the essential character of Cabernet Sauvignon—a character further protected by aging in neutral German oak ovals; considerable varietal and geographic blending at Louis M. Martini, on the other hand, produced agreeable wines ready to be drunk early and with less regard for varietal purity; and at Beaulieu, of course, American oak was used to dramatic effect on intense, unblended Cabernet Sauvignon to create the Private Reserve of Georges de Latour.

The contrasts in these familiar styles were etched in my memory at a dinner in the fall of 1979 when the 1951 Cabernet Sauvignons of Beaulieu Vineyard and Louis M. Martini were served with a 1956 Charles Krug and a 1941 Inglenook. The wines were presented to us in receding order of vintage—first the Charles Krug, with fruit so persistent and finish so soft that the wine left a sweet impression against which the Louis Martini seemed at first to be austere. The Louis Martini was certainly less direct than the others, but eventually revealed a youthful, berrylike bouquet that softened the wine and flattered the palate. The Beaulieu Vineyard Private Reserve that followed, richly preserving all those characteristics associated with Rutherford, with Cabernet Sauvignon, and with American oak that André Tchelistcheff combined into one of the most particular and consistent wines made anywhere, brought us more bluntly to the essence of Cabernet Sauvignon; and that was carried on by the Inglenook 1941, an immense, muscular wine, dark almost to the point of blackness, yet with bouquet unexpectedly fresh and elegant. Despite its size, there was no burn of excessive alcohol, no distortion of flavor or character: It had the perfect balance then characteristic of this estate.

These extraordinary wines of the forties and fifties, with an occasional glimpse or guess at pre-Prohibition production, remind us that Cabernet Sauvignon has a history in the state, and is certainly not a product of the recent wine revival. They provide a perspective in which we can better judge the potential and what seems to be the natural style of Cabernet Sauvignon in California. True, preoccupation with the grape is fostered by its associations with the great classed growths of Bordeaux (though none uses it to the exclusion of all others), a challenge as compelling to any winemaker as the Matterhorn is to a mountain climber, but that would soon be over if the wines to which Cabernet Sauvignon contributes did not so frequently touch our highest expectations of red wine.

~ ~ ~

In his *Bordeaux Antique,* R. Etienne suggests that evidence enough exists to show that today's Cabernet Sauvignon grape descends from Biturica, which in turn descended from Balisca, brought to Bordeaux in antiquity from the eastern shore of the Adriatic, where modern Albania now is. Pliny the Elder was familiar with Biturica in the first century and wrote

(I quote and translate loosely) that "it flowers well, is resistant to wind and rain, and does rather better in cool than in warm regions," all of which makes sense to us today. Columella (according to René Pijassou of the University of Bordeaux: I have searched for the exact quote without success) confirmed Pliny's observation that Biturica stood up well to rain, and added another attribute familiar to us—it gave wine that kept well and improved with age.

Cabernet Sauvignon vines grow not exuberantly, but vigorously, and, when properly cultivated, yield sparingly. Their buds open late, an advantage in areas prone to spring frost, as are both the Médoc and the floor of Napa Valley. The dark green leaves are indented deeply in a way that causes the lobes to overlap slightly, a varietal characteristic. Its fruit is most appreciated by winemakers for reliable acidity and for the intensity of color and flavor inherent in the tough, resistant skin. Bunches are small and irregularly shaped, but the berries are perfectly spherical, black, and tightly packed together. They have a high proportion of seed and little juice.

Cabernet Sauvignon grapes give a wine that is distinctive, and most who have tasted it would recognize it again even when blended with other grape varieties. The characteristic smell and flavor bring forth references to violets, black currants, eucalyptus, tar, and, in older wines, chocolate and charcoal. In California, vocabulary has recently been extended to include vegetables of various kinds, perhaps through a misconception of the French tasting word *végétal,* which means "vegetable" only in the sense that we distinguish plant life from animal and mineral. It should not be surprising to find echoes of fruits and flowers in Cabernet Sauvignon, however: All wines share at least traces of most of the acids, alcohols, and esters occurring in everything from pineapple to roses. It is Cabernet Sauvignon's richness in this respect that makes the variety such an important component of a great wine.

But Bordeaux has always been more concerned with terrain, with the "best sections" of a vineyard and what to plant there than with grape varieties as such and where to plant them. The great growths of

Bordeaux, and therefore Bordeaux wine as we know it today, evolved from the discovery that a knoll of sand and gravel at Haut-Brion, though barely different from land that surrounded it, nevertheless produced wine of greater distinction. John Locke, the philosopher, went there in 1677 to see for himself, and described in his journal "a little rise of ground, lieing open most to the west. It is noe thing but pure white sand, mixd with a little gravel." He continued: "One would imagin it scarce fit to beare any thing. . . . This, however, they say, & that men of skill and credit, that the wine in the very next vineyard, though in all things seeming equall to me, is not soe good." Arnaud de Pontac, the owner of Haut-Brion at that time, was a man of influence and wealth, able to ensure exposure of his wine to those best able to appreciate and recommend it. The style of winemaking in Bordeaux changed to accommodate this newly understood potential as much as to adjust to new market needs, and claret was transformed from the uneven beverage it had been since the Middle Ages to what the *London Gazette*, in the early eighteenth century, referred to repeatedly, and with determined fascination, as New French Claret. But "if the *régisseurs* gave great importance to the role of the soil," says René Pijassou, in his 1980 treatise *Le Médoc,* "they gave no recognition to the virtues of grape variety as a factor of quality." In the carefully detailed working instructions left by Berlon, Château Margaux's great *régisseur* at the time of transformation, there was no indication at all of which grape varieties were to be used. At that time, white grapes were freely mixed with black in the château's vineyard (the white vines of Château Latour were grafted to black only in 1813), and Merlot was still unknown in the vineyards of the Médoc.

The emergence of Cabernet Sauvignon as the preferred grape of Bordeaux, after 1815, was probably due more to the properties of the vine than to the quality and style of the wine produced from it. Writing in 1850, Edouard Lawton, the well-known Bordeaux broker of the period, said that Cabernet Sauvignon (then referred to as Carmenet Sauvignon) had been planted in the vineyards extensively during the preceding twenty-five years because the variety budded late, a protection from spring frosts, and was resistant to flower-drop in wet and cold seasons. As late as the 1830s, Château Latour continued to experiment with all manner of grapes, including Syrah from the Rhône, and only in 1849 was there a policy established that, since terrain was of prime importance, selection of grape varieties was to be made in accordance with soil compatibility. Most Bordeaux châteaux today still use grape varieties in proportions dictated by the soil composition of their vineyards. Rarely do they plant varieties specifically with a predetermined style in mind, disregarding soil. It is in this sense, above all, that the soils of a Bordeaux château dictate the recognizable style of its wine. Bordeaux still thinks vineyard first and vine variety second. Though by 1970, Cabernet Sauvignon dominated the Médoc through the style it imposes, it represented only 48.6 percent of the vines planted there, and an even smaller proportion of the vines of Saint-Emilion and Pomerol.

In California, on the other hand, emphasis on winemaking rather than on grape growing has allowed, indeed encouraged, more play to a winemaker's expression of the character inherent in specific grape varieties, than to the style and quality dictated by a particular vineyard site. It is a difference of attitude accentuated by giving grape and wine the same name in California, creating an assumption, at least, that one should faithfully reflect the other. For some varieties, particularly most whites, depending on fruit aromas and flavor for their character and style, that might be justified. But Cabernet Sauvignon develops through the transformations of age, acquiring grace and subtlety, flavor and bouquet not present in its early youth. We value mature Cabernet Sauvignon wines because they *are* so much more than the fermented juice of a particular grape.

Yet even in those instances where much is made of origin—Martha's Vineyard in the Napa Valley, for example—its importance seems to lie in the extent to which it brings out the character of Cabernet Sauvignon planted there. Few California winemakers would be comfortable expressing the style of a particular vineyard, using without concern whatever grape variety or varieties seemed most apt to the location. Most, consciously or not, seek out growers whose vineyards give the greatest opportunity to express best the variety of special interest to them. This is notably true of Cabernet Sauvignon. Joe Heitz, a distinguished proponent of vineyard identification, says, nevertheless, that he "tries to make a first-rate California Cabernet Sauvignon, one that reflects the character of the vineyard." He does not say that he "tries to make a first-rate Martha's Vineyard, one that reflects the character of Cabernet Sauvignon." He thinks Cabernet Sauvignon, makes his wine from Cabernet Sauvignon alone, and is impatient with those who prefer to blend. "They look to France," he says, "when our soils and our climate are different." In one respect, at least, Michael Rowan of Jordan Vineyard in Alexander Valley agrees. "Vineyards in Bordeaux are traditionally on meager soils. Producing fine wine from richer California vineyards is a new art. We cannot rely on the experience of Bordeaux. The expression of Cabernet Sauvignon is changed here, and we learn as we go." Ric Forman, previously with Sterling Vineyards, also accepts that California's climate, in particular, brings out greater richness, but complains that it has been too often presented in a heavy-handed way, just for effect. "It is an added quality that we should use," he says, "but not to the extent of wrecking the inherent finesse of Cabernet Sauvignon. Bigger is not better."

The "heavy hand" originated in a system by which growers were paid for grape sugar rather than grapes. In 1975, for example, when a cool, slow ripening season delayed sugar formation, there were stories of growers who cut the canes to allow dehydration to concentrate low sugar in the grapes. Today, wineries often agree in advance to pay the price for twenty-four degree Brix grapes, marginally high for elegance, if they can retain the right, should they prefer, to have the grapes picked at a lower sugar concentration for the same price. In the early seventies, a "heavy hand" also reflected the eagerness of a new generation of winemakers to explore the extent to which they could push the varietal's intensity. A key sentence in the edition of Amerine and Joslyn's *Table Wines* then in use as a standard text at the University of California may have spurred them on. "The most common defect of California wines," ran its message, "is their lack of distinctive aroma or bouquet rather than the presence of any specific disease or defect." Whether or not that was true of wines of the Central Valley, the mass-production area closest to the Davis campus, it probably was never intended to refer to the limited production of coastal Cabernet Sauvignon wines.

"It was a time," says Warren Winiarski of Stag's Leap Wine Cellars, referring to the early seventies, "when California winemakers were asking what Cabernet Sauvignon grapes *could* give, as opposed to what they *should* give." Massive, often charmless wines found ready acceptance among those who, often new to wine, allowed themselves to be impressed by scale before they had learned to recognize standards of balance, subtlety, and just plain drinkability. Dense, oversized wines matched the abundant enthusiasm typical of the newly converted. But such wines crushed any balanced, restrained wine tasted alongside them, so that the rosettes, medals, and endless accolades bestowed on them by county fairs, newsletters, and tasting groups further encouraged excess. The public, lacking guidance, accepted the rosettes and medals as recommendations, and were disappointed to find so many of them attached to wines that were unacceptably harsh and coarsely flavored. It was no consolation to be told that the wines would "live" forever.

~ ~ ~

Fortunately, the tradition preserved by Martini, Krug, Inglenook, and Beaulieu, now strengthened and extended by others, continued without fanfare to provide balanced wines that perceptibly evolved from, and maintained, earlier styles. The point at which balance was again recognized as the key quality of a California Cabernet Sauvignon, as it is of any wine, was marked by the 1976 tasting in Paris at which Winiarski's Stag's Leap Wine Cellars' 1973 Cabernet Sauvignon was acknowledged the peer of any in the world. Stag's Leap had had some recognition in

California, too, but the benchmark there at the time was still set by intense, exceedingly tannic wines that overwhelmed Stag's Leap in any direct comparison. European tasters had few preconceived ideas of how California wines were supposed to taste, and even fewer of the criteria by which they were being judged so articulately in California. Winiarski claims that he did not aim at any particular style for his 1973, but admits at least, on reflection, to having sought moderation in all decisions along the way. Balance and moderation are now his consciously defined goals, increasingly shared by most other winemakers in California, however diverse the paths they use to arrive at them.

Balance in wine starts in balanced grapes, and Louis P. Martini says "perfect grapes, grown in a perfect spot, would need little help. But not much in this world," he is quick to add, "is perfect." Martini blends to achieve the particular balance he prefers in his wines, bringing Cabernet Sauvignon grapes from his old vines in the Mayacamas mountains between Napa and Sonoma to add strength and a certain soft richness to the flowery, more pointedly acid, fruit of equally mature Cabernet Sauvignon vines grown in the cool Carneros region close to the Bay. He uses Merlot, too, to round out his blends, but only enough to arrive at the balance he seeks. Though it is an article of faith with him that no wine need be undrinkable when young in order to age, a Cabernet Sauvignon, he believes, is better for having all the Cabernet Sauvignon that balance and harmony will allow.

To Joe Heitz, "all the Cabernet Sauvignon" means *only* Cabernet Sauvignon. He feels that in the otherwise imperfect world lamented by Louis Martini, his own perfect grapes are indeed grown in perfect spots. "Blending," he says, "is all right for those who have to buy up lots here and there of what they can find. But the best wines are vineyard wines made from grapes where everything necessary is there within the fruit." André Tchelistcheff would once have agreed with him. Unblended and clearly defined Cabernet Sauvignon from designated vineyards was, and is, what Beaulieu Vineyards' Georges de Latour Private Reserve is all about. But though Tchelistcheff feels that a classic like the Georges de Latour Private Reserve must meticulously maintain its consistency of style, he now believes that softer, less assertive, more complex and more pleasing wines can be made from California Cabernet Sauvignon by blending, especially with 10 to 15 percent Merlot.

It is a philosophy widely shared in California; indeed, those using 100 percent Cabernet Sauvignon for production of fine wines seem to be in the minority. But with less than 2,600 acres of Merlot vines bearing in 1980, compared with over 22,000 acres of Cabernet Sauvignon, it is clear that California is far from the proportions of Merlot and Cabernet Sauvignon often common in Bordeaux. Freemark Abbey adds 12 to 15 percent Merlot to the Cabernet Sauvignon of its Bosché Vineyard wines. Charles Carpy, claiming that it enriches and rounds out the Cabernet Sauvignon, says "it also adds a hair of color," acknowledging that in California, at least, Merlot is often more deeply colored, stronger in alcohol, and richer in texture than is Cabernet Sauvignon. That is exactly what Michael Rowan likes about Merlot: "its concentrated, almost candy-like, fruit." "It is a flavor," he says, "that gets under the Cabernet Sauvignon and seems to push it forward, making it both more vibrant and more accessible." He uses roughly 10 percent Merlot in all his blends.

The strength and richness of California Merlot is a problem to Cathy Corison of Chappellet. She seeks a lean style for her Cabernet Sauvignon, picking carefully to keep grape sugar under control so that no Chappellet Cabernet Sauvignon need ever exceed 12.5 percent alcohol. "Merlot," she explains, "is sometimes bigger than Cabernet, and I trial-blend to check proportions to suit each vintage." But despite the problems, she would not want to work without the extra dimension of flavor and texture that Merlot brings.

In Monterey County, Bill Jekel, of Jekel Vineyard, uses no Merlot at all. He would, he says, if he felt his wines needed some softening influence, but learning to adapt to conditions in Monterey County—"so different from Napa and Sonoma"—he has also learned how to draw the best from the grapes of his Cabernet Sauvignon vines. A number of new factors came together in Monterey: Ungrafted new clones of heat-treated Cabernet Sauvignon were set in a cool climate with low rainfall on soils that varied from sand and gravel to hard adobe clay. Greater control of water through irrigation was both a blessing and a disaster until the growers had learned how to handle it. On their own roots, Cabernet Sauvignon vines in Monterey were vigorous, but those who tended them, often new to viticulture, did not understand that the vines needed to be stressed at certain critical periods. Some say that improvement in Monterey Cabernet Sauvignon is due to maturing of the vines over the past decade, but Jekel disagrees. "We have learned how to handle the vines," he explains, "how to adapt our winemaking to the grapes produced here." He refers to better water control, fermentation techniques that drive off excessive aromatics, and aging procedures that bring out a distinctive style for Monterey Cabernet Sauvignon. "I don't see why Monterey Cabernet Sauvignon must taste like a Napa wine. All that is important is that it should be enjoyable. Local identity is part of the pleasure of wine."

Accepting such differences has not been easy in California. At recent public hearings that preceded labeling regulation changes for California (and all other U.S.) wines, one wine enthusiast, a lawyer, argued that he liked best Beaulieu Vineyard Private Reserve and fell into the common error of assuming that what he preferred must be, in some way, intrinsically superior. When he found that the wine was made from 100 percent Cabernet Sauvignon, he decided to campaign in favor of 100 percent Cabernet Sauvignon for *all* California Cabernet Sauvignon wines so that they could *all* taste like the Private Reserve. He was insensitive to the many variants possible and permissible in California Cabernet Sauvignon, and expected them all to conform to some predetermined type. As Peter Quimme (the *nom de plume* of John Frederick Walker and Elin McCoy) said in *American Wine,* no one should "hold a wine's own unique character against it as if it were a defect."

The unique character of a California Cabernet Sauvignon, whatever it owes to the region where the grapes were grown and the proportion of other varieties introduced, is also based on the wood in which it is barrel-aged. The neutral German oak ovals brought to Inglenook by its founder, Finnish sea captain Gustave Ferdinand Niebaum, continued in use throughout the years from 1939 to 1964 when his widow's grand-nephew, John Daniel, was in charge. Bordeaux wines, too, had been aged in Baltic oak until the early nineteenth century. Perhaps it was the British naval blockade of the Napoleonic era that first forced Bordeaux growers to use wood from their own forests. Whatever the cause, the effect was to add a further strand to the flavor of a fine Bordeaux wine. In California, French oak was first used consistently, as every-one knows, at Hanzell Vineyard in the 1950s. Until then, redwood vats and American oak barrels had been the standard aging vessels. Both Louis Martini and Charles Krug had used well-seasoned barrels to avoid oak flavor, whereas Beaulieu Vineyard had deliberately included a proportion of new oak for the Private Reserve. "I liked the vanilla aroma of American oak," says André Tchelistcheff. "It brought a richer and distinctive style to the Georges de Latour." Beaulieu Vineyard Private Reserve still spends two years in American oak before bot-tling. Paul Draper of Ridge also uses American oak to enrich his Monte Bello Cabernet Sauvignons, and at Jordan Vineyard, too, American oak plays an important stylistic role. After normal fermentation in stainless steel, the Cabernet Sauvignon is racked into large American oak vats for malolactic fermentation before transfer to small French oak barrels and American oak barrels for aging. Michael Rowan finds the charac-ter that each wood gives complements the other, and each brings out a different strain of fruit and flavor in Cabernet Sauvignon. Ric Forman and Robert Mondavi use French oak alone, and both study carefully the type and condition of the wood they use. Mondavi tries to ensure that his top reserve wines go into new wood, as do the Bordeaux first growths. "I find it gives backbone and vitality to the wine," he claims, and uses it for the same reason that he prefers Cabernet Franc to Merlot in his blends (though he uses both). "Working with the French," he says, "has taught me that elegance and vigor can go together. I have learned what can be done to sculpt a wine and give it structure."

The different uses of woods, the what, how much, and if-at-all of blending, the choice of yeast and control of fermentation itself, the varied microclimates and terrains of California—all play their part in determining the style of an individual wine. It is easy to generalize and claim that California Cabernet Sauvignon is richer than its Bordeaux counterpart, and then be silenced by a comparison of Clos du Val's classically reserved style with the exuberance of La Mission Haut-Brion. It is easy to suggest that California Cabernet Sauvignon is "forward" and less durable than Bordeaux and then remember the Rixford La Questa '36. It is easy to imagine that California Cabernet Sauvignon, as if there were only one, cannot match the variety of Bordeaux. Easy, that is, until we try to imagine what that one wine would be.

Originally published as "California Cabernet Sauvignon" in *The Book of California Wine,* eds. Doris Muscatine, Maynard A. Amerine, and Bob Thompson (Berkeley, London: University of California Press / Sotheby Publications, 1984).

Since this was written, Professor Carole Meredith of the Department of Viticulture and Enology at the University of California at Davis and her graduate student at the time, Dr. John Bowers, have shown through DNA analysis that Cabernet Sauvignon is the offspring of a natural cross between Cabernet Franc and Sauvignon Blanc. The use of different kinds of oak has continued to evolve. Beaulieu Vineyards, for example, has gradually dropped American oak in favor of French for aging the Georges de Latour Private Reserve. Cathy Corison is no longer with Chappellet but has her own winery in Napa Valley, where she continues to make particularly elegant Cabernet Sauvignon.

A MORNING TASTING
WITH JOE HEITZ

Joe Heitz called me one morning early in January to ask me to join him and a few friends at his Napa Valley winery the following Saturday to taste the 1970 Cabernet Sauvignon he was about to release. He was also releasing small quantities of some earlier vintages that he had held back for further maturing, and we were to taste these too.

It was a good day for a tasting. I left the Bay fog behind at Yountville and arrived at the Heitz winery under a blue sky. There were six of us, including Joe and his son David, and we set out nine Heitz Cabernet Sauvignon wines, covering the five vintages from 1966 to 1970, and three "outside" wines of the 1970 vintage as a comparison base for the latest Heitz wine. All the bottles were carefully masked and identified only by number, and when we each had our twelve glasses ready we set to work.

We were asked to rank the twelve wines according to preference, not an easy thing to do when judging wines of different vintages. Should one prefer a younger wine for obvious potential, if it is there, or a mature wine, less fine, perhaps, but which makes more satisfying drinking now? The passion for introducing an element of competition between wines—other than at official fair judgings—is something I still find difficult to accept, but in a way I suppose it is what we do every day when we decide to purchase one bottle rather than another. I am bothered by the system of evaluating wine in California, which is much more structured than the practice I am used to. In France, for example, where I have frequently served as a judge, a wine can earn a maximum of fifty points: ten for color and clarity, twenty for bouquet and aroma, and twenty for flavor and finesse on the palate. These broad divisions give considerable flexibility to the judge, who is even free to ignore a small technical fault if the overall quality, style, and delicacy of a wine are outstanding.

California tends to employ a twenty-point system developed for classroom work at the University of California at Davis. The division of points is particularized quite carefully: one point each for sugar and body; two points maximum each for color, appearance, acescency, flavor, astringency, total acid, and general quality; and four points maximum for aroma and bouquet. It is an excellent system for teaching because it trains the taster to pay consistent attention to individual aspects of the wines he is evaluating, and, provided the wines under consideration are all straightforward, everyday wines, it is as fair a method to rank them as any other. But it was not designed to classify outstanding wines, only to indicate, by award of the maximum extra points for aroma and general quality, that a wine is outstanding. If, under this system, a bottle of quite ordinary but fault-free wine were judged against one of the finest bottles to be found, the fine wine might take a point or two more for bouquet, possibly one for flavor, and perhaps another for general quality, but it is likely that both would obtain at least the seventeen points necessary to qualify for the "outstanding quality" description that Davis awards to wines in the seventeen- to twenty-point range. Rigid application of the Davis point system in situations for which it was not designed can lead, and has led, to bewildering and misleading consequences.

Fortunately, we were not asked to use any point system, but were left to resolve the cross-vintage comparisons as we thought best. It took about an hour to complete the tasting, and, when the bottles were finally unmasked and the results compared, we were all keen to taste the wines again—this time with knowledge of what was in each glass.

Heitz is one of a band of California winemakers (there are quite a few others, including Robert Mondavi, Richard Graff, Paul Draper, and

André Tchelistcheff) who impose a personal stamp on any wine they make. Regardless of the nuance of the vintage or the characteristics of the particular varietal, there is an individual style recognizable in wines made by these men. Mondavi, for example, makes racy, elegant wines and often succeeds in achieving the degree of finesse that he seeks above all else. Tchelistcheff's hallmark is a classic, fine-wrought stateliness that is sometimes out of place in his whites, but that has won his red wines a place among the most respected in California—and in the world. The Heitz style is partly a matter of scale—the wines are as big as the conditions of the vintage will allow—and there is always an echo of the wood in which he matures them. They are large, comfortable wines, with a warm, subtle gleam of flavor. Boldly self-assured, they rarely lack elegance and always have a certain bravura. When I taste them I am put in mind of richly polished and extravagantly carved Victorian mahogany furniture.

In addition to his regular Cabernet Sauvignon, Heitz bottles a separate vatting made exclusively from the vines in nearby Martha's Vineyard (a confusing name for Easterners). We tasted four vintages of the regular wine and five of the Martha's Vineyard. Of the nine wines, there was little doubt that the 1968 Martha's Vineyard was best if judged on the basis of present drinkability. By general consensus, in fact, it was rated the best overall wine of the twelve sampled that day. Perversely, I had preferred the regular Cabernet, Lot C91, of the 1969 vintage. The 1968 was soft, with a delightful aroma of Cabernet. On the palate it seemed to expand, releasing a whole series of flavors with a decided vanilla overtone. The 1969 Lot C91, however, seemed to me to be potentially greater, better even than the Martha's Vineyard of the same year. There was unusual strength in every aspect of the wine: a deep color, a bold black currant fruitiness redolent of certain Pauillacs, and the tough presence of tannin, which underscored the body of the wine. Yet there was perfect, graceful balance. I placed the Martha's Vineyard wine of 1969 immediately behind the 1968, third in my overall rating. It had a fine harmony of flavor, tannin, and acids, and I feel that it will match the complexity of the 1968 wine when it has had more time in bottle. When judging wines all of which are of outstanding quality, the choice is entirely subjective. Lot C91 of the 1969 vintage had a swagger that I found hard to resist—a personal preference in the final analysis.

Both 1970 wines—the vintage that was at the heart of the whole exercise—were of good quality. It was a difficult year in the Napa Valley. The winter of 1969–70 had been very mild. By April the vines were showing their new growth when a severe frost occurred. Most vineyards lost half their prospective crop. The summer was very hot, for once echoing conditions in Western Europe. (It is one of the idiosyncrasies of the wine world that rain in Bordeaux, and its subsequent effect on the quality of the vintage there, can handicap the reputation of wines made in the same year as far away as Australia.) The flowering of the vines was followed by such high temperatures that many of the newly formed grape berries shattered, further reducing the crop. More heat in July and August burned the grapes. These conditions were far from ideal, especially for the white wines, but the reds that survived have shown exceedingly well. With rare exceptions they are big wines with richly complex flavors. Heavier than the 1969s, some of them seem clumsy at present, and apart from those wines specially brought on for early drinking, it is a year that will need time to develop. Nor is this true only of the traditional long-keeping varietals like Cabernet Sauvignon. Even Zinfandel and Gamay Beaujolais of the 1970 vintage are heavier than usual, and a 1970 Petite Sirah of Robert Mondavi that I had wanted to serve at dinner a few weeks ago had to be decanted to help it aerate and stretch, or it would have been disagreeably hard to drink.

~ ~ ~

Of the two 1970 Heitz wines, the Cabernet Sauvignon from Martha's Vineyard was plainly superior to the regular bottling. Its color was deeper and richer; the nose, though seeming less mature than that of the regular bottling, was stronger and more complex. On the palate it was a solid wine, astringently tannic and harshly unripe, but clearly with a good future. Roughly on a par with the 1970 Martha's Vineyard were the 1970 Cabernet Sauvignon Private Reserve of Beaulieu Vineyard and the 1970 Cabernet Sauvignon of Mayacamas, both of which had been included blind. It is of small significance when comparing such peak wines, but I ranked the Beaulieu wine marginally ahead of the Martha's Vineyard and the Mayacamas wine marginally behind it. The other tasters seemed to like the Beaulieu Vineyard wine too, although the majority placed it after rather than before the Martha's Vineyard.

I found a lack of support from the others for the Mayacamas. It revealed little of its varietal character and no charm. But, in a way, I was reminded of the closed, hard style of certain Bordeaux classified growths when first bottled. Its structure and balance were perfect, indicating sound winemaking, and gave a good base for development. Since we had not been told what the outside wines were (nor, of course, which they were) I had assumed this one—so clearly not of the Heitz stamp—to be a young red Bordeaux; and although we had not been asked to guess which were the cuckoos in the nest, I had marked it as a possible Bordeaux on my tasting sheet. The others were disturbed by an "off" flavor that I could not find, and I began to wonder if perhaps they were put off by the wine's strangely withdrawn character. In the context of the other wines, all so positive and assertive, its low profile could easily have seemed a distortion. When the wine was identified, I remembered that I had tasted it a few months earlier. In checking my files later, I found that I had previously noted its good balance, but had then found its hefty scale inelegant.

Of the two older vintages, the 1966 was preferred to the 1967. They were both lighter than the younger wines, and although the 1966 Martha's Vineyard in particular showed deep color and a finely shaded bouquet of Cabernet with citrus tones, they had not reached—and would not reach—the peak already arrived at by the 1968 Martha's Vineyard. They were destined to be overshadowed by the 1969 and 1970 wines.

When we went into the house to eat one of Alice Heitz's delicious luncheons, we took the bottles with us so that we could go on discussing as we tasted (and drank, let it be said) the wine with the food. I made a mental note to watch which bottle became empty soonest, sometimes a more telling evaluation system than any other. But in the relaxed atmosphere inevitable around such a friendly table, with good food and wine, I must confess that my mental "work" department closed down, and this valuable evidence is lost forever.

Originally published as "A Morning Tasting" in *Gourmet,* May 1975.

BEAULIEU VINEYARD'S GEORGES
DE LATOUR PRIVATE RESERVE

A year ago this month a group of French men and women—professionals in wine, marketing, and law—met in Chinon in the Loire Valley to ask themselves which was preferable: adapting classic wines when necessary to meet fluctuations in consumer preferences or using marketing skills to persuade consumers to accept and appreciate such wines as they are. A classic wine in Europe is usually identified by the name of the place from which it comes. Its production is controlled by statutes based on established local traditions of winemaking. Not surprisingly, the consensus of those present in Chinon seemed to be that, though even a wine with a controlled appellation evolves over time, a deliberate change in style or quality could be achieved only by breaking this tie between origin and winemaking tradition. No matter how delicious the wine that took its place, the classic wine itself would then cease to be.

Such questions—is a wine created for consumers, or are consumers created for a wine?—would have been irrelevant to Georges de Latour, a Frenchman turned U.S. citizen, when he was again allowed to sell wine freely from his vineyard in Napa Valley after the repeal of Prohibition in 1933. Fourteen years of restriction had reduced the wine industry to tatters. If there had once been a classic California wine of determined style and quality for Georges de Latour to protect and promote, the Volstead Act would have swept it away. On the other hand, consumers denied access to wine by Prohibition (which began in many states earlier than 1919) and deflected from its use by ceaseless propaganda long before it was banned had little understanding of wine and no preferences to be gauged and met.

Born in Bordeaux and raised in Périgord, de Latour studied chemistry in Paris and then came to California in 1884 to seek his fortune in the gold mines. He soon decided there was greater opportunity in collecting and processing the cream of tartar going to waste as a by-product of the burgeoning California wine industry. Establishing himself first in San Jose (in those days Santa Clara was a more important wine county than Napa) and later in Healdsburg, in Sonoma County, his business flourished.

By the end of the century he had married and bought a small farm—120 acres, mostly wheat and orchards—in Rutherford, Napa Valley. His wife gave it the name Beaulieu. (No matter how the French pronounce it, in California the word is *boh-lyoo.* Nor is that particularly odd. After all, the English call Beaulieu in Hampshire, England, *byoolee* and will feign not to understand if a visitor says it any other way.) Vineyards were planted, and a former grain store on the property was converted into a small winery. De Latour's daughter, Hélène, the Marquise de Pins, remembered in a 1966 memoir that from his first crop of what she called "ordinary grapes" her father made five barrels of wine.

In 1908 de Latour brought back from a trip to France a selection of varietal cuttings that he planted on a property adjoining his own, which he bought for the purpose. They included a fair quantity of Cabernet Sauvignon and other Bordeaux varieties. It was about then that he hired Joseph Ponti, a newly arrived Italian immigrant, as his right-hand man in both the winery and the expanding vineyard.

At about that time, too, San Francisco's Archbishop Riordan, a close family friend, asked de Latour to begin making altar wines for him. Initially a small matter, the altar wine business, together with that of "wines prescribed for medicinal purposes," grew and saved the Beaulieu vineyard by allowing the winery to continue in production throughout Prohibition. While others pulled out their vines and sold their land, de Latour acquired and planted more. In 1923 he moved into the former Seneca Ewer winery on the Rutherford highway opposite his home vineyard and pulled down the old grain store that had served him as winery until then. The handsome Ewer building—today a venerable pile of ivy-covered brick and stone—had gone up in 1885, and it is still Beaulieu's winery.

The vines de Latour had planted in the home vineyard, the one known today as BV No. 1, were fully mature by the time Prohibition ended and were giving fruit of high quality and intense flavor. The wine he made from this fruit in 1936 took the Gold Medal award at the 1939 World's Fair on Treasure Island in San Francisco Bay. Though it had been made mostly from Cabernet Sauvignon grapes, it had to be presented—and was acclaimed—as Beaulieu Burgundy. To post-Prohibition consumers red wine was Burgundy, and that was that.

In her 1966 memoir, Hélène de Pins described the scene in which her father first opened a bottle of this particular wine in the dining room of the family's home in San Francisco: "I recall as though it were yesterday—it was a wine of such splendor that it totally filled the room with its perfume."

It was not until the spring of 1940 (after Georges de Latour's death), when this award-winning wine was ready for sale, that his widow decided to accept the suggestion of the winery's general manager, Nino Fabbrini, and rename it in honor of her husband. That is how, fifty years ago, Beaulieu Vineyard's first Georges de Latour Cabernet Sauvignon came into existence.

The grapes had been harvested and the wine made by Joseph Ponti, counseled by Leon Bonnet, a Frenchman and a professor of enology at the University of California. Bonnet retired in 1937, and there arrived at Beaulieu to take his place in time for the 1938 vintage a Russian-born research assistant from the National Institute of Agronomic Research in Paris named André Tchelistcheff. In his book *The Wines of America*, Leon Adams said that, in bringing Tchelistcheff to California, Georges de Latour did as much for the state's winemaking as a whole as he did for the wines of Beaulieu.

Tchelistcheff's role at Beaulieu seems to have been at first ill-defined. An article in the *American Wine & Liquor Journal* of May 1941, describes Joseph Ponti as winemaker and André Tchelistcheff as chemist; but, in 1942, Joseph Ponti was described in a *Country Life* article as supervisor of the vineyards and winery, and André Tchelistcheff as enologist. When Tchelistcheff retired in 1973, his title was technical director and vice-president. But regardless of the confusion of titles, Tchelistcheff was effectively responsible for the wines of Beaulieu Vineyard for more than thirty years.

In a conversation with me a few years ago, Tchelistcheff referred to the first release of Georges de Latour Private Reserve '36. "It was an elegant wine," he said, "aged in French oak. We had even bottled it in secondhand Bordeaux bottles. But the style was different from what the Private Reserve later became. We decided to make a bigger style of wine, using nothing but Cabernet Sauvignon aged in American oak barrels. I thought American oak would bring to the wine a richer and more distinctive character." Actually, in 1940, Tchelistcheff had little choice but to use American oak if he wanted to age a red wine in barrel: France was at war and might even have already fallen by the time this was being considered. He had more latitude in the matter of grapes, though, had he wished to use it.

Beaulieu lacked only Cabernet Franc in the 1940s; all the other Bordeaux blending varieties—Merlot, Malbec, and Petit Verdot—were available to him. Robert Gorman, in his 1975 book, *California Premium Wines* (an elegantly written, incomprehensibly neglected masterpiece, a snapshot of the California wine industry at an important moment of change), said that Tchelistcheff found Beaulieu's Malbec too neutral, contributing nothing to the wine; that the Petit Verdot failed to ripen to his satisfaction, a problem most years in Bordeaux, too; and that the Merlot provoked a maturing of the wine too rapid to allow adequate development. Tchelistcheff, in using only Cabernet Sauvignon, departed from the Bordeaux tradition of blending.

In the design of the Private Reserve no one, not even Tchelistcheff himself, can now say for certain how much was judgment, how much was the constraint of circumstances, and how much was plain good luck. But that marriage of American oak barrels with Cabernet Sauvignon from mature vines nurtured in a uniquely favored vineyard in Napa Valley gave Beaulieu a wine that has become in every sense a classic ("of the highest class; being a model of its kind; excellent ... " begins the definition of that word in my *Webster's*). The Private Reserve meets the expectations of such a wine anywhere in the world: Like the French wines being considered last year in Chinon, the consistency of style and quality in a Georges de Latour Private Reserve is imposed by its Rutherford origin and by the spirit in which it has come to be made.

In 1936 there were perhaps two hundred acres of Cabernet Sauvignon vines in California. Today there are more than twenty-six thousand. The Georges de Latour Private Reserve remains an important stylistic benchmark, a definition of what we mean by Cabernet Sauvignon in California, even though it now takes its place among the many others that were encouraged—indeed, inspired—by its success.

What is that definition, that stylistic benchmark? If asked to give in few words an impression of the Private Reserve style, I would certainly put "opulent" among them. There is also a robust vigor about the wines that make them almost a metaphor for California itself. Others have described the wines as huge, dense, and concentrated. There have been references to their overwhelming bouquet (a quality mentioned by Hélène de Pins in her memoir), to their power, and to their intense black-currant flavor. In one vintage or another I have been able to find all of these characteristics, but not necessarily all in the same wine at the same time. Being that most of these words give an impression of heft, let me say that though the most successful vintages of Georges de

Latour are indeed rich and full, the balance of every one is impeccable, the proportion elegant, the total effect harmonious. A mature bottle of any particularly successful vintage of the Georges de Latour Private Reserve is, to me, one of the most cogent arguments for drinking wine at all.

Given the unique status of the wine, there was considerable concern when the family sold the Beaulieu winery, together with most of the vineyards (but not BV No. 1) and the rights to its brand name, to Heublein in 1969. Lamentations were premature: No one now disputes the superiority of the 1970 over both the 1964 and the 1966, for example. The 1970 vintage, made after the winery had been acquired by Heublein, stands as one of the best Private Reserves ever made. Later it was whispered that all would be over after Tchelistcheff retired; yet everyone now accepts that the 1976, the 1982, and the 1985, all made by his successors, are great vintages and in perfect concord with the wine's traditional style and quality.

Tchelistcheff has favorites among the thirty-odd vintages for which he was responsible. "Of the forties' vintages, I liked 1940, 1942, and 1948," he once told me. "1958 was my favorite of the fifties—1951 was rather alcoholic—and, although 1964 was very elegant, 1968 was my favorite among vintages of the sixties."

I, too, have favorites. One of them, the 1970, had just been released when I came to California in 1974. Back then I wasn't able to get my hands on any from under the counters of San Francisco. But I could find it on trips back to New York City, where in those days California wine still lacked cachet and Georges de Latours were available to anyone with the sense to buy them. I would lug them by the case back to the West Coast.

Of vintages in the fifties and sixties, my favorites in some instances differ from those of Tchelistcheff. For example, I preferred the 1951 to the 1958. I first tasted the 1951 only about ten years ago, when it was one of four Napa Valley Cabernet Sauvignons of the forties and fifties served at a dinner in San Francisco. I described it then as "richly preserving all those characteristics associated with Rutherford, with Cabernet Sauvignon, and with American oak that André Tchelistcheff combined into one of the most particular and consistent wines made anywhere."

I could have said much the same about the 1951 when I tasted it again last year. The bouquet had what we call "tar," because it seems precious to write of an amalgam of roasted coffee, charcoal, prunes—and old wine. Though drying a little, it was still both smooth as silk and splendidly vigorous. I tasted the 1958 only once, a few years ago. It was in perfect condition but lacked the intensity of the 1951. I doubt that the extra years of aging alone had made the 1951 so much more memorable.

On the other hand, I agree with Tchelistcheff about the 1968, even though it is drying a little now. Its flavor has always been distinctly exotic: fruitier, spicier, more lush than that of other great years of the Private Reserve but lacking none of the vibrant richness. I also enjoyed the 1966 on both occasions when I tasted it; but either the two bottles had matured in different ways—not as unusual as one might think—or the wine of this vintage had changed dramatically between 1984, when I first tasted it, and 1989. In 1984 the bouquet was fresh and the wine was lively, but the bottle I tasted in 1989 had the evocatively sad-sweet smell of dried moss and faded flowers. The wine was still fairly full on the palate, but the flavor was as romantically melancholy as the bouquet—damp woods, dried apricots, a hint of past glory. I was in the right nostalgic mood for the wine and found it delicious.

~ ~ ~

It is said that a Georges de Latour Private Reserve defines the style of its vintage in Napa Valley. The wine itself is basically so consistent that variations in it from year to year point up the local weather's diversity. That certainly seems to be true of the three most distinguished of recent vintages. The 1976 Private Reserve is richly charged, a product of the first of the seventies' drought years in California. Many less successful Napa Valley Cabernet Sauvignons were heavy that year: condensed, tannic, even tough.

The 1982 crop in the valley had the advantage of a long, cool growing season but was then almost washed out by heavy rains in September. Fortunately, an Indian summer in October raised sugar levels in the Cabernet Sauvignon. Flavors were already intense thanks to the drawn-out ripening. That year, almost a write-off for many whites, was successful for late-picked reds. They were bigger than expected, with intense, tight flavors—much in the style of the 1982 Private Reserve.

The 1985 Private Reserve, released last year, is perfectly, elegantly balanced. The growing season was slow and long, like that of 1982, with moderate temperatures helping to intensify flavors. There were no surprises, no downpours, no dramatic heat waves. Indeed, after a summer such as growers pray for, the vintage is one of the best of the decade for Cabernet Sauvignon in Napa Valley.

This month Beaulieu Vineyard will release the 1986 Georges de Latour Private Reserve, and, although—strictly speaking—this will be the Private Reserve's fifty-first vintage, it marks the fiftieth anniversary of the release of the first of these extraordinary wines, back in 1940.

Perhaps this is an appropriate time, then, to remember that Beaulieu's tradition has always been a progressive one. The BV No. 1 vineyard, for example, owned by Georges de Latour's granddaughter but managed by Beaulieu, was first replanted in the 1940s and has since been replanted twice, in the 1960s and in the 1980s. The success of the Private Reserve encouraged the winery to use for the most recent replanting essentially the same clone of Cabernet Sauvignon that has been so successful there for the last fifty years. However, there have been increases in the proportions of two other clones: one because it was found to add more color and a greater intensity of flavor, and the other because it gives fruit with a richer, more definitely black-currant taste and contributes a more supple, more elegant, more forward quality.

Beaulieu has also been experimenting with American oak barrels specially made for them in a variant of the French manner. (Put very simply, the main difference between French and American oak barrels, apart from the variety of oak, is that French barrel staves are handsplit, air-dried, and then made pliable over a fire that toasts them as the barrel is made; whereas American barrels are usually machine-cut, oven-dried, and then made pliable in steam tunnels. It is thought that much, though not all, of the difference between the way American and French barrels affect the taste of wine has less to do with the oak itself than with the way it is handled.) The oak barrels used for Beaulieu's Private Reserve are always two or three years old. They are always first used for the Beaulieu Vineyard Rutherford Cabernet Sauvignon before graduating to hold the Private Reserve. The winery feels that this wine should not be exposed to the shock of raw new wood. American oak barrels assembled from air-dried and lightly toasted oak staves have been arriving at Beaulieu for the past few years now, and some of these slightly modified barrels were used for the 1986.

These small changes—the strengthening of some characteristics in the vineyard and of others in the barrel—will intensify the familiar style of the Private Reserve while allowing the wine more grace. They will be perceived negligibly, if at all, in the 1986 Georges de Latour, where the greater influence will be the unusual weather conditions of that year. Though the vines sprouted leaves quite early, and all signs pointed to an early vintage—as 1981 had been, and 1984—the warm weeks of early summer gave way to an August that grew cooler and cooler. Grapes that had been expected to reach optimum sugar levels rapidly went into slow motion. But having had the benefit of a warm start (heat after flowering often thickens the grape skins, improving flavor and color no matter what happens subsequently) as well as the advantages of a slow ripening, 1986 is expected to be the equal of 1985 and perhaps even better. This wine will be one classic that no one will have to be persuaded to buy.

Originally published as "Beaulieu Vineyard's Georges de Latour Private Reserve" in *Gourmet,* October 1990.

The "small changes" to the Georges de Latour Private Reserve I refer to have continued. A little Petit Verdot and Malbec have been introduced into the Cabernet Sauvignon (which still accounts for 93 percent of the *cuvée*). The greatest change has been a gradual move away from American oak to French with now a small amount of Russian oak in addition. The winery is now part of Diageo.

Here is Jeffrey Stambor, director of winemaking, writing specifically on the 2007 vintage: "The 2007 Georges de Latour is 93 percent Cabernet Sauvignon, 4 percent Petit Verdot and 3 percent Malbec. It was aged in 93 percent French oak [barrels] and 7 percent Russian oak. This was the first year that we experimented with barrel-fermenting the Cabernet [Sauvignon] and the third year that we were making Georges de Latour in small (six- to seven-ton) lots with berry sorting after destemming, very gentle handling, and the use of a basket press. With these small lots we were able to identify sections of a block to keep them separate and [could] avoid end vines and border rows which exhibit different ripening characteristics. The gentle handling allowed us to extract tannins when and how we wanted to. I believe that the barrel-fermented portion has given us seamless barrel integration and allows us to maximize the extraction without any rough edges. We were able to get maximum extraction of supple tannins and retain enough acidity to ensure long aging. As a result, the 2007 Georges de Latour is a wine with well-developed ripe aromas, a rich attack, broad mid-palate, and a super-long finish."

And here is my own brief tasting note of the same wine on July 14, 2010: "Attractive fruit. Silky tannins, good balance. An elegant wine."

SANTA CRUZ MOUNTAINS

Ingenuity and Tenacity

I had never before been asked, prior to sitting down to dinner, to sign a release absolving my hosts from responsibility for any subsequent "discomfort or distress." But then this was the first time I had been invited to the annual feast of the Fungus Federation of Santa Cruz, held this year at India Joze restaurant on Center Street, where local chefs had gathered to show what they could do with *Dentinum repandum* and *Pleurotus ostreatus.*

As might be appropriate in Santa Cruz, a sort of Berkeley-by-the-Sea, India Joze, an airy café popular with everyone for miles around, usually specializes in what I can only call Third World cuisines: a north Indian version of scrambled eggs, for instance; falafel; Armenian-style chicken breasts marinated in paprika yogurt; local snapper prepared *à la turque;* Balinese chicken; Greek prawns; tofu Malaysian-style with a hot bean sauce; Coptic chickpeas; and, for Carnival night, an all-Brazilian menu (with samba lessons). Given the weakness of the dollar, I suppose it was inevitable that the eclectic menu should now extend to classic American folk dishes like eggs Benedict and hash-browns.

For the Fungus Feast, however, we ate hors d'oeuvres of chicken wings stuffed with morels and ginger, crab and horn-of-plenty mushroom canapés, and oyster mushrooms quickly fried in a light beer batter. No distress so far, and none likely with David Bruce's California Blanc de Blanc sparkling wine. A salad of marinated chanterelles and hedgehog and oyster mushrooms with fennel and slivers of Parmesan led us to a cream soup of shiitake and morels, by which time we were ready for a choice of 1986 Monterey Chardonnay from Bonny Doon or 1986 Mendocino Sauvignon Blanc from Obester.

Dishes of chicken braised with *boletes* and red bell peppers arrived, along with a steaming couscous studded with more chanterelles. Doubtless as a special gesture to the household gods of India Joze, there was also a quickie world tour in the form of "Turkish style, wok-braised vegetables with tomato and fresh rosemary." Ahlgren's 1984 Cabernet Sauvignon from the Bates Ranch near Gilroy and a 1983 Cronin Pinot Noir from Ventana Vineyards in Monterey County were offered with the chicken. Guests could drink either or both.

Dessert was a *Linzertorte* with candy cap mushrooms. In my innocence I assumed candy cap to mean mushrooms of the genus *Confectioneris* and was amazed to discover the existence of a comparatively sweet fungus, *Lactarius fragilis*. A 1986 Monterey Muscat Canelli from Devlin Wine Cellars brought the evening to a fine conclusion.

Perhaps it was an effect of the mushrooms or of the music, which drifted amiably all evening from a neighboring room, but guests at the crowded tables seemed to be a much jollier lot than the wine buffs I usually consort with. Mycologists, to their credit, simply reached for their wine as part of the evening's pleasure. They weren't overly zealous about mushrooms, either. I couldn't imagine anyone at my table proposing a comparative tasting to judge the *Craterellus cornucopioides*. In fact no one at the Fungus Feast judged anything. They didn't sniff at the *Lentinus edodes* or suggest the *Cantharellus cibarius* might be over the hill. They ate everything and enjoyed themselves, swapping recipes and good-humored stories, lapsing into the obscurely elliptical talk common to wine gatherings only when pressed to reveal the *exact* glade where they found such plump chanterelles.

Those with sharp eyes will have noticed that none of the wines offered by the Santa Cruz wineries represented at the dinner were made with grapes actually grown in Santa Cruz. The next morning, after a sound sleep disturbed by neither discomfort nor distress (nor, for those who are wondering, by psychedelic dreams), I set off to talk to some Santa Cruz winemakers to find out why.

~ ~ ~

Santa Cruz, on the Pacific coast about eighty miles south of San Francisco, is at the northern end of a bay that sweeps to the Monterey peninsula. It is a pretty town that has preferred, in recent years, to hide itself in the blur that most visitors see between San Francisco and Carmel. Nevertheless its boardwalk is an inherited concession to tourists, and its old pier (known as the Wharf), swarming with shops and restaurants perched over the water, rivals the commercial enterprise of a medieval bridge.

Behind and above the town, roads twist into hills covered by magnificent redwoods that have replaced, for the most part, virgin forest logged when the area was first settled. But there is little agriculture, and none is encouraged. The county supervisors pursue a no-growth policy that, by rare coincidence, is supported both by the environmentalist student vote of Santa Cruz's large University of California campus and by Silicon Valley executives, who, fond of the trees that screen their houses, have no wish to see them exchanged for noisome tractors and Quonset huts. In any case, forested hillside land is not only expensive to buy but costly to develop and cultivate. It is difficult to make grape growing pay.

Not surprisingly, then, even though the federally defined Santa Cruz Mountains Viticultural Area is extensive, spreading beyond the county to include the east flank of the mountains in Santa Clara, where barriers are less political than they are economic, and north along the ridge to embrace the high ground of San Mateo, fewer than three hundred of its acres are planted with vines presently bearing grapes. Of those, Santa Cruz County itself has thirty-eight acres of black grapes—mostly Pinot Noir—and thirty-six acres of white: a mere seventy-four acres in all. In comparison, Monterey, a county adjacent to Santa Cruz, grows twenty-six thousand acres of vines.

Ironically, and some might say tragically, California's most distinguished wines were, in the past, grown in Santa Cruz Mountains vineyards; but it is now a struggle for Santa Cruz wineries even to promote themselves collectively because a Santa Cruz address counts for little on labels boldly qualified with appellations like Mendocino, Sonoma, and Monterey, the sources for most of their grapes.

Santa Cruz wineries are small. Except for Bargetto, a winery founded in time for Prohibition but revived in 1933, they are mostly businesses begun with the enthusiasm of expensive hobbies over the last twenty years or so. Two or three acres of vines, an extension to the garage, and some basic equipment are enough to produce the three or four hundred cases of wine that can be sold without need of employees, let alone a marketing plan. A few wineries still operate on that scale, selling through a limited mail-order list and at the premises on Saturday afternoons. Others, having grown to a few thousand cases, are in a double bind. While needing to establish a Santa Cruz identity to distinguish their products in a market awash with California wine, they are unable to find an adequate supply of Santa Cruz grapes—County or Mountains—to do so.

Desperate for grapes, Bargetto started to use local plums and apricots to make wines back in the 1960s and is now proud of its reputation for fruit wines (and pleased with the cash flow they generate). But its winemaker, Paul Wofford, greatly respected by other winemakers in the area, is nervous that, with fruit wines still accounting for 25 percent of Bargetto's business, the quality of its Santa Cruz Mountains Cabernet Sauvignon and of other varietal wines could be overlooked or obscured.

David Bruce, whose wines were once known for their idiosyncratic style, is now so mainstream that, with a production of roughly forty thousand cases, his has become the largest winery in Santa Cruz County. But he makes no secret of being obliged to buy the bulk of his Chardonnay and Cabernet Sauvignon grapes from Sonoma County, selling the wines made from them with a catchall California appellation. Bill Frick is thinking of relocating his winery to Sonoma County because of the difficulty of obtaining Santa Cruz grapes. Chuck Devlin grew up on the property south of Santa Cruz where he has his winery and hopes, one day, to have twenty acres of vineyard there. For the present, however, and although he is able to buy the Chardonnay he needs in Santa Cruz County, both the Zinfandel that provides the bulk of his business and the Merlot that has won him most acclaim are grown outside the area. Silver Mountain's Jerold O'Brien, a retired Air Force pilot, had hoped to be self-sufficient in grapes when he bought seventeen acres on the Santa Cruz ridge. The lot was an abandoned orchard that had been a vineyard before Prohibition, but he was nevertheless obliged to provide an environmental study of the impact of his proposal on flora and fauna. Delays lasted three years. He was eventually able to build his winery and plant his vineyard, but he ran out of money before his vines were bearing, and so for the time being he too is obliged to buy grapes from growers elsewhere.

~ ~ ~

Some wineries, like Bonny Doon and Roudon-Smith, have managed to grow or find at least enough grapes in Santa Cruz to establish the local character of their wines even if they must then supplement them with grapes bought elsewhere. Both are particularly imaginative, however, even in their quest for alien grapes. Bonny Doon Vineyard's Randall Grahm, California's only winemaking literary philosopher, has reached as far as the Willamette Valley in Oregon to find Pinot Noir. He has scoured California to find the needed proportions of Syrah, Cinsault, Grenache, and Mourvèdre to reproduce, in his Cigare Volant wine, the quality and style of a Châteauneuf-du-Pape. ("It has a bouquet of ultraviolets," claimed Grahm in one of his tongue-in-cheek newsletters.) When I arrived to chat with him last February, he was crushing a batch of frozen Muscat Canelli grapes for ice wine.

Ice wine in Santa Cruz? It is perfectly possible if the winery assists nature by putting the freshly picked grapes into a freezer and leaving them there until calm returns after the rest of the harvest is fermented and racked. "We can then make ice wine in a civilized way," Grahm explained. "None of that getting up at four o'clock in the morning before the sun gets on the grapes and thaws them. We pull one press load a day from the freezer and give it all our attention."

The Bureau of Alcohol, Tobacco, and Firearms had disallowed Grahm's attempt to label an earlier batch of his ice wine *Vin de Glace*, and it is now refusing to acknowledge the appropriateness even of *Vin de Glacière*. Ever resourceful, Grahm will surely find a way through this thicket of regulation for the sake of regulation.

Understanding the need for focus and recognizing the difficulty Santa Cruz wineries have in using a local geographic identity for that purpose, Grahm pursues instead his interest in wines made from grapes associated with the Rhône Valley. Apart from his Cigare Volant (a "flying cigar" is what the French call a flying saucer; the commune of Châteauneuf-du-Pape once passed a *cigare volant* ordinance forbidding such vehicles to land on local vineyards), Grahm makes a deliciously fruity Grenache each year under the name Clos de Gilroy that out-nouveaus most Beaujolais. He has planted the elusive Viognier and makes a Marsanne-Rousanne blend (the formula, if you like, for Hermitage Blanc) under the name Le Sophiste: Cuvée Philosophique. (In time even Grahm will get bored with these insider jokes, but meanwhile the rest of us must be indulgent. His wines are superb, the work is hard, and the rewards are largely illusory.)

Bob Roudon and Jim Smith's winery is hidden among redwoods and rhododendrons in a setting that would make convinced environmentalists of the EPA. Through a network of contacts, these two manage to find small batches of Santa Cruz grapes. "Every so often someone with a house and a few acres will come up with the idea of starting a small vineyard. So, although it is true that most of the county opposes vines, every year a few people discreetly plant an acre or two. Plantings on such a modest scale usually go without remark." Roudon and Smith have also been creative with a Rhône variety. "I found this vineyard of Petite Sirah in San Luis Obispo," Bob Roudon told me. "The vines were about ten years old then, which was back in 1978. The fruit has got better all the time. I tried blending a little Chardonnay—just 5 or 10 percent, depending on the year—to give some finesse. We've built quite a clientele for it."

Blending a few white grapes with black for red wine is still a current practice in some Rhône areas (and elsewhere: remember the touch of white grapes in Chianti). Until the nineteenth century it was a practice almost universal in France, and for the same reason that Roudon and Smith add Chardonnay to their Petite Sirah: finesse. Roudon-Smith's 1984 Petite Sirah, aged for a while in American oak, has both elegance of structure and length of flavor. I am not surprised it is the winery's most popular red wine.

I made my last call at the Santa Cruz Mountain Vineyard itself. Its thirteen acres of Pinot Noir and single acre of Chardonnay are planted on a choice section of the old Jarvis vineyard, established on Vine Hill in 1863. In those days, there were said to have been several thousand acres of vines in the Santa Cruz Mountains. Ken Burnap dry-farms his vines and uses only gravity in his hillside cellar (I watched while a cellarman gently raised one barrel on a forklift and siphoned the contents over to another barrel.) For fermentation he relies strictly on the natural yeast that arrives with the grapes from the vineyard, for his pressed pomace is returned there to build an indigenous yeast population. His wines have character; but whether that character is stamped on them by this gritty, mountain terrain or imposed by the vigor of Ken Burnap's personality is hard to say.

I drove back to San Francisco over the Hecker Pass into Santa Clara County because I wanted to see the southern extension of the Santa Cruz Mountains Viticultural Area, one of the few sections where vineyards, like those of the Bates Ranch, are expanding. It was depressing even there, though, to find myself almost immediately in the spreading community of Morgan Hill and, soon afterward, lost in the concrete sprawl of San Jose. I'm not sure about the future of Santa Cruz fungus, but I could see why Santa Cruz wineries, poised between preservers of manzanita scrub and builders of shopping malls, will need all the ingenuity and tenacity in the world to survive.

Originally published as "Santa Cruz" in *Gourmet,* July 1988.

India Joze restaurant closed in 1999. It reopened in May 2010 with the same chef but at a different location in Santa Cruz.

ZINFANDEL

California's Own

The table in my kitchen is small and round; no more than two, per-haps three, can eat there together comfortably, a limit that allows me to open—for what is often an impromptu meal—one of those bottles we all hoard but that could never be stretched to a dinner party. I share some of my best wines in the kitchen.

Though curiosity sometimes prompts us to seek out wines we know will be difficult to appreciate, wine is never intended to be anyone's jousting partner. And, especially in the kitchen, it should comfort and be companionable, whatever its pedigree: cheer rather than challenge. Few wines show these qualities as consistently, as comprehensively, and as exuberantly as *good* Zinfandel.

The qualifier is important, because there is a mass of not very in-teresting Zinfandel too. Twenty years ago it was usually a simple, and often dull, red jug wine. Now it's more likely to be a simple, and often dull, white (well, pink anyway). We also had a spell of late harvest monsters that would have amply satisfied anyone's fancy for demand-ing, challenging, and intimidating wine. But during all that time, and particularly since the late sixties, there has also been a subculture of distinguished Zinfandels, almost all produced in wineries far out of the mainstream, using fruit grown on what I can only describe as California's viticultural fringes.

For years these wines were hardly known beyond the circles of those who made a cult of them. But the secret's been out for quite a while now, and, as production has slowly increased, these handcrafted Zinfandels have become available to anyone prepared to take the trouble to look for them. In price they range from as little as seven dollars a bottle, though most are from ten to fifteen, and a few of the most celebrated are now pushing toward twenty.

~ ~ ~

The potential for outstanding Zinfandel quality was always there, of course, even when there were few wines to provide confirmation of it. In his 1880s book, *Grape Culture and Wine Making in California*—the standard text in California until well into this century—George Husmann said he had "yet to see the red wine of any variety [that he preferred] to the best samples of Zinfandel produced in this state." Some sixty years later, in 1941, when the California wine industry was struggling to recover from the years of Prohibition, Frank Schoonmaker wrote in his classic work, *American Wines,* "[Zinfandel] deserves more respect than it generally gets . . . [it] reflects so obviously, in the quality of its wine, the soil on which it was grown. . . . "

When Schoonmaker wrote that, few Americans gave much thought to the idea of a wine reflecting the soil on which it was grown. Accustomed to using the same name for a grape and for the wine made from it, Americans expected no more than that one should reflect the other. It was left to Europeans, who name their wines geographically rather than varietally, to concern themselves with a soil, with the climate that goes with it, and with a pattern of winemaking intended to resolve incompatibilities between the two.

However, leaving aside such idiosyncrasies as White Zinfandel and Zinfandel Nouveau (no matter how successful commercially, they could hardly have been what Schoonmaker had had in mind), most California winemakers working seriously with Zinfandel would agree with Husmann that, when grown on appropriate sites and handled with the care given other varieties in California, Zinfandel can give red wine at least as fine as any in the state. They would also accept Schoonmaker's view that Zinfandel reflects its physical environment in ways that impose distinct variations on the wine from one region of California to another.

~ ~ ~

Tasting my way recently through almost 150 California Zinfandels, almost all of them of the 1990 and 1991 vintages, I began grouping the wines by style to get an easier grasp of what I had before me. It quickly became clear that by doing so I was in fact also sorting them into regions of origin—wines from Dry Creek Valley here, Sonoma Valley there—though that had not been my intention.

In California much is made of geography (witness the American Viticultural Areas, the officially delimited wine regions like Carneros or Stags Leap District or Sonoma Valley) when it suits a marketing strategy. Otherwise, little more than lip service is paid to the differences of style and taste imposed by location. Producers who buy grapes from various parts of the state know very well what these differences are—they base their buying decisions on them. But too often they then allow regional distinctions to disappear in the blending vat. Some of the Zinfandels on my tasting table had clearly been made that way. Though not necessarily less attractive than the others, they were less focused, less collected.

Most of the wines, however, were clearly defined by the regions from which they came. For example, the Zinfandels from Sonoma Valley were the hardest, the most tannic, and the most astringent. Those with a bright, crisp style—an edge of acidity, rather than tannin, that was coupled with the clear, forward berry-fruit aroma and flavor we most associate with California Zinfandel—were likely to be from Dry Creek Valley, Russian River Valley, or the Lytton Springs region, where the previous two areas meet. Wines from the upper part of Dry Creek Valley or from Alexander Valley, across a watershed, were more mellow, had a more complex—or at least a deeper—flavor, and were generally more plump.

Though no less bold, the fruit of Zinfandels from Amador County in the Sierra Foothills comes across as plum rather than berry and sometimes as dried fruit rather than fresh, with hints of apricot and prune.

Zinfandel grapes, known for their tendency to ripen irregularly within the bunch (some berries have already become raisins while others are barely ripe), accumulate sugar in a rush just before picking. So their alcohol, most often in the 13 and 14 percent range, is usually higher than the average for table wine in California. In Amador County Zinfandels, the alcohol can be particularly generous, and it is the headiness of these wines, combined with their spicy, dusky aromas and flavors, that makes them so richly and so appealingly exotic.

Napa Valley Zinfandels are the opposite: well-structured, well-bred, and impeccably straight-backed. Though vigorous, they have perfect balance and show a patrician restraint. Nothing is to excess. Their aromas and flavors, while at times quite powerful, have finesse and delicacy. Sometimes one can detect in them a touch of the cassis one associates with Cabernet Sauvignon. But, then, it's not unknown for the producers of Napa Zinfandels to add a little Cabernet Sauvignon to the blend, in proportions that the law allows, to give exactly this effect.

Zinfandels from the hillside vineyards above Napa Valley—from Howell Mountain, Stags Leap, and Atlas Peak on the east side of the valley and Spring Mountain and Mount Veeder on the west—have characteristically tighter flavors. Closed when the wine is young and then, as it develops, opening to an unexpected (sometimes even medicinal) intensity, the flavors are nevertheless all of a piece with the wines' lean and forthright hillside style.

Such differences within a single region are not at all uncommon with Zinfandel; they are further confirmation of the way this variety adapts to and reflects every changed circumstance of growth. In Mendocino there's an equally wide divide between the tense and concentrated Zinfandels produced from old vines planted by turn-of-the-century Italian immigrants who settled the exposed, high ridges between Anderson Valley and the Pacific and the subtly urbane wines from vineyards almost as old but planted in milder and better-protected sites around Ukiah and in the adjacent McDowell and Redwood valleys.

Jed Steele of Steele Wines, a man who knows the vineyards on the Mendocino ridges better than anyone, says of them, "The vines there have never been irrigated and they yield very little. Even when the fruit is really ripe, the acid is always good. There is never a hint of the raisining common in late-picked Zinfandel elsewhere. That's why the flavor is so pure and seems to be etched into the wines despite their opulence." To see the difference between the two styles of Mendocino Zinfandel, one need only compare the inherently wild qualities of a wine from the ridge with the supremely civilized Private Reserve Zinfandel from Lolonis Vineyard in Redwood Valley.

I found the Zinfandels from around Paso Robles, in San Luis Obispo County, the hardest to pin down. They were all supple and agreeable (except when too much oak had been dumped on them), but in the end I recognized them more for what they weren't than for any particular characteristics they shared. They were amiable rather than assertive and seemed to vary more in response to winemaking technique than anything else. Charm made up for their low profile, and Paul Draper, Ridge Vineyards' winemaker, told me that their very reticence was a quality readily accepted in many markets. As far as his own wines were concerned, he said, Europeans in particular preferred the relative quiescence of Ridge Vineyards' Paso Robles Zinfandel (a wine I nevertheless found more concentrated and more muscular than other Paso Robles Zinfandels) to the high vivacity of his Lytton Springs wine.

Zinfandels from the Arroyo Grande Valley at the opposite end of San Luis Obispo County (I know only of those from Saucelito Canyon Winery and Santa Barbara Winery) are remarkably engaging and sweetly harmonious—they've not a note out of place. In some ways they come close to the bright-berry style of Dry Creek Valley, but they are both more tightly woven and more supple. The intense fruitiness of these wines makes them irresistibly delicious.

～ ～ ～

Zinfandel is California's own grape, but it's also California's mystery. Its history, both before and after its arrival in the state in the 1850s, has been continually revised in the light of both serious research and enlightened speculation. There seems little doubt that Zinfandel's name has come to us from the Zierfahnler grape by way of its Czech-language variant, Cinifadl. The name was used for both white and black grapes grown in the nineteenth century in the vineyards of a region that spilled across what until recently was the Austrian-Hungarian-Czechoslovakian border. The black version—Blauer Zierfahnler—is thought to have been either the Kadarka grape or the Kékfrankos, both of Hungary. But that doesn't necessarily tell us anything much about California's Zinfandel because there is no certainty that its connection with the Blauer Zierfahnler goes further than the name.

Zinfandel came to California from nurseries in New England where vines of that name (or slight variants of it) were already being grown and offered for sale in the 1830s. But either there or after its arrival in California, Zinfandel could have become confused with Black St. Peter's, a vine of similar appearance bearing similar grapes, developed from seed in eighteenth-century England (it's mentioned in William Speechly's *Treatise on the Culture of the Vine,* published in 1790). Black St. Peter's was introduced to California from East Coast nurseries at the same time as Zinfandel, and its wines started winning awards in California as soon as the first vines came into production. We know that cuttings of both Zinfandel and Black St. Peter's were sent in the late 1850s to General Mariano Guadalupe Vallejo, the last military commandant of what had been Mexican northern California, for his vineyard near the old Sonoma mission—a vineyard that was itself the source of cuttings for the establishment of many vineyards elsewhere in the county.

But no matter whether today's California Zinfandel is still the variety that arrived as such in the state or is Black St. Peter's with a change of name, we know from genetic fingerprinting that it's related to the Primitivo di Gioia, a black grape grown in Apulia, the heel of Italy. For a while after the Primitivo connection had been established, it was assumed that Zinfandel's mystery was solved and that one must have come from the other. But Primitivo was introduced into Italy only in the late nineteenth century, when the vines indigenous to Apulia had been destroyed by the vine pest phylloxera. That was long after Zinfandel had been brought to California. All that can be said with certainty is that Zinfandel and Primitivo are related and that they have a common connection, possibly a common ancestor, in the Plavać Mali, a grape grown on the Adriatic coast of Croatia. Croatia, of course, was part of the Austro-Hungarian Empire until 1918. And that, perhaps, brings us back full circle to the Zierfahnler.

The revival of California Zinfandel as a serious varietal wine began with the rediscovery of forgotten patches of old vines such as those on the Mendocino Ridge, most of them tucked away among hillside orchards. ("Rediscovery" might not be the appropriate word: When I used it once to Ken Deaver, a Zinfandel grower in Amador County, he stared at me and said, "We didn't know we'd been lost.") These old vineyards were always small because there was no point then in a man planting more vines than he could cultivate alone by hand. In any case, those who had planted vines had done so mostly to nourish their families. Wine was as intrinsic to the diet of most immigrants settling on the land at that time as it had been in Europe, and they sold, more or less haphazardly, only the wine that was surplus to their needs. (In a recorded oral history of the Mendocino coast, Joe Scaramelia, a former mayor of Point Arena, describes how, as a boy, he was given Zinfandel every day to take to school to moisten the otherwise dry bread that served as his lunch.)

Age gives a Zinfandel vine many important advantages. Once established, the vine's extensive root system protects it from climatic adversity: rarely, if ever, does it need to be irrigated. It is always head-pruned—an old system of shaping and training a vine low to the ground in the form of a fistful of spread fingers with the support of neither stakes nor wires—with leaves and fruit open to sun and air to help the grapes ripen more easily. "It's interesting if you look at what they [the growers] are doing today with leaf trimming, opening up the center of the vine to let light onto the fruit," Michael Martini of the Louis M. Martini Winery recently told *Wines & Vines,* a trade publication. "That's exactly what happens with a head-pruned vine naturally."

The yield of old, head-pruned vines is limited—partly because of the age of the vines but also because it's more difficult to overcrop head-pruned vines than vines supported on wires. For that very reason the regulations for some French controlled appellations stipulate that vines must be head-pruned and their shoots left unsupported.

Perhaps the most significant advantage of all, however, is that California's old Zinfandel vines are of a type giving small bunches of small berries that can be relied on to produce wine with character. Though cuttings from these old vines are once again being used for the propagation of new—anyone with an old vineyard is trying to extend, duplicate, or preserve it—most of the Zinfandel vineyards established in recent years were planted with a clone selected and developed by the Department of Viticulture and Enology of the University of California at Davis. It's a clone that gives generous crops of large bunches of big berries—appropriate, perhaps, for White Zinfandel but for little else.

Old vineyards have something more in their favor: a generous sprinkling of other black varieties, most commonly Petite Sirah, Carignan, and Grenache, that the "little old winegrower" of yesteryear planted at random in his vineyard to add interest to his finished wine and, more importantly, to compensate for any possible lack of color, alcohol, or finesse. A few years ago Ridge Vineyards went through the vines it leases from the Trentadue family at Geyserville and found that the proportion of Zinfandel there was actually less than two thirds (the balance was made up of roughly even proportions of equally ancient Petite Sirah and Carignan vines). Having made successful wines from the vineyard exactly as planted for almost thirty years, Ridge Vineyards has chosen to continue as before, but it now sells the wine simply as Geyserville, with no varietal designation. The 1990 Geyserville is so remarkable that it lent considerable excitement to the California Grill at Bordeaux's Vinexpo last June.

A few of the old vineyards had been abandoned, but most were still being cultivated for fruit to be used by the owners or sold to home wine-makers or to the large producers who could always accept another ton or two for their big volume blends. Jed Steele had started to make wine from old Mendocino Ridge Zinfandel vines at the Edmeades winery in Anderson Valley in the early 1970s, but David Bennion and his partners at Ridge Vineyards had stumbled onto the possibilities of old Zinfandel vines almost ten years earlier. The founders of Ridge Vineyards, colleagues at the Stanford Research Institute, had bought their mature Cabernet Sauvignon vineyard on Monte Bello Ridge in the Santa Cruz Mountains, south of San Francisco, in 1958. On their drives up and down the mountain they'd often stopped to buy Zinfandel made by their neighbors the Picchetti family. (The Picchettis had been making wine from their Zinfandel vineyard since 1877, selling it mostly at the winery gate.)

In his book *Angels' Visits,* an inquiry into California Zinfandel published in 1991, David Darlington describes what happened next. Darlington has a keen eye for the telling detail (and, although not evident in the excerpt below, a wicked skill in allowing the characters in his saga to skewer themselves on their own offhand remarks). His book is one of the most entertaining (and honestly informative) on wine to have appeared for many years. This is what he has to say: "In October 1964 the [Ridge Vineyards] families were nearly finished with the Monte Bello harvest when they learned that the Picchettis were giving up the wine business—ordered by the county health officials to put in a concrete floor, the younger generation, insufficiently enamored with winemaking to comply, abandoned plans to pick their grapes. The '64 Monte Bello Cabernet crop had been short, so the Ridge owners leaped into the lurch. They harvested the Picchettis' Zinfandel (at twenty-four degrees Brix, a sugar level that the owners considered overripe) and fermented it according to their traditional methods. 'It was so good right from the beginning,' Dave Bennion recalled, 'that when we needed a wine for dinner, I'd just go get some from the barrel and put it in a flask. Our Cabernet couldn't be quaffed that way. I saw right then that Zinfandel could be our bread and butter.'"

The next year Bennion arranged to buy more Zinfandel grapes from old vines in a Paso Robles vineyard that still supplies Ridge Vineyards to this day. He also agreed to help finance the restoration of the badly neglected Zinfandel vines in the Jimsomare vineyard, another property on Monte Bello Ridge. In 1966, Bennion contracted to purchase grapes from old Zinfandel vines in the Trentadue vineyard that is now the source of the winery's Geyserville *cuvée* mentioned above. All those early Ridge Vineyards Zinfandels were provocatively different from other wines then being made in California. Sometimes they were overbearingly clumsy, but they were always impressive. Ironically, by the time Ridge Vineyards had left that more or less experimental stage of their winemaking behind them, others seemed to be taking Ridge's early wines as models for their own.

Those others did not include the late Joe Swan, a Western Airlines pilot who had made a hobby of wine for years before a transfer from Los Angeles to San Francisco allowed him to buy a vineyard near the Russian River planted in the old-timers' classic mix of Zinfandel, Petite Sirah, and Carignan. He made his first Zinfandel in 1968, and the wines his Joseph Swan Vineyards continued to produce through the 1970s and 1980s are as much a part of California legend as the man himself.

Joel Peterson of Ravenswood—now perhaps the leader in California Zinfandel—served an apprenticeship of sorts with Joe Swan in the mid-1970s. Peterson had been raised with a broad knowledge of wine (he sat in at his father's distinguished twice-weekly tasting group from the age of nine) and brought to winemaking a sophisticated palate, a scientific training as a biochemist, and a confident insouciance.

Acknowledging his debt to Swan, he told David Darlington, "[Swan] tended his fermenting wine as if it were a newborn child. He was so meticulous. He smelled every barrel in the winery, made sure everything was clean to his nose; he never rushed, never did anything unconsciously."

Peterson made his own first Zinfandel with Swan's equipment in 1976. His Zinfandels from the Dickerson Vineyard in Napa Valley and Old Hill Vineyard in Sonoma Valley are now among the finest wines—regardless of variety—produced in California; few, at any price, are as thrilling as they. (On the day after my big Zinfandel tasting I passed up a chance to drink a Léoville-Las-Cases '70 with my lunch, preferring to take a glass from the opened bottle of Dickerson Vineyard '91 instead.)

Peterson follows Swan's precepts: He chooses fruit from old, head-pruned vines with low yields and ferments it with its natural, indigenous yeast in old open redwood fermenters that are wide rather than high—the mass of skins and pips that floats on the surface is then more shallow and easier to punch down for flavor and color extraction. "We let the fermentation get quite warm," he told me, "and, depending on the fruit and the year, we let the skins macerate when fermentation is finished for anything from three to five weeks. For the size of our operation, we have a large cellar staff. That's important, too. You need to stay close to the wines. You mustn't let them get away from you."

Ridge, Ravenswood, and Rosenblum Cellars—the last a winery in Alameda, across the bay from San Francisco, founded and run by Kent Rosenblum as a sideline to his veterinary practice—are known among enthusiasts as the big *R*s of Zinfandel. Of the three, Ridge Vineyards' Zinfandels have classic measure, Ravenswood's are flowingly romantic, and Rosenblum's are gorgeously, dramatically florid. If Ridge Vineyards is the Bach of the Zinfandel world, Ravenswood is the Brahms, and Rosenblum the Strauss—Johann, of course, not Richard.

Originally published as "Zinfandel: California's Own" in *Gourmet*, February 1994.

Since this was written, Professor Carole Meredith of the Department of Viticulture and Enology at the University of California at Davis, working with colleagues in Croatia, revealed through DNA analysis that what we in California call Zinfandel is the same variety as the Crljenak Kaštelanski of the Dalmatian Coast.

WINE AND FOOD

The Myth of a Perfect Match

Raymond Oliver, distinguished chef and proprietor of Le Grand Véfour in Paris, once wrote, "Apart from a few rare and gross mistakes there are few wines and dishes which really do not marry." Most would agree. For my own part, I have endured my share of awful food and miserable wines, but I have yet to be confronted with truly well prepared food and delicious wine in a combination so bizarre that either or both were actually ruined. Wine and food can be mutually enhancing, but in any case they have a natural affinity and are tolerant of each other to a broad degree. On occasions when I have had cause to reflect on a particularly fine wine failing to show at its best, the obstacle has less often been the food than lack of judgment in serving the wine on the wrong occasion or in selecting an inappropriate wine (or none at all) to precede it.

Yet seeking a perfect fit of wine and food risks becoming one more complication thrown in the path of those who simply want to enjoy a bottle of wine. The few traditions we lean on, though reassuring, are of dubious value. The pairing of wine and food is a subject that none of the gastronomic writers of the past, from third-century Athenaeus to nineteenth-century Brillat-Savarin, have even cared to discuss. For despite the filler pages in diaries that used to caution us to drink Muscadet with oysters and a glass of dry Madeira after the soup as if failure to do either could bring the social opprobrium normally reserved for those who omit to turn down the appropriate corner when leaving calling cards, there neither are, nor were there ever, rational rules to guide or restrain us in matching wine and food.

Formal meals were once differently composed, of course. Instead of today's well defined progression of courses that allows all guests to be eating the same thing at the same time, for centuries grand occasions attracted a multitude of dishes to the table in a series of arrangements that seemed to lack cohesion and meaning, seen in the structured context of the way we eat now. Each time the table was reset with a stylized pattern of new dishes, those present might choose to taste all, a few, or none. The dining table itself was a visible menu, starting with half a dozen soups or a dozen unrelated first courses from which guests helped themselves and each other. With their removal, eight or ten varied entrées would arrive, followed by an assorted selection of roasts, another of vegetables and side dishes, and so on. Fish and meat, sweet and savory, could arrive on the table together, just as today they might be alternative selections on a printed restaurant menu, and, if one guest chose to eat prawns from among the first group of dishes while another helped himself to a sauté of kidneys, how could a host have hoped to plan a series of wines that would progress logically and match the food?

The answer is that he didn't, and nobody seemed much to care. Paintings of such banquets confirm that neither glasses nor wine—whether in bottle or decanter—shared the table with the elaborate food until the late eighteenth century. Wine bottles usually stood in coolers on the floor or were kept with glasses on a sideboard. When a guest asked for wine, he or she was brought red or white with a glass to drink from. Water was usually mixed with the wine according to preference. The glass, always emptied at one draft (no swirling, sniffing, and sipping), was then either handed back to the server or placed upside down in a rinser.

After the French Revolution, Grimod de la Reynière, a former aristocrat who lived well to compensate himself for physical deformities, instructed the new masters of Paris in the art of living, by writing extensively on eating and drinking. His work, which inspired the far less useful but more widely known *Physiologie du Goût* of Brillat-Savarin, his contemporary, provides details of a way of life de la Reynière's pre-Revolutionary peers had taken for granted and never, therefore, would have recorded for themselves. Drawing on his privileged experience under the *ancien régime,* he explained everything from the way a menu for sixty should be planned to the manner of carving or dividing each kind of bird, fish, or joint of meat. He instructed those eager to know how to eat boiled eggs in polite society always to crush the empty shells, inspired in them a passion to eat purée of woodcock ("the greatest ecstasy—having tasted it one might as well die," he said, innocently bequeathing a phrase still haunting us in Valley-talk), and told them, doubtless with no greater success than our parents, to keep their elbows off the table. He gave excellent directions (would that they were compulsory reading today!) on how to accept or decline invitations with prompt courtesy and counseled his readers not only on what could safely be discussed at dinner in the presence of strangers, but why they should avoid houses where they risked paying at cards four times the value of the meal they had eaten.

Of particular interest are his comments on wine. He explained that the beverage wines served during a meal—a Chablis for the white, perhaps, and a Mâcon Rouge for the red—should be drunk undiluted only if there were to be no lingering over fine wines later. By the time he published his *Manuel des Amphitryons* (*Hosts' Manual*) in 1808, the beverage wine, water, and glasses had moved from sideboard to table, where guests, free to serve themselves, could follow their own tastes rather than that of a lackey who often premixed the wine and water in proportions to suit his own whim or in accordance with the size of tip he had in view.

With or without water, however, Grimod de la Reynière expected guests to drink copiously. At a lunch for twenty-five, for example, he recommended providing a dozen bottles each of an ordinary red and an ordinary white wine, to be supplemented at the final service of sweet and savory entremets and dessert with four bottles of fine red Bordeaux, four of Beaune, four of Clos Vougeot, four of white Saint-Péray, two each of the sweet wines of Cyprus and Málaga, and, for good measure, a bottle each of Rivesaltes and Lunel, golden dessert wines from the south of France—all of which would have been drunk without the addition of water, of course. Essentially, de la Reynière shows us that in his day, in the society familiar to him, wine—or wine and water—was quaffed without much thought during the progress of a meal. But what we might consider a tasting of a few select fine wines followed at leisure with appropriate delicacies at the meal's close.

In eighteenth-century England, a diet mainly of bread and red meat was washed down with copious drafts of Port, then still a coarse wine and hardly the classic it has since become. Lady Mary Wortley Montagu, wife of the British ambassador to the Turkish sultan in Constantinople, found, on the other hand, that in Vienna in 1716 a prepared list of the wines to be offered with dinner—"often as many as eighteen"—was laid with the napkin on each guest's plate. She doesn't tell us, however, whether each wine was served successively on such occasions, whether the list was intended to provide guests with the means to select the appropriate match for any one of the variety of dishes tasted at each course, or whether guests were advised precisely of the extensive choice available merely to ensure that each would find within it a wine to meet his or her particular preference.

But regardless of the ceremony of Paris, the monotony of London, and the ambiguity of Vienna, it has been suggested that the rich bourgeoisie of Hamburg were already fumbling toward matching wines and specific dishes as early as the 1770s, even though published references to their efforts are less than reassuring. They include Málaga partnering fresh herring, Burgundy with peas, and Port with salt fish. I imagine there has been compounded confusion either in the retelling or in the translation.

The possibility of serving wines in sequence, each linked to a specific dish, came only as formal dinners changed in the course of the nineteenth century from a series of gastronomically incongruous set pieces to what was referred to as service *à la russe*, whereby servants carried the dishes round one at a time, offering them to guests who helped themselves.

Surviving diaries and menus show, however, that little thought was given to wine and food compatibility despite what had become feasible. At a dinner in England in 1847, provision of wines for seventeen diners consisted of ten bottles of Sherry, two bottles of Port, and one bottle of red Bordeaux, a selection that speaks for itself regardless of what was to be eaten. Mrs. Beeton, in her *Complete Etiquette for Gentlemen* of 1876, makes no bones about recommending Sherry as the appropriate wine for dinner, and even the venerable Professor Saintsbury, whose *Notes on a Cellar-Book* is holy writ to most modern wine drinkers, says brightly that "Manzanilla [Sherry] will carry you nearly through dinner, and others of the lighter class will go all through. . . . "

Saintsbury does not discuss wine in the context of food (except to make a passing reference to sparkling Moselle with sardine sandwiches taken as an undergraduate at Oxford), but the menus with which he closes his book show that, though he preferred always to start with Sherry followed perhaps by a glass of white wine, on special occasions he served his guests Champagne until red Bordeaux, Port, or both appeared to bring the meal to a close. In 1899 Colonel Newnham-Davis, gastronomic correspondent of the *Pall Mall Gazette,* complained that, "In Paris no man dreams of drinking Champagne, and nothing but Champagne, for dinner; but in London . . . ninety-nine out of a hundred Englishmen . . . turn instinctively to the Champagne page of the wine-card." Anthony Trollope, the novelist, writing as a traveler in the United States in 1862, said that Americans in hotels drank mostly at the bar before they ate, but they, too, drank Champagne with dinner on the rare occasions when they did not drink water.

So much for inspiration from our gastronomic past.

~ ~ ~

Though good wines and food do have a natural affinity and a broader mutual tolerance than we usually admit (except to ourselves when we dine alone and reach for the bottle we most want to drink without jumping through gastronomic hoops), it is also true that there is special satisfaction in achieving a compatibility so harmonious that it seems unthinkable to have paired either wine or dish in any other way.

The mistake most commonly made is to look for such congeniality by the matching of flavors difficult, if not impossible, to define. Talk of Gewürztraminer wines, for example, accompanying spicy dishes to advantage is based mostly on the rationalization that *Gewürz* means spice. The delicate aroma of a Gewürztraminer—more like the smell of damask roses than any spice I can think of—would be overwhelmed by the pungency of Madras cooking and becomes an irrelevant, even irritating, flourish when imposed on the carefully self-contained balance of most Chinese dishes.

Essentially, the response between wine and food depends on texture, intensity, and scale. The texture of a dish is more often established by a sauce or the method of cooking than it is by the density of the basic ingredient. A light, white wine that happily accompanies a plain grilled sole, for example, might taste thin and pointless if served with the same sole under a creamy Mornay sauce. Charts that recommend specific categories of wine with fish, chicken, or veal rarely allow for applied variations in texture, which can make one and the same wine appear to be unexpectedly full or disappointingly light.

A California Riesling, often thought difficult to match to food because of its forward fruitiness and slight sweetness, presents few problems if the modest residual sugar is recognized as part of its textural balance. This natural sugar fills the wine out and makes it a match for dishes in which a ripe texture and hint of sweetness will find an echo—a grilled veal chop garnished with slightly caramelized confit of onions or a blanquette of veal or young lamb.

Intensity and persistence of flavor in wine and food must be symmetrical or one will make the other seem fleeting and inconsequential. Veal in a cream and mushroom sauce, for example, presents a rich texture but mild flavor. It calls for the combination of full body and restrained flavor peculiar to barrel-fermented, lees-aged Chardonnay. A dish like

Richard Olney's chicken with garlic and fennel, on the other hand, though without the texture to support a heavy wine, needs one with sustained, exuberant flavor: new Beaujolais, young Chianti, Mendocino Zinfandel. It matters less that the flavor of wine and food should echo each other (how could they?) than that they balance each other. Fish is particularly tricky because we think of it always as light and delicate, but when steamed over ginger, poached with garlic and saffron, or grilled with herbs, the flavor expands and can accept a more assertive wine.

Scale, a combination of texture and flavor intensity, is more than a sum of its parts and harder to define than either. A wine with scale is imposing: One can either match it or play up to it. A sumptuous 1978 Châteauneuf-du-Pape, for example, can be matched by a truffled pheasant ("stuff it with 3 oz. pork fat pounded with a few truffles," recommends Auguste Escoffier in *Ma Cuisine*) or be supported by a simple but succulent fillet of beef. In matching an imposing wine, one must be careful not to overreach; and in playing up to it, the dish must be bold even if simple. Something or other luxuriantly *financière* might upstage even the most imposing of wines, whereas two lamb chops and a mess of zucchini would be weak and niggardly.

When serving particularly fine, old red wines it is best to err toward food with lightness of texture to allow the wine to seem contrastingly full, and to aim for moderation of scale so that the wine's delicacy of flavor is not overwhelmed. Food lacking texture, flavor, and scale altogether would be inappropriately insipid to accompany a special bottle, however, so careful judgment is needed.

White wines rarely age to the same advantage as red. Those that do will lose their youthful aroma but acquire a deeper flavor—what one might call a grain—allowing them to partner dishes of greater scale. An old-fashioned, mature Italian white wine, usually slightly oxidized, can be a revelation with pasta in a creamy Gorgonzola sauce. (Oxidation is a fault when it is plainly identifiable. Until then, like so much else purists think of as defective in wine, it adds complexity. It is a question of degree.)

Because food affects the appreciation of a wine far more than a wine can possibly influence the taste of food, the time given to assessing how the texture, intensity, and scale of a finished dish, as opposed to its principal component, will modify a wine is better used, surely, than it would be searching through a thousand tasting notes to find a wine with an herbal aroma or an alleged hint of clove in its bouquet to support an ingredient or garnish. One man's herb is another man's green leaf, this one's hint of clove is another's geranium finish. Looking for specific and identical matching flavors in food and wine is the way to madness and perdition.

Once the principles of texture, intensity, and scale are understood, mentally checking the probable harmony between wine and food becomes automatic and uncertainties are easily resolved. In any case, there is never only one correct choice. There are usually several choices that will work very well and an almost infinite number that will work tolerably well.

A wine and a dish might work well together and still be an inappropriate combination for the occasion, however. If, for instance, a few friends are invited to a dinner of plain, broiled steaks, the vigorous and unpretentious Gigondas recently discovered will work as well as the last, treasured bottle of Mouton-Rothschild '53 left in the cellar. In one case, however, the evening becomes an informal, relaxed get-together. In the other, the steak plays up to the Mouton-Rothschild, which therefore looms in importance and cannot be ignored. Its presence could introduce an unintended focus at the table, and possibly an unwelcome formality. The choice of wine, always assuming it to be compatible, dresses both the dish and the occasion up or down.

There are times when the wine adds its own sheen to an occasion. Raymond Oliver, in *The French at Table*, wrote, "I like a wine to be presented in a given context: the vintage of a friend's year of birth, a shared memory, an anniversary or some such reason. Then the wine becomes a symbol whose value lies outside the accepted canon."

Any exaggerated or even obvious effort to coordinate such a wine diminishes rather than enhances its special role. As in so many situations, success is assured by knowing what *not* to do. If it is an imposing bottle, never match it, always play up to it. If the wine is comparatively simple except for the memories it is intended to shake loose, don't compensate by elaborating the food unnecessarily. Let the food be simple, too, but think of subtle ways in which it can be made to reinforce the wine's message.

A special wine, no matter how defined, will be appreciated all the more if a preceding bottle establishes criteria for it. Often an occasion to drink one remarkable wine is expanded into an occasion to drink two, or even more; unfortunately, rarely is one of them adequate preparation for the others. Use the first wine as a curtain raiser, to set the mood and establish a standard that will then be gloriously excelled by the special wine of the evening. A simple, light red wine, preferably one that has lost or is losing its youthful fruitiness, will show off an older red wine of great delicacy far better than an initial white wine can. On the other hand, a massive wine with subtleties that could be missed in reaction to its scale, should be preceded by a robust but straightforward wine that will make scale itself less remarkable.

Unfortunately, this preparatory sequence does not work well among white wines. In fact, I would serve one white wine with another only if there was a particular reason to do so. When young, white wines rely more than red on varietal aroma for their distinction, and, though the contrast of one young varietal against another might be interesting at the tasting bench, it is meaningless at the table. An older white wine, on the other hand, no matter how magnificent, is reduced to being merely an older white wine when seen against a younger one.

More important than remembering all these principles and examples, however, is to bear in mind that wine and food, in any combination, taste better with amiable companions. Start there, I find, and everything falls into place.

Originally published as "Wine and Food" in *Gourmet,* December 1987.

CHARDONNAY

Buds, Twigs, and Clones

At the last count, there were forty-two thousand acres of Chardonnay vines in California. That is more than double the acreage in Burgundy, Chardonnay's home. The rising flow of California Chardonnay has coincided with a change in the way the state's wineries are handling this popular varietal. They are turning away from the chunky oak-and-fruit style that has served, brashly enough, for the last decade or two, and, with Burgundian tradition as their example and restraint as their new watchword, they are placing greater emphasis on balance and texture. But because, in the flood of brands and labels, the wineries need more than ever to be distinctive, no matter how discreetly, subtle differences among Chardonnay's varietal clones and selections are now matters of serious concern. In Healdsburg and Saint Helena, where wise heads once talked late into the night on the relative merits of light-toasted Vosges oak barrels and heavy-toasted Allier, conversation is now larded with references to Rued and See's and Old Wente.

For years I had been puzzled by references to Chardonnay clones. Occasionally, when curiosity got the better of me, I searched for information on the Curtis clone, the Spring Mountain clone, the Martini clone, and all the rest. There was nothing on Chardonnay clones in print, not the smallest reference to them even in Winkler's *General Viticulture*, the standard California teaching text.

Just when I had more or less given up trying to make sense of them in favor of the less abstruse tangles of Eastern European politics, I received from Simi Winery a newsletter with a neatly drawn plan of a test vineyard they have planted on Diamond Mountain, above Napa Valley. It showed alternating rows of seven Chardonnay clones. In the accompanying text were two key sentences: "The concept of choosing a plant according to intended use is familiar to gardeners who plant plum tomatoes for sauce and beefsteak tomatoes for sandwiches. . . . For several years we have been working with selected Chardonnay clones to determine if there are aromatic or flavor differences between them which might be the basis for varying styles of Chardonnay wine."

Perhaps it's because every vine is propagated from sprouted bud wood— a twig taken from another vine—and never from seed that the term *clone,* from the Greek word for *twig,* has come to be applied so loosely. (In much of California the bud wood is grafted, on a bench or in the vineyard, onto phylloxera-resistant rootstock.) Professors Carole Meredith and Michael Mullins of the Department of Viticulture and Enology of the University of California at Davis define a clone as a distinct subtype within a wine-grape variety.

"Differences between these sub-types are genetic differences—they are stable and they are maintained through propagation," they wrote in a leaflet, "Romancing the Clone," published by the university in cooperation with the U.S. Department of Agriculture. "These differences are thought to arise as the result of mutations, very small changes in the DNA, the genetic blueprint in each cell that governs every process and structure that makes up the vine. Such changes are natural and normal and occur from time to time in all cells of all organisms. If such a change takes place in a grapevine cell that is destined to give rise to a bud, then the shoot that eventually develops from that bud will be genetically different from the rest of the vine. (This is called a bud sport.) Cuttings or buds taken from that shoot for propagation will give rise to entire vines that are now slightly different from the original vine but identical to each other. A new clone is born."

A mass selection of Chardonnay, on the other hand, is the result of a mass of bud-wood cuttings taken from a great number of vines throughout a vineyard that were in turn propagated from a similar mass of bud wood cut in another vineyard. If each time there is a deliberate effort to seek out and take bud wood from vines with specific attributes, whether yield, aroma, or some other quality, such repeated selections of selections, even when taken from a large number of vines, can eventually lead to some common characteristics. But no matter how homogeneous such a collection of vines might then be, they do not constitute a clone. And because the individual vines do not share a single genetic origin, the reaction of each to cultivation methods in a shared environment is likely at times to be surprisingly different.

I called Diane Kenworthy, Simi's viticulturist, about that newsletter. It had seemed to offer hope, at last, of practical information on the subject. She told me the winery had planted three standard clones from the University of California at Davis and was testing them against others taken from commercial vineyards with both specific styles and distinguished records, to see to what extent their qualities would be consistent when transferred. "We want to see if we can find anything among these clones that's better than what we already have," she said.

Four of the Simi clones were new, each propagated from a single vine chosen from among the many similar or complementary vines within one of the specific and acknowledged Chardonnay selections. Diane Kenworthy was well aware that a clone propagated from just one vine of such a selection did not necessarily carry overall the mass selection's characteristics, "but we need a controlled experiment," she said.

One of the mass selections from which Simi has propagated a clone is popularly referred to as Spring Mountain. It is widely used in Sonoma County.

Merry Edwards first brought it into the county when she was at Matanzas Creek, I was told. "The muscat-like strain in its aroma comes across as no more than a heightened fruitiness when it's used with restraint in a blend," said Diane Kenworthy. "The Rued selection—not one of those we are testing here—has an even more intense aroma, one we already know carries over wherever the selection is planted."

When I called Merry Edwards, now the winemaker at both Merry Vintners and Domaine Laurier, to ask where the Spring Mountain selection had come from, she told me she had taken cuttings from Spring Mountain Vineyard's old Wildwood Vineyard on Silverado Trail in Napa Valley. "I had gone there for cuttings of the Mount Eden Vineyards clone. I had understood there were Mount Eden vines there. But it was winter and difficult to see what was what. The vineyard manager must have misdirected me. I've been told that what I took is probably related to the Chardonnay Musqué of Burgundy, and might even be the same vine. It certainly gives a very perfumed wine."

The Rued selection, named for Paul Rued's vineyard near Graton in the Russian River Valley, "is also highly aromatic," Merry Edwards added. "But it's supported by better texture and depth of flavor. I would never use Spring Mountain alone, but Rued gives a balanced wine of real interest."

Paul Rued has little light to shed on the origin of his vines. "We bought them from a nursery in Calistoga in 1971. There was quite a demand for Chardonnay at the time. This was what they had."

Whether or not Rued and Spring Mountain owe their aroma to Chardonnay Musqué, they exist as selections because growers have segregated cuttings from aromatic vines and propagated them. Larry Hyde, a grape grower in the Carneros, the cool district by San Francisco Bay where Napa and Sonoma run together, found his aromatic vines through mass selections cut in the Long Vineyard in Napa Valley—a vineyard propagated from Stony Hill vines that lead us back to Wente, as we shall see. Sixty percent of his vineyard is planted with such vines. "Wineries rely on me for aromatic fruit," he told me.

I was ignorant of "the Chardonnay Musqué of Burgundy." I eventually found a reference to this particularly aromatic subvariety of Chardonnay as a footnote in a French scientific directory of vines. Trying to trace it in California was even harder. Records of who had brought which variety, and when, were never very extensive, and many of those that did exist were destroyed during Prohibition, when the majority of wineries closed. Charles Wetmore, while president of the State Viticultural Commission, was responsible for some of the first Chardonnay to arrive in California in 1882, directly from Meursault in Burgundy. He distributed its bud wood in the Livermore Valley, where he had established his own Cresta Blanca Winery. Some of that wood went to the Gier vineyard at Pleasanton.

Thirty years later, Ernest Wente persuaded his father to bring in some Chardonnay, along with other *vinifera* cuttings, from the vine nursery of the distinguished wine school at the University of Montpellier in the south of France. He also acquired Chardonnay cuttings from the Gier vineyard that were drawn from Wetmore's original importation from Meursault. It would therefore appear that the Wente vineyard, later to be a key source of Chardonnay in California, contained from the start at least these two distinct selections.

Paul Masson was said to have imported Chardonnay for his La Cresta Vineyard, in the Santa Cruz mountains south of San Francisco, directly from Burgundy in 1896. The property passed to Martin Ray when he bought the Paul Masson company in 1936. Ray took cuttings from it for a new vineyard of his own nearby when he sold the company and La Cresta to Seagram in 1943. His widow, Eleanor Ray, seems to think on the other hand that he might have imported his own fresh cuttings at that time—she mentions as the source Louis Latour's vineyard at Corton-Charlemagne—but the war makes it unlikely.

Others have suggested that the original Chardonnay at La Cresta was supplied to Paul Masson by his father-in-law, Charles Lefranc, founder of Almaden, who had brought it to California in the 1870s. There are, indeed, several contemporary references to Chardonnay existing at that time in Santa Clara County's Almaden. But whatever its path to Martin Ray's vineyard, that strain of Chardonnay, now planted at Mount Eden Vineyards, has remained distinct, it is generally agreed, from the other Chardonnays that converged on, and later were to spread from, the Wente vineyard in Livermore Valley. The only commercially viable acreages of Chardonnay to survive Prohibition, according to an orthodox reading of California history, were those in Ernest Wente's and Paul Masson's vineyards.

To help me in my quest for Chardonnay Musqué, John Wetlaufer, a wine merchant and amateur historian in Calistoga, put me onto an old and out-of-print account of California vines by Professor Harold Olmo of the Department of Viticulture and Enology of the University of California at Davis, published by a now-defunct wine advisory board. In it, he made a brief reference to Chardonnay Musqué having been imported by a Captain J. H. Drummond of Sonoma Valley in the 1870s. "It was probably lost," Olmo wrote, "during the vineyard removals of the Prohibition period."

I hunted for other references to Captain Drummond and found one only in several effusive paragraphs of Frona Eunice Wait's book *Wines and Vines of California,* published in 1889. She made no specific mention of Chardonnay Musqué but did commend Captain Drummond for having "all that is rare in the fruit kingdom."

John Wetlaufer told me that Captain Drummond had been step-father-in-law to Frederic Bioletti, the man responsible for the first attempts at clonal research at Davis prior to Prohibition. And Bioletti was himself mentor to Professor Olmo, the man who has since continued his work and who had written with such assurance of Chardonnay Musqué's presence in Drummond's vineyard.

Even in France, apparently, Chardonnay Musqué is considered a rare oddity. If it had been planted in Drummond's vineyard, is it not likely that neighbors, for whom Drummond was always "demonstrating the advisability of fine varieties of grapes," according to Frona Eunice Wait, would have asked for, and been given, a little of its bud wood? And is it not probable that cuttings from their patches of vines—perhaps considered too insignificant to be pulled during Prohibition or counted afterwards—strayed into other Chardonnay vineyards, letting loose the muscat element now prevalent in the Rued and Spring Mountain selections?

~ ~ ~

Tracking with certainty any Chardonnay clone or selection would be difficult enough even if better records had been kept. The trail is further obscured, however, because of confusion on both sides of the Atlantic between Chardonnay and Pinot Blanc. Chardonnay has existed as a distinct variety in France for centuries, but it was always referred to under other names (and in some parts of France, still is) and was assumed to be identical with, or at least no more than a variant of, the Pinot Blanc with which it was often promiscuously planted. The Chardonnay name began to appear, spelled in a variety of ways, only in the mid-nineteenth century. Even then it was used as if it were a synonym for Pinot Blanc.

Jean Lavalle's 1855 book, *Histoire et Statistique de la Vigne et des Grands Vins de la Côte d'Or*, is so highly regarded for its accuracy of observation that as recently as the 1930s it was used as the primary source for the definitions of controlled appellations in Burgundy. Yet even Lavalle, director of the Dijon Botanical Garden, refers to "*chardenet ou pinot blanc*" as if they were a single vine variety.

The experts now agree that Chardonnay is not a member of the Pinot family at all, though it is evident from past confusion that it has not been easy to distinguish one from the other. In California, where there was yet more muddle caused by the practice of referring to Chenin Blanc as White Pineau until the 1950s, the distinction between Chardonnay and Pinot Blanc was thought finally to have been settled until a recent finding that vines in the state formerly accepted as Pinot Blanc are in fact Melon de Bourgogne. Melon is more commonly known as the Muscadet grape and in France is used extensively to make a wine of that name in the low-lying vineyards south of Nantes at the mouth of the Loire.

This can only mean that true Pinot Blanc, certain to have reached these shores along with those early cuttings of Chardonnay, is probably still out there somewhere, like the Chardonnay Musqué, misidentified and contributing to those surprises in the Chardonnay vineyards.

Alex Vyborny grows grapes in Sonoma County and manages vineyards for absentee owners there. He has worked extensively with the Spring Mountain selection and told me there were "several kinds," implying that it is inconsistent—as one might expect from a mass selection, as opposed to a clone. He more or less dismissed the Spring Mountain selection and said he preferred to work with See's clone, anyway.

See's clone takes its name from what had once been Charles See's vineyard in Napa Valley, now part of Silverado Vineyards. Vyborny thought it had been propagated from cuttings taken there from Sterling Vineyards, where vines had been propagated from bud wood taken from the old Wente vineyard in Livermore Valley. See's sounded to me more like a mass selection than a clone, and Jack Stuart, the winemaker at Silverado Vineyards, agreed.

"The vines are inconsistent," he told me, "Grapes from some vines taste quite muscaty, but others not at all. Taken as a whole, though, fruit from the See vineyard brings a roundness to our wine and a touch of apricot or peach flavor. That vineyard is aging now and is in decline, suffering from leaf roll. Perhaps because of that, the fruit seems to be less aromatic than it was and could be less aromatic than the fruit of young vines that have been propagated elsewhere from our bud wood."

Sterling Vineyards was far from the first to get bud wood from Wente. Fred and Eleanor McCrea had taken cuttings there long before, in 1948, for their new vineyard at Stony Hill, above Napa Valley.

"Herman Wente stood at the door of his house and said to us: 'There it is. Just go take what you want,'" Eleanor McCrea remembers. "We knew nothing. There were no peas greener than we were. No one talked about *clones* in those days. We just went in and took cuttings from all over."

Others who subsequently took bud wood from the vines propagated by the McCreas at Stony Hill would refer to their own vines sometimes as Stony Hill selection, and sometimes, knowing where the Stony Hill vines had come from, as Wente.

Louis Martini was among those who referred to the cuttings he had taken from Stony Hill as "Wente." In 1951 or 1952 he had marked thirty Stony Hill vines that interested him. When they were dormant he had gone back to take cuttings from them, propagating twenty vines from each on a new Martini family property on Stanly Lane in the Carneros. He allowed the Department of Viticulture and Enology at Davis to use his six hundred Chardonnay vines for trials.

"Davis would come over every year to measure them, take samples of the grapes, and make wine," Louis Martini recollected recently. In 1955 Professor Olmo made a selection from the "Wente" vines for the university's clonal propagation program.

Professor Olmo, who still has an office on the Davis campus of the University of California, told me that the Department of Viticulture and Enology released healthy bud wood from that selection before it had been through the hands of the plant pathologists. When the pathologists had indexed the bud wood—viticultural jargon meaning it was tested for plant viruses—but had not at that stage heat-treated it to ensure its being virus-free, it was rereleased.

Unfortunately, the pathologists worked with numerical references of their own, according to Professor Olmo, and the result is still confusion. The indexed material they released has been referred to by some as clone 2A, yet the viticulturists say it should have carried a series of numbers in the sixties. It is astonishing, to say the least, that records even at the university should be so vague. But whether as one clone or as a series of them, this bud wood, too, was widely referred to as "Wente clone."

Both this original material available from Davis and the mass selections taken directly and indirectly from the original Wente vineyard are all dubbed indiscriminately now with the name "Old Wente clone." Not surprisingly, vines so called vary considerably. A characteristic they share, according to Bill Dyer, the winemaker at Sterling, is their "pumpkins and peas" look of large and small berries jumbled together in their bunches. But other characteristics—particularly those of flavor and aroma—have come to distinguish one group of these mass selections from another. Depending on the specific vines chosen for their bud wood, mass selections can differ markedly, even when taken from the same vineyard. When the characteristics of one mass selection are preferred to those of another, growers need rough-and-ready ways to indicate which is which, and new identities are created for them. Hence, Rued, See's, and Spring Mountain.

Wente Brothers, not inappropriately, were the first to have, on their new property in Monterey County, a certified block of a heat-treated version of a Davis clone released by the university under the reference 108. That clone has now been redesignated as two separate ones, 4 and 5, to distinguish two different durations of heat treatment, according to some, and to designate two different vine sources, according to others. (I was beginning to learn why there was so little in print on the subject of clones. Academic angels had refrained from treading where inconsistency, contradiction, and incoherence lay in wait at every turn.)

In the late 1960s, millions of cuttings of clone 108 bud wood were being used to plant half the present Chardonnay vineyards of Napa Valley and most of those in the state of Washington. It was referred to colloquially as "the Wente clone," and "for a while," Eric Wente said recently, "we were making more money from its bud wood than from its grapes."

Later, bud wood of that same clone began to circulate from vineyards on the Curtis ranch, north of Napa (the property of Bill Jaeger—a partner in Rutherford Hill Winery, whose mother was born a Curtis—now renamed the Jaeger Ranch). That wood was referred to as the Curtis clone. For the record, it is synonymous with the Davis clone 108, a.k.a. the Wente clone.

But whatever they call them, winemakers have sometimes been leery of these Davis clones, believing that their healthy yield capacity is at cross-purposes with quality. Yet Bill Dyer said he always got good quality from the clone 108 planted on the hillsides of Sterling's famous Winery Lake Vineyard in the Carneros, provided he controlled the crop. And although Merry Edwards thought that the Davis clones had been propagated to give healthy yields, she confirmed Dyer's observation. "If you let them, they tend to be highly productive of grapes with low-flavor intensity," she said. "But growers who hold down their crops to no more than three or four tons to the acre can get satisfactory quality from them."

The Mount Eden Vineyards Chardonnay strain—by now who can say whether it is a clone or a selection?—seems to be the only one that does not lead back to the Wente vineyard in Livermore Valley. There are still twelve acres of it at Mount Eden Vineyards, where some of the older vines, affected by phylloxera, will soon have to be pulled. Small amounts of the strain might well have been mingled into other selections, but the only vineyards in California known to be planted with it exclusively, other than those at Mount Eden itself, are at Congress Springs and Cinnabar, both nearby in the Santa Cruz Mountains, and at Kistler Vineyards, on the Sonoma side of the Mayacamas.

All who have worked with the strain enthuse over it, despite its lack of vigor, its virus, and its low yields. Merry Edwards, who knew it well from her three years as winemaker at Mount Eden, said that the tight, conical bunches of tiny berries give a wine that shows its complexity only after several months in barrel. She describes a Mount Eden Vineyards Chardonnay wine as richly textured, well rounded, impeccably integrated.

Jeffrey Patterson, the present winemaker at Mount Eden, is struck by the change he finds in wine produced by Kistler from what are essentially the same vines in the different environment of the Mayacamas. "The Mount Eden Vineyards clone never gives an overtly fruity wine," he said, "but the wine of Kistler Vineyards has orchard-fruit tones—apples and pears—quite distinct from ours."

David Ramey, a distinguished California enologist formerly associated with Chardonnay research and development at Simi Winery, and winemaker at Matanzas Creek after Merry Edwards, describes the

Mount Eden Vineyards strain as "classically Burgundian" and says that the Kistler Estate Vineyards Chardonnay made from it is presently "perhaps the best Chardonnay in California." (He would be too modest to say so, but the 1987 he himself made at Matanzas Creek wasn't bad, either.) Kistler has so far released commercial quantities only in 1987 and 1988 from their estate, and both wines are still difficult for some of us to judge. They clearly have great promise but for now show qualities best described as Episcopalian—discreetly elegant, if a bit fleshy, and not overly forthcoming.

Patterson's remarks point up the difference that site can play in moderating clonal distinctions. Dale Hampton, the leading grape grower in Santa Barbara County, says site is everything. "Clones change with the environment," he told me. "I can take one clone, put it in five different places, and get five different qualities from it."

Craig Williams, winemaker at Joseph Phelps Vineyards in Napa Valley, partly concurred. "The more I make wine," he said, "the more respect I have for differences of soil and environment, even though they were always played down [in California] before."

~ ~ ~

Questions of winemaking and site, selection and clone, are pointed up in the recent history of the Robert Young Vineyards in Alexander Valley. The vineyard first gained a reputation in the seventies when Richard Arrowood, winemaker at Chateau St. Jean, began to release a succession of highly prized wines with labels that identified this vineyard as the source of the grapes. Encouraged by the success of Arrowood's wines, other winemakers bought grapes from Robert Young. A similarity in the wines they made was at first attributed to the vineyard itself, later to the selection of Chardonnay grown there, and eventually to the marriage of the two. Another explanation, of course, could have been that winemakers drawn to buying grapes from the Robert Young Vineyards were those who, admiring the wines already made from them, would be likely to have adopted as their goal what they perceived as a "Robert

Young" style and would therefore have been following similar wine-making procedures to achieve it.

Like so many others in the 1960s, the vineyard was planted with bud wood brought there from the old Wente vineyard. Robert Young's son, a recent graduate of the Department of Viticulture and Enology at Davis, made selections of cuttings from their best vines a few years ago and took them to be tested for virus by the university's Foundation Plant Materials Service. One selection showed virus-free, and from that one vine the Youngs have since propagated two blocks of vines, which they have designated the "Robert Young clone." It is therefore distinct, of course, from the general selection of their Robert Young Vineyards, and, like both the transformation of wood from the early Wente selection in Louis Martini's vineyard into Davis clone 108 and the experimental lots on Simi's Diamond Mountain vineyard, it is a further example of a selection giving rise to a clone.

We shall see more of such transformations as growers, eager to take advantage of the concentrated flavor and distinction of the older, non-heat-treated selections but anxious to avoid the drawbacks of virus-ridden vines, follow Robert Young's example. Selecting the best from the selections they have, they are checking for "clean" wood and beginning to propagate new clones.

The University of California, too, is conducting clonal tests in their experimental vineyards in Napa Valley. Fortunately, similar work has been conducted for more than twenty years by Raymond Bernard, regional director in Dijon of the Office National Interprofessionnel des Vins de Table. Some of the Chardonnay clones proved by him to be successful have been imported through the plant quarantine service of Oregon State University and are beginning to find their way into California. There is also rumor of a Burgundian clone on the loose in one or two vineyards in California, brought in from France by a less circuitous route. Whether we shall be better off with "controlled" clones than we are with the chance of our present random selections, who can say? We must hope, though, that someone, somewhere, is keeping accurate notes on all this activity. Otherwise there will be scope for more conjecture in the year 2090. Watch this space.

Originally published as "Chardonnay: Buds, Twigs, and Clones" in *Gourmet,* May 1990.

By 2009 the acreage of Chardonnay in California had doubled to almost ninety-five thousand acres. Meanwhile, the Chardonnay planted in the former See vineyard, now part of Silverado Vineyards, had been pulled out and the vineyard replanted with Cabernet Sauvignon. Merry Edwards now has her own eponymous winery. Professor Harold Olmo died in 2006, at age ninety-six.

HAUT-BRION

A Most Particular Taste

"A little rise of ground, lieing open most to the west. It is noe thing but pure white sand, mixed with a little gravel. One would imagin it scarce fit to beare any thing. . . ." John Locke's words are taken from his journal entry for May 14, 1677. At that time a philosopher's journey to view a vineyard at first hand and to write down his impression of it was as unlikely as the visit today of an eminent intellectual to ponder the significance of a cabbage patch. Locke's curiosity confirms a singular achievement of Arnaud de Pontac, the richest and most influential man in Bordeaux, first president of its parliament (a configuration of law courts rather than a legislature), but best remembered as Château Haut-Brion's owner from 1649 until his death in 1681.

Samuel Pepys, later to be secretary of the admiralty in London, had first noticed "a sort of French wine called Ho-Bryan which hath a good and most particular taste" in a London tavern in 1663, but Locke makes clear that what had been a novelty to Pepys had become, in a very few years, a wine so esteemed in England as to be almost an object of cult. Significantly, Locke's journey to report on Haut-Brion underlines how identification of Pepys's "Ho-Bryan" wine with Arnaud de Pontac's vineyard at Château Haut-Brion helped bring about such status. It is a vineyard-to-wine relationship we would take for granted today, but one that required new perception when wines were still as broadly anonymous as other agricultural products.

De Pontac's great-grandfather, Jean de Pontac, a general trader descended from a pewtersmith, had acquired land at Haut-Brion in the village of Pessac outside Bordeaux through his marriage to Jeanne de Bellon in 1525. In the course of a long life (he was still sound of mind and limb when he died at 101), he filled all those legal and administrative offices, for king and city, most likely to enrich and advance a man in a contentious age. While acquiring two further wives, fifteen children, and the largest fortune in Bordeaux, he had found time to enlarge and embellish his property at Haut-Brion long before it came, through the usual chain of inheritance, into Arnaud de Pontac's hands.

Arnaud de Pontac paid close attention to the family estate at Haut-Brion. He introduced there the practice of regular racking from barrel to barrel, separating young wine from its coarse and mischievous early lees, and was among the first to realize that frequent "topping up" to compensate for evaporation allowed wine in cask to improve rather than spoil—simple usages that allowed him to reveal to the full the inherent advantages of his vineyard.

The general lack of such care in an absence of what we might consider basic cellar hygiene normally led wine to deteriorate so rapidly in the sixteenth century that new wine commanded a substantial premium over old. A buyer at that time concerned himself less with the fine points that preoccupy us today than with a wine's soundness and reliable drinkability.

Though this preference for new wine over old continued into the seventeenth century, there were by then, even among new wines, some more prized than others, the most highly regarded being those associated with powerful families, including the de Pontacs, but with little attention paid by buyer or seller to specific vineyards. René Pijassou, of the University of Bordeaux, comments that consumers seemed to see a connection between a wine's quality and the financial strength and fame of its producer, a phenomenon not unknown today and one that might be justified by the care made possible by greater resources. The seeming lack of concern about vineyard of origin might have been no more than a worldly assumption that the families of the newly powerful administrative class would have their vineyards in privileged sites. But even if that were the case, there is no doubt that Arnaud de Pontac was the first to emphasize the relevance of his vineyard's unique *terroir* to the style and quality of his wine. And, in attaching Haut-Brion's quality and distinction firmly to the site where its grapes were grown, Arnaud de Pontac fathered a model, widely emulated, that is still responsible for Bordeaux's luster three centuries later.

De Pontac realized, of course, that his wine would sell at a price to justify the pains he took only if distinguished from the general mass. But the urge both to raise quality and to sharpen distinction was itself a response to changed circumstances for Bordeaux wines in London. Though England had lost possession of Bordeaux two centuries before, it remained a vital, if not the principal, market for Bordeaux wine. With the restoration of the English monarchy in 1660, Arnaud de Pontac and his peers had probably looked for a strengthening of that market after years of puritan restraint. But even before the return of Charles II, chocolate houses and coffeehouses had already made their appearance in London, and, with the encouragement of the king's pleasure-loving court, the reconstruction of the city after the Great Fire of 1666, and the new riches that flowed from the country's mercantile success in winning leadership at sea from the Dutch, the purveyors of these novel and exotic luxuries proliferated and prospered.

London society, euphoric and, to put it bluntly, energetically opportunist, found in the coffeehouses not only a revival of political and literary vigor after Cromwell's "grim constraint of compulsory godliness" but also the possibility of commercial and financial adventure, as some of these establishments evolved into the embryonic exchanges from which London's financial institutions have sprung; while others, through a process of exclusion, ripened into the city's great political and literary clubs. Is it any wonder that fashionable London was seduced from the simple pleasure of a pitcher of Bordeaux wine in a tavern?

To win them back, de Pontac sent his son François-Auguste, together with the chef from his own Bordeaux mansion, to open London's first restaurant. It was elegant, expensive, and roaringly successful; and in that perfect setting the de Pontacs presented their Haut-Brion wine to a clientele best able to appreciate it, to pay for it, and to further its cause.

Though he could have known little of marketing theory, and even less of its jargon, Arnaud de Pontac had used his wealth, political clout, and social connections to do more than reconstruct and reposition his product: He had transformed it into the very coinage of prestige.

∼ ∼ ∼

Because de Pontac's strategy was quickly adopted by others, he secured the future of the Bordeaux wine trade in providing for the success of Haut-Brion. The war that erupted between England and France in 1688 was followed by almost two centuries of unrelieved hostility, when punitive levels of duty imposed on all French wines, and sometimes their outright ban, restricted availability. Yet so thoroughly had the new style of wine initiated by de Pontac captured London's fidelity that, whereas country squires made do and made merry with the cheaper Port urged on them by the government's new alliance with Portugal, there were always Englishmen willing to pay the high duty, and others prepared to resort to subterfuge, rather than be deprived of Bordeaux.

Americans, after 1776 no longer bound by English policies hostile to France, were free, of course, to do as they pleased with regard to Bordeaux. Thomas Jefferson, standing in 1787 where John Locke had stood a century before him, echoed the philosopher's words in his description of the vineyard at Château Haut-Brion as "sand, in which is near as much round gravel or small stone and a very little loam."

The *terroir* had not changed. But the world had turned with the success of the policies initiated by Arnaud de Pontac. Where once the price of Bordeaux wine had dropped by nine-tenths as soon as wine of the new, and therefore more reliable, vintage was available, Jefferson reported a dramatic annual *increase* in the price of wine as it aged and as demand responded to its quality.

Wines of the 1783 vintage of the great growths (which by then included Margaux, Lafite, and Latour as well as Haut-Brion), he said, "sell now [in 1787] at 2,000 livres the tonneau; those of 1784, on account of the superior quality of that vintage, sell at 2,400; those of 1785, at 1,800 tho they sold at first for only 1,500." For comparison, wines of the 1783 vintage had first sold at 1,350 a tonneau, the 1784 at 1,300, and the 1785 at 1,100, while standard red wines of the region then sold for 200 to 300 livres a tonneau, a differential that has become only more marked in recent years.

On return to the United States from his tour as ambassador in Paris, Jefferson continued to order wines from Bordeaux, asking the U.S. consul in Bordeaux in 1790, for example, to arrange a shipment of eighty-five cases of wine, some for himself and some for George Washington ("packed and marked G.W."). But, with other priorities and, no doubt, with other tastes, the young republic was not immediately an important customer for Bordeaux. Madeira had attracted lower duties in the English colonies, as Port had in England, because of the Anglo-Portuguese alliance, and the habit thus established stayed with Americans for many years, even when the Crown and its use of import duties for political ends had lost power in the United States.

The de Pontac heirs lost Haut-Brion along with their heads at the time of the French Revolution, and, although the property was eventually restored to their successors, the sustaining continuum had been broken. In 1801 it was sold to Talleyrand, Napoleon's foreign minister, who knew that diplomacy was built on a well equipped kitchen and a well stocked cellar. But he was rarely at Haut-Brion, and in selling the estate to a Paris banker in 1804, Talleyrand set in motion a chain of ownership that swung from banker to merchant. If Arnaud de Pontac had turned commercial instinct to the advantage of his estate, those who then gained control of Haut-Brion too often turned the estate to the advantage of their commercial instinct. Jullien, in his *Topographie de Tous Les Vignobles Connus*, complained that Haut-Brion lost its reputation for some years because the vineyards were overfertilized—if true, doubtless to boost profitability by raising yields. "But the care of the new proprietor has improved it," he said, "and it has regained its place among the first growths with the 1825 vintage." He was referring, presumably, to Beyerman, a Dutch wine merchant established in Bordeaux, who had taken over the property in 1824.

The estate changed hands again in 1836, however, acquired by Eugène Larrieu, a retired banker, whose son, Amédée, was as devoted to restoring the grandeur of Haut-Brion as Arnaud de Pontac had been in first creating it. So far did he succeed that not only did Haut-Brion retain its rank of first growth in the 1855 classification still binding today but by the end of the century its wine could, and did, command prices above those of the other three first growths—Margaux, Lafite, and Latour. The 1899, particularly, opened at a price almost 20 percent above that of Margaux and had a reputation that still reverberates. Charles Walter Berry of Berry Bros. and Rudd, the London wine merchants, tells in his book *In Search of Wine* of refusing to allow Christian Cruse to order for him a bottle of the 1899 at an impromptu lunch in Paris in 1934 simply because it *was* "one of the most famous and expensive wines to be bought." (His sense of decorum was rewarded: At a dinner party that same night he was served the 1899 Haut-Brion with a fresh, truffled pâté de foie gras. It was, he wrote, "a dream—I would like to be Rip Van Winkle, and take a bottle of this to bed with me.")

Recently I too had an opportunity to taste the 1899 Haut-Brion at the climax of three days of tasting and drinking twenty-six vintages of white Haut-Brion ranging from 1985 to 1916 (the Château produces about a thousand cases of white wine a year from a small parcel of Sauvignon Blanc and Sémillon vines) and forty-nine vintages of red. Marvin Overton, a Texas surgeon, rancher, and wine lover, had organized this mammoth event at his ranch as his own very original contribution to the 150th anniversary of the state.

He succeeded in proving that Haut-Brion Blanc can be as greatly enjoyed with catfish eaten at a bench in the shade of an open shed as with turbot in a private dining room at Taillevent; and that the red wines of Haut-Brion can be as much at ease as we were with barbecued pig and wild rice, cowboy stew, and make-your-own kebabs in a field full of bluebonnets and longhorn steer.

Above all, Overton succeeded in showing us, with the help of an illuminating commentary from Haut-Brion's manager, Jean Delmas, how an Haut-Brion personality—precise, refined, and intense, like the sound of a silver flute in the hands of a master—could be traced unfailingly despite the vicissitudes of wars, changes in ownership, and the annual uncertainty of vintage.

Haut-Brion had faltered early in this century when ownership passed to two godchildren of the last of the Larrieu family and ended up as the retirement settlement of André Gibert, a director of the Société des Glacières of Paris. He took control before the 1923 vintage—"a pretty wine, one of the most beautiful of that very charming vintage," according to Maurice Healy, an Irish barrister devoted to the idea that Haut-Brion's name had somehow descended from a seventeenth-century compatriot. Perhaps that explains his serving a series of Haut-Brion vintages at a Saint Patrick's Day dinner in 1931, an occasion when his friend André Simon, founder of the Wine and Food Society, commented that the 1923 was "almost too ready," later qualifying his remark by adding, in his book *Tables of Content,* that "the same thing was said of the 1871s and 1875s; they were ready at a very early date and did last: in fact they are still lasting." The 1871s might indeed have lasted sixty years, but I have to report, with regret, that in 1986 the 1923 had not. The best I can say is that its strangely scented bouquet was not unpleasant.

Gibert's 1924 and 1926 were impressive, however, and have been praised over the years. André Simon, at that same Saint Patrick's Day dinner, had found the 1924 Haut-Brion preceding the 1923 "too green to drink with due respect" but said it showed great promise and concluded that he would be "very much surprised if it does not turn out to be a very fine wine." (How agreeable to have lived at a time when experienced men refrained, even seven years after the vintage, from being dogmatic about a wine's future. Today grapes are hardly picked before someone or other is telling us with insolent confidence how a wine will be ten, twenty, and thirty years on.) Simon was right about the 1924. It was still superb when we tasted it at Overton's ranch, with the strength and richness of bouquet—vanilla and sealing wax—that I remembered from tasting it on one other occasion, in 1979. But the 1926, though equally forceful, was marred by the dry, hard finish that Edmund Penning-Rowsell, our most distinguished contemporary chronicler of Bordeaux, has described as "typical of that vintage."

Penning-Rowsell could find nothing kinder than "poor" to say about the 1928 Haut-Brion and gave a head-shaking "not very good" to the 1929. The years must have tempered the 1929; I found it drying out but fairly full and still deep of hue. Its fading bouquet of plums and violets had a nostalgic charm. Time had done little to help the 1928, however. It too was still big and dark, but its astringency was aggravated by an aftertaste others have described as medicinal but that was most likely mercaptan: an ineradicable smell and taste with a sulfur component (that fact alone will help those unfamiliar with it to imagine its effect) most often caused by delay or lack of care in racking a young wine from its lees, an ironic footnote to Arnaud de Pontac's endeavors in initiating the practice of regular racking of wine at Château Haut-Brion.

The vintages that followed must have tested sorely whatever commitment André Gibert had to Haut-Brion. After visiting him at the close of 1934, Charles Walter Berry wasn't much impressed with the 1933 and would risk saying nothing of the 1934 beyond "it may conceivably be an improvement on the previous vintage." Faint praise, perhaps, yet praise to some extent justified. Of the three vintages of the thirties at our giant tasting, the 1934 was the best, and it had worn better than many of which more had been expected. Nevertheless, Gibert had had enough, and, when his offer of the estate as a gift to the city of Bordeaux had been refused, he sold Château Haut-Brion in 1935 to the American banker Clarence Dillon, whose family, still owning and controlling it today, have worked with the tenacity and intelligence of the de Pontacs and the Larrieus to restore and extend its reputation.

The first result had to wait until the end of the war, but then the 1945 Haut-Brion was one of the most praised of a much praised vintage. In Marvin Overton's barn it was still alive, full flavored, and superb. Other successful vintages followed, most especially the 1952 and 1953, the latter an epitome of Haut-Brion's "precise, refined, and intense" personality. (In Texas, unusually and unfortunately, our bottle of 1953 was slightly oxidized, and the wine was overwhelmed by the 1952.) Neither the 1955 nor the 1959 was as firmly structured as the 1952, but they shared both its scale and the whiff of sealing wax typical of Haut-Brion in its bigger years.

~ ~ ~

The sixties were a decade of transition at Haut-Brion. In 1960 the Château was the first to install stainless-steel fermenting tanks, the better to control the fundamental process of fermentation, and in 1961 Jean Bernard Delmas succeeded his father, Georges, as *régisseur.* The modification of style that then occurred was perhaps little more than adaptation to a series of difficult vintages, each of which presented varied problems of some magnitude. On the other hand, could the new tanks have made possible a noticeably leaner, tighter style? Or was it the result of a new philosophical direction given to, and supported by, the particularly able and perceptive new *régisseur,* a man who had been raised at Haut-Brion and understood its significance and potential?

Whatever the cause, from that time a new delicacy and restraint underlined Haut-Brion's precision, refinement, and intensity. Though the new style was already obvious in the 1961, it could, and can still, be seen to even greater effect in the 1964—a disappointing year for many Bordeaux properties because of October rain on a late vintage but a triumph for Haut-Brion.

Whereas weather conditions in 1972 and 1977 were also difficult for Bordeaux, other years of that decade, particularly 1971, 1975, 1978, and 1979, encouraged a widespread winemaking change toward fuller, more robust red wines that has continued into the eighties. It was obvious from the wines tasted at Marvin Overton's, however, that while respecting the bigger characteristics imposed by those years, Haut-Brion has succeeded both in preserving the personality that evolved over centuries and in retaining its new, faultless elegance of style. The unity of these various strands can be seen most perfectly in the 1971: a seamless wine of impeccable balance that is all the de Pontacs, the Larrieus, and the Dillons could have hoped for as justification of their efforts. The 1979, 1981, and, especially, the 1983 seem each to possess similar harmonies of quality.

To crown our last evening with the 1899, we had tasted backward through the years, delighted that the 1921, the praises of which we had so often read, was still able to flatter with its light cherry color and fresh bouquet and that the 1907, though fading, had retained its Haut-Brion sealing-wax hallmark after almost eighty years.

Finally we came to Charles Walter Berry's dream wine, a wine that Hugh Johnson more recently compared to the pediment of the Parthenon. (It's never difficult to tell when wine fanciers are enthusiastic.) It was faded, of course, but surprisingly fresh and smelled of thyme. The flavor, too delicate to analyze, was astonishingly long. By then, as one might have expected, we were tired and exhilarated, so perhaps I only imagined hearing the voice of Arnaud de Pontac expressing satisfaction.

Originally published as "Château Haut-Brion" in *Gourmet,* February 1987.

JUDGMENT OF PARIS

California's Triumph

In the early 1970s Steven Spurrier, an English wine merchant, and
Patricia Gallagher, his American partner, had a small wine shop
in Paris in a cul-de-sac near the Place de la Concorde, where, in an
adjacent building, they also gave courses in wine to their enthusiastic
customers. Almost inevitably, Spurrier and Gallagher developed a considerable clientele among expatriate Americans. The U.S. Embassy was
a block or two away, the substantial offices of IBM were almost next
door, and American law firms were scattered all around them. Through
word of mouth, their Caves de la Madeleine became a regular stop for
California wine producers and others making the rounds of the French
wine scene. Often these visitors brought a bottle or two with them, and
Spurrier was able to taste what he has described as "some exceptional
[California] wines."

At their shop Spurrier and Gallagher dealt in French wines (except for
a few of the most ordinary commercial blends, there were no California
wines available in Paris at that time), but they decided to use the excuse
of the United States's bicentenary to show a selection of California wines
to French journalists and others connected with the wine world. They
were sure that they would make a good impression on the French and
thought they might even surprise them. They hoped, too, that any stories generated in the press might bring in a new client or two.

With their bicentenary plan in mind, Gallagher visited California in
the fall of 1975 and Spurrier followed in the spring of 1976, during which

time he picked out six Chardonnays and six Cabernet Sauvignons, all of recent vintages, that he thought would give a fair picture of what was going on in California. He needed two bottles of each, and, assuming he might have difficulty bringing two cases of wine through French customs, he arranged for a group of twelve tennis enthusiasts on the point of leaving for a wine and tennis tour of France to carry two bottles each in their hand baggage.

To give the wines a context and ensure they would be judged without prejudice, he decided to offer them for tasting in unidentified, wrapped bottles and to mix in among them a few white Burgundies and red Bordeaux. He knew he would have to choose among the very best of these or risk the suspicion that he and Gallagher had set up the California wines to score off the French. He knew, too, that because he would be showing the wines blind—that is, unmarked—and asking the tasters to rank their preferences, the credentials of those participating would have to be impeccable; otherwise any approving nods toward California might be dismissed as stemming from a lack of familiarity with the niceties of French wines.

The tasting took place at the Inter-Continental Hotel. The panel members—experienced and of high repute—were all French: Pierre Brejoux, then chief inspector of the National Institute of Appellations of Origin; Aubert de Villaine, part-owner of Domaine de la Romanée-Conti; Michel Dovaz, a wine writer and enologist; Claude Dubois-Millot, from *Le Nouveau Guide;* Odette Kahn, editor of the influential *Revue du Vin de France;* Raymond Oliver, the celebrated chef and owner of Le Grand Véfour; Pierre Tari, owner of Château Giscours, a *cru classé* of the Médoc, and secretary-general of the Syndicat des Grands Crus Classés; Christian Vannèque, head sommelier of Tour d'Argent; and Jean-Claude Vrinat, owner of Taillevent.

The Chardonnays brought by Spurrier's tennis players from California bore the labels of Spring Mountain '73, Freemark Abbey '72, Chalone '74, Veedercrest '72, Château Montelena '73, and David Bruce '73. He added to them four white Burgundies: Meursault-Charmes Domaine

Roulot '73; Beaune Clos des Mouches '73, from Drouhin; Bâtard-Montrachet '73, of Ramonet-Prudhon; and Puligny-Montrachet Premier Cru Les Pucelles '72, from Domaine Leflaive.

Spurrier's Cabernet Sauvignons were Clos du Val's '72, the 1971s of Mayacamas and of Ridge Vineyards' Mountain Range, Freemark Abbey's '69, Stag's Leap Wine Cellars' '73, and Heitz Cellars Martha's Vineyard '70. I wondered why he had not included wines such as Robert Mondavi's 1969 Cabernet Sauvignon or the Georges de Latour Private Reserve '70—both of these wines yardsticks by which other California Cabernet Sauvignons were being measured at the time.

"I simply didn't get to taste them," he told me recently, whereas he had already tasted a number of the wines he did select, and the rest had been chosen based on visits to wineries made on the advice of friends.

Nothing was left to chance in his choice of Bordeaux to put alongside the California reds. They were Château Mouton-Rothschild '70, Château Haut-Brion '70. Château Montrose '70, and Château Léoville-Las-Cases '71. A formidable group of wines.

Members of the jury knew only that some of the wines were French and some from California. Once they had graded the ten white wines—poured from their wrapped bottles—on a scale of twenty points, they did the same with the reds, and a group order of preference was determined. Among the journalists present as spectators was the Paris bureau chief of *Time,* and in the magazine's international edition of June 7 he announced the group's decisions to the world.

Among the white wines, California's Château Montelena headed the list, followed by the Meursault-Charmes, Chalone, Spring Mountain, Beaune Clos des Mouches, Freemark Abbey, Bâtard-Montrachet, Puligny-Montrachet, Veedercrest, and David Bruce. A California wine, the Stag's Leap Wine Cellars '73, was first among the reds, too. It was followed, respectively, by the Château Mouton-Rothschild, Château Haut-Brion, Château Montrose, Ridge Vineyard Mountain Range, Château Léoville-Las-Cases, Mayacamas, Clos du Val, Heitz Cellars Martha's Vineyard, and Freemark Abbey.

In California, growers took the news calmly—"Not bad for kids from the sticks" was the reported response of Château Montelena's owner, Jim Barrett. But in France, and particularly in Bordeaux, there was consternation and, one might say without exaggeration, a degree of shock. It was not that California's success diminished in any way the real quality or value of the French wines—they had been used, after all, as the measure by which the others were judged—but the published results challenged the French in a field where they had assumed their superiority to be unassailable.

The French experts who had participated in the tasting, greatly embarrassed, felt a need to excuse themselves: Sophisticated arguments were put forward to explain away their choices. But, even allowing for every extenuating circumstance and accepting—as Spurrier has since said repeatedly—that another jury, or even the same jury on another day, might have placed the wines in a different order, it was clear that California had arrived. Regardless of the statistical reliability of the point system Spurrier had used to establish the group preferences, serious California wines, tasted seriously by serious judges, had at the very least stood shoulder to shoulder with French wines produced from similar grape varieties.

The tasting gave California a shot of confidence and earned it a respect that was long overdue. But it also gave the French a valuable incentive to review traditions that were sometimes mere accumulations of habit and expediency, and to reexamine convictions that were little more than myths taken on trust.

They were soon all over California—a place they had until then largely ignored—to see what was going on. In no time at all the first of many of their sons and daughters had enrolled in courses at Davis or begun working a crush in California, just as many young Americans had always done in France. And within the year, Baron Philippe de Rothschild, of Château Mouton-Rothschild, was in deep negotiation with Robert Mondavi to form the joint venture we know today as Opus One.

In a recent article in the British publication *Decanter,* commemorating the twentieth anniversary of the tasting, Steven Spurrier said that the recognition given California twenty years ago was recompense for the state's investment in research and equipment. To some extent he is right. As a consequence of Prohibition, California vineyards had been replanted with coarse shipping varieties, winemaking standards had been seriously compromised, and most wineries had fallen into disrepair. The University of California had had to send its professors on the road to show vintners who had missed traditional father-son instruction how to make clean, flawless wines again. They never claimed to be teaching the art of making fine wine; their task—much more basic—was simply to reestablish the essentials of the craft, to reconnect post-Prohibition wine producers to a heritage that had been lost.

Certain vineyard sites that today are recognized for the quality of the wines they yield may well owe their survival to the professors' tours—but in fact many were first cultivated a century ago. Robert Mondavi's Reserve Cabernet Sauvignon is essentially the product of a vineyard, To-Kalon, originally planted by Hamilton Crabb in the 1880s. Spring Mountain now occupies the winery built by Tiburcio Parrott in 1884. (Parrott's house is familiar to viewers of "Falcon Crest"; in the 1890s he produced there an exceptional Cabernet Sauvignon.) And, as our subject is about recognition, the Liparita winery on Howell Mountain, now active again, took a gold medal for its Cabernet Sauvignon at the Paris Exposition of 1900—then, too, in competition with French wines.

A few weeks ago I saw the actual scores awarded each wine by individual members of the 1976 Paris jury—as opposed to the final rankings published at the time. I was struck first by the fact that all nine judges had given their highest scores for white wine to California—either to Château Montelena or to Chalone. That, it seemed to me, was indeed an endorsement—at least for young wines—of California grape maturity, technique, and hygiene.

And yet something about Spurrier's attribution of California's success to equipment—to technology—bothered me. I thought, for example, of Richard Graff's Chalone Vineyard as I had known it in 1974. Graff had always been a maverick among California wine producers. His vineyard, waterless and difficult to reach, was planted with an old clone of Chardonnay that he had cultivated vine by vine. Neither his methods of cultivation nor his winemaking had much to do with modern California technology. Chalone had little equipment to speak of; in 1974 it was still generating its own limited supply of electricity. And most important of all, at a time when California was only beginning to flirt with oak barrels, Graff had spent a year in France researching a treatise on oak and, probably alone in the California of that period, was fermenting his Chardonnay in the barrel and aging it on the lees. Now, more than twenty years later, that is commonplace.

Mike Grgich, then winemaker at Château Montelena, was born into a winegrowing family in Croatia and had perfected his craft first with Lee Stewart at the old Souverain winery on Howell Mountain (now the home of Burgess Cellars). A legend in California in the 1950s and 1960s, Stewart, self-taught, was obsessed by the details of winemaking. For him, it was the small things that counted. "I learned from Lee to watch over a wine as I would a baby," Grgich told Richard Paul Hinkle in a recent, anniversary interview for the trade publication *Wines & Vines*. From Stewart, Grgich moved on to André Tchelistcheff, the man behind the success of Beaulieu Vineyards's Georges de Latour Private Reserve, "who taught me to look at wine from the vineyard," and then to Robert Mondavi, "who made me aware of temperature control and French oak." When Grgich went to Château Montelena, he applied what he'd learned. "By then I knew how to handle a wine gently," he told me. "To disturb it as little as possible." The grapes for his winning 1973 had, like Graff's, also come from an old Chardonnay clone.

The Stag's Leap Wine Cellars Cabernet Sauvignon was the only California red to place among the first four. Surely it is more than coincidence that Warren Winiarski, the man who made it, should also have been an alumnus first of Lee Stewart, "a fastidious man who applied himself to every aspect of his wine," then of André Tchelistcheff, and, finally, of Robert Mondavi. "André gave us the soaring, the poetic vision. He had the gift of articulating what wine was to be, raising our horizons," Winiarski told Hinkle. "Robert provided the push, the thrust to get things done. Details and vision are nothing without the will to execute them."

It took a while longer for California's new crop of younger winemakers to learn these same lessons: to free themselves from technology; to abandon their expensive high-speed pumps and centrifuges; to reassess what "cellar hygiene" means (it doesn't mean keeping nature at bay with laboratory-prepared yeasts, preventing contact between a wine and its lees, and avoiding malolactic fermentation, the bacterial change that softens a wine and draws its disparate elements together); and to understand that fine wine is indeed made in the vineyard. In fact, it was a traditional, low-tech California that was honored that day in Paris in 1976. What the French recognized in wines they'd never tasted before was not equipment and rampant technology. It was the quality inherent in mature California vines; the skill and artistry of men like Richard Graff, Mike Grgich, and Warren Winiarski; and the vision of those who had gone before them.

Originally published as "The Judgment of Paris Revisited: A California Triumph" in *Gourmet,* January 1997.

A SILENT REVOLUTION

Organic and Biodynamic Wines

How good are organic wines? For a start, there are far more of them out there than you might suspect. They're not in some fringe niche either: They include, for instance, Château Margaux, the Médoc first growth, the wines of the Domaine Leroy in Burgundy, those of Robert Sinskey Vineyards in Napa Valley, and certain bottlings from the Penfolds vineyards in South Australia's Clare Valley.

The question, then, would seem to answer itself, but there's a catch: Wines like these rarely display the word "organic." Sometimes it's to avoid having the wine perceived as funky, or bought for what the grower believes is the wrong reason. Robert Sinskey says he doesn't want people to think first about the way he cultivates his grapes and then about the quality of the wine. "We want the customer to buy our wine because it's good. The way we nurture the vines is simply part of our effort to make it that way."

Robert Gross of Cooper Mountain Vineyards in Oregon also insists that quality is the point of the wine and that organic cultivation is simply a technique. Gross does use the words "organically grown" on his label because he knows there are people looking for it. "But it can also be a turnoff," he said. "Some wine drinkers see it and think we're being preachy."

Many producers of wine from organically grown grapes keep mum on the subject to leave their options open in the vineyard. Organizations that certify organic compliance sometimes impose parameters based on philosophically wholesome principles rather than on the practical needs of viticulture. In an extreme emergency, growers might be faced with the choice of spraying, as innocuously as possible, or losing a crop. They argue that it's better not to carry an "organic" statement at all—even when the vineyard is certified—rather than find themselves obliged to explain, in such a situation, why it had to be dropped. And then there are the many grape growers of California who ignored the chemical revolution of the 1950s and continue to do what they have always done. As bemused as Monsieur Jourdain—the character in Molière's *Le Bourgeois Gentilhomme* who discovered he'd been speaking prose all his life—they now learn that they have long been practicing organic viticulture without having once given it a thought. "They just don't make a big deal of it," Bob Blue, winemaker for the Bonterra organic wines of Fetzer Vineyards, told me. "They don't even bother to sell their grapes as 'organically grown.' But that's probably because they'd have to get involved with the maze of certifying organizations and state regulators to do it. And the fees can be heavy for a small producer."

Aside from those who had never grown grapes in any other way, the return to organic practices, both in California and in Europe, began in the early 1980s. I remember my surprise, sometime about then, when I found Ulysses Lolonis of Redwood Valley in Mendocino County dumping buckets of predator ladybugs among the vines in his family's vineyard. He says he started because of concern about the pesticides being proposed to him. "Eventually we found we didn't need them at all," he told me recently. "If we left enough grass between the rows of vines to serve as bug territory, it soon had a mixed population of insects keeping themselves busy devouring each other without bothering us.

"We've come a long way since then. Now, rather than grass, we grow a nitrogen-rich cover crop to feed the soil when we plow it under. The bugs are just as happy, and we can do without pesticides, herbicides, and fertilizers. Do these organic methods enhance the flavor or quality of our wine? Well, they don't seem to take anything away from it." (In fact, Lolonis's Zinfandel is one of the best in California.)

~ ~ ~

John Williams of Frog's Leap Winery in Napa Valley is more forthright. He is convinced that organic cultivation does make a difference to wine quality. "The first vineyard we purchased in 1987," he said, "had been farmed by an old-timer on what we would now call organic principles. Wanting to do things right, we retained a firm to test the vines and the soil and make recommendations to us. They found many things wrong, but fortunately were able to supply us with all the chemical supplements they said we needed. The effort was grandly expensive and soon led to a general decline in the vineyard, the quality of its fruit, and the wine we made from it.

"I was urged to talk to an organic-farming consultant. Amigo Bob [Cantisano] certainly looked the part—ponytail, shorts, and tie-dyed T-shirt. What he said made sense, and we decided to give it a try in a couple of test areas. We now have nine growers in Napa Valley producing organically grown grapes for us.

"We found that a soil rich in organic matter absorbs and holds moisture better—so we were able to go back to dry farming, the old way of growing grapes in California, instead of relying on irrigation. We discovered that plants fed by compost and cover crops, rather than chemical fertilizers, draw in nutrients in a measured way that helps control growth. Our vines are therefore strong and healthy and give balanced fruit. We've learned to think about the causes of problems rather than react with a quick fix to each one as it comes up. It's made us better farmers. In doing all this, I'm not trying to save the world. I just want to make good wine."

There are others who farm organically simply because they don't like the idea of using industrial products in the vineyard. Jean-Pierre Margan of Château La Canorgue in the Côtes de Luberon (Peter Mayle country) told me he was taught in his viticulture courses which synthetic fertilizers to use and what and when to spray. "I never liked the idea," he said. "My father and grandfather had made good wine in the traditional way, and when my wife and I started to revive her family's dormant vineyard, I decided to do the same. It wasn't an act of defiance.

"But confronting nature directly means you have to be vigilant. You must look ahead—mistakes are difficult to correct organically. You become more efficient because you have to stay on top of every detail of every vine—and perhaps that's why the wine is better.

"Though the 'organic' aspect of the vineyard is simply the way we work, I put it on the label to allow those who want wine from organically grown grapes to find us. But there should be no need for me to say anything. Organic cultivation is and should be the norm. It's those who use chemicals that should have to identify themselves.

"I'm not alone in the way I work. There has been a tremendous awakening among winegrowers in France. Usually it starts with the growers getting involved with a program of reduced reliance on synthetic sprays and fertilizers and the reintroduction of more benign techniques—but they soon see the difference in their vineyards and move increasingly toward the freedom that organic cultivation allows."

That awakening has been greatly accelerated by the work of Claude Bourguignon, whose highly influential book, *Le sol, la terre et les champs* (*The Soil, the Land and the Fields*), is now in its third edition. Almost every French winegrower I've talked to in the past several years has at some point introduced Bourguignon's name into our conversation. Now he's one of the leading French experts in soil analysis—his client list includes Domaine de la Romanée-Conti and Château Latour and reads, in fact, like an honor roll of French viticulture. Much of what he has to say comes down to the essential role of microorganic life in the soil. He expresses regret, in the introduction to his book, that the issues involved have become noisily politicized.

In the second edition of his book *Burgundy,* Anthony Hanson describes a visit to Bourguignon's laboratory, north of Dijon. Having collected a random sample of earth from a flower bed, Bourguignon shook it with water, added a coloring agent, then put it under his microscope for Hanson to look at. "I shall never forget the sight," Hanson writes. "Tiny specks of solid particles (clays and other inanimate matter) were bathed in liquid which teemed with swimming, turning, thrashing, pulsing little organisms—bacteria, yeasts, microbes of all sorts."

In an ounce or two of healthy soil, Bourguignon will tell you, there are billions of such microorganisms. They transform mineral elements in the soil to make them available to plants that could not otherwise assimilate them. They attach iron to acetic acid, for example, forming the iron acetate that a plant can absorb. This symbiotic relationship allows a plant to function properly, to capture the energy in sunlight. That's where the energy-into-matter and matter-into-energy food chain starts. Soil bacteria need no human presence to flourish and do their work. It's sobering to be reminded that our lives depend on them.

～ ～ ～

Biodynamic farming takes organic cultivation one step further by paying special attention to soil bacteria and to harnessing the rest of the energy in the cosmos in ways that strengthen the vine. It has developed from theories expounded by Rudolph Steiner, the Austrian social philosopher, in the 1920s. Those who practice it are used to the skepticism, even the mockery, of others—there's an air of both New Age mysticism and Old Age witchcraft about it. But it works.

Robert Sinskey, who is heading toward biodynamic certification for all his vineyards, got interested because of a specific problem with one vineyard in particular. "The soil was as hard as rock," he told me. "It was dead. It was planted with Chardonnay, and the wine from those vines was always green and lean. We put in a cover crop and began using biodynamic sprays to encourage the development of microorganisms in the soil. Gradually we brought that vineyard around, and the wine is now so appealing and distinctive that we will soon be bottling it with a special designation."

Robert Gross, a physician whose interests include alternative medicine, is also moving toward biodynamic certification for his vineyards at Cooper Mountain. "It brings the vines into harmony with their environment," he told me.

Two of the biodynamic sprays—500, a very dilute solution of cow manure that has been aged in a cow horn placed underground through the winter and then stirred into blood-warm water with a motion calculated to maximize its effect; and 501, a similarly dilute solution of powdered silica—are basic to the system. Other sprays, mostly homeopathic teas of herbs and flowers, are used by some and not by others. Working in accordance with phases of the moon and reserving certain days for spraying, pruning, or planting to take advantage of propitious movements of the planets are ideas that some accept and others reserve judgment on.

Farming with due provision for the gravitational pull of the moon is ancient wisdom. Jim Fetzer—who started the program of wines made from organic grapes at Fetzer and is now owner of the Ceago Vinegarden, a fully accredited biodynamic vineyard estate in Mendocino County—said he never has to explain any of this to his Mexican workers. "They're used to the idea that various aspects of agricultural work should coincide with the phases of the moon," he said. "It makes sense: If the changes in atmospheric pressure associated with the moon's waxing and waning can affect the rise and fall of oceans, you can be sure it affects the position of the sap in the vines." As for the special days, Alan York, Ceago Vinegarden's biodynamics consultant (and consultant to Joseph Phelps and Benziger, among others), put it to me this way: "We don't know why or how the plant responds to the changing positions of the planets. It's like surfing. There's this force and you try to ride it."

There is much more to biodynamics than homeopathy and "root" days. A key element is the systematic introduction of other plants among the principal crop. There is a rich diversity of them growing among the vines at Ceago Vinegarden, including olive trees, lavender, and buckwheat—habitat to tiny wasps that lay their eggs inside the eggs of leafhoppers and stop that problem before it starts. When I was young, I took it for granted that most vines in Italy and France had peach trees and even a line or two of corn planted among them. I thought it was to make full use of the land, but now I know better.

"Biodynamics is neither a recipe nor even a specific technique," says Nicolas Joly, owner of Coulée de Serrant, the white-wine jewel of Loire Valley vineyards. "It can't be applied mechanically. It demands a complete understanding of what is happening in the life cycle of a plant and the formation of its fruit so that the functions can be enhanced."

Joly, an articulate advocate and proselytizer, condemns completely what he sees as the sins of modern viticulture. "Herbicides and pesticides annihilate the microbial life peculiar to any particular soil, and synthetic fertilizers then standardize the vines' nourishment and thus the character of the fruit. What is the point of talking about *terroir* in such circumstances?"

There is a wide gap between biodynamics and conventional viticulture, and a considerable one even between standard and organic practices. Part of that difference is cost. The abuse of pesticides, herbicides, and synthetic fertilizers can create an imbalance ever more expensive to address. But the considerable handwork involved in organic viticulture is also costly—and justified economically only if higher quality attracts a better price for the wine.

In the detailed report on its experiment of organically cultivating roughly 125 acres of vineyard on its Clare Valley estate over the past ten or twenty years, Penfolds (owned by Southcorp Wines) shows that the cost of cultivating those blocks of vines was as much as 50 percent higher than that of cultivating similar neighboring blocks by conventional methods. Australia has high labor costs, and that accounts to some extent for this startling difference; but, when expressed as cost per ton because of the smaller yields when compared with conventional viticulture, the cost of Penfolds' organically grown grapes becomes 100 percent higher.

In the face of such numbers, we can't ignore the fact that whatever satisfaction growers may get from the quality of their products and from their stewardship of the land, they accept the risk inherent in growing a crop as fragile as grapes in order to make a fair return.

~ ~ ~

In most parts of the winemaking world, particularly in California, there are programs designed and supported by growers' associations to help members wean themselves from dependence on synthetic chemical treatments and to combine organic farming principles with a sound and limited use of environmentally safe products in a cost-effective manner. The program run by the Lodi-Woodbridge Winegrape Commission, financed by an assessment on grape production voted by the growers themselves, includes a step-by-step workbook that encourages growers to meet regularly in small groups for mutual support and the exchange of information, and to constantly survey every aspect of their work. They evaluate their progress in sowing cover crops, for example, and installing nesting boxes near their vineyards for predator barn owls. There are similar programs organized by the Central Coast Vineyard Team, and still more are being developed on a smaller scale in Amador and Lake counties.

These programs encourage growers to check their vines closely and, by thinking ahead, to discover new options for dealing with problems. They lead them to a system of fully sustainable agriculture—or beyond—and at the same time help them steadily improve the quality of their wines.

Paul Pontallier, manager of Château Margaux—where herbicides, pesticides, and synthetic fertilizers are rarely used—commented to me recently that there's much to be said for organic farming and for biodynamic viticulture, whatever the circumstance, so long as the approach is always practical. "The danger comes," he said, "when some particular way of doing things is turned into an ideology."

Originally published as "A Silent Revolution" in *Gourmet,* September 2000.

A MEMORABLE WINE

"What was the best wine you ever tasted, the one you will always remember?" It's a question I'm often asked when someone newly introduced first realizes how I spend much of my waking time. How to answer? I think I'm expected to château-drop, to say something glamorous about a Margaux '53, a Cheval-Blanc '47, or a Mouton-Rothschild '45—a monumental wine, by the way, still flamboyantly vigorous when poured for me at a dinner at Mouton itself a couple of years ago. (There's a real château-drop for you.)

But how does anyone compare that Mouton-Rothschild with a Cheval-Blanc '47, last tasted in the 1970s, to decide which was "better"? And what would be the point anyway? Such wines are almost always impressive, and usually memorable. But that isn't the same thing as "always remembered," is it? In any case, one's memory of a wine is rarely a mere abstraction of aroma and flavor. Often it seems to reflect so well a particular context that later we are never quite sure whether we remember the circumstances because of the wine or the wine because of the circumstances. At times, the two can even be ludicrously at odds.

Not long ago, helping a friend clean up an apartment from which the movers had taken his furniture just hours before, I came across a bottle of Barossa Valley Cabernet Sauvignon, a 1981 from the Hill-Smith estate, overlooked by the packers. We were tired and more than ready to stop. Fortunately, one of us had a corkscrew, and there were paper cups in a kitchen cupboard. We sat on the floor, our backs to the wall. The wine was more than remarkable: It was patrician and elegant beyond anything I'd expected. At that moment, it was the most delicious wine in the world.

~ ~ ~

When mountains labor to bring forth a mouse, that can be memorable, too. In the 1960s, when my then-company in London imported and distributed the wines of Henri Maire—an important but highly promotion-driven wine producer in the Jura, in eastern France—I was asked, at short notice, to arrange a small dinner at a distinguished restaurant (my choice) for a few distinguished guests (my choice). The principal dish (Henri Maire's choice), prepared by none other than Raymond Oliver, at the time still reigning at Le Grand Véfour, was to be flown over from Paris hours before the event.

The object was to show—in London and Paris simultaneously, and with precisely the same dish—a wine that Henri Maire had shipped in barrel around the world. In the eighteenth century it had been a custom to send certain Sherries to and from the tropics in the hold of sailing ships; the journey was thought to age fortified wines advantageously. Names of certain blends—Fine Old East India, for example—still allude to the practice. The wine Henri Maire had chosen to be dispatched for two years before the mast, so to speak, was an Arbois rosé. He called it Vin Retour des Iles and proposed to offer it to his numerous guests at the Grand Véfour (and to my much smaller group in London) to demonstrate—I think—that Arbois rosé was a serious wine and not to be confused with the pretty tipples in designer bottles then increasingly popular at restaurant lunch tables.

I chose to hold my dinner in a private dining room at Prunier's on St. James's Street. Simone Prunier, a consummate restaurateur, was a resourceful woman of limitless discretion, and I knew I could rely on her to pull together what seemed to me to be an adventure fraught with risk. We knew nothing of the dish to be sent from Paris except that it was to be *marcassin* (young wild boar) accompanied by a sauce. It would need only to be reheated.

We composed a menu around this dish—Champagne and canapés to greet the arriving guests; a plain poached turbot with hollandaise (Prunier's, after all, was renowned for its fish, but we did not want to upstage Raymond Oliver); cheeses from the Jura area—the Franche-Comté—to follow the *marcassin;* and a sumptuous pineapple ice, to be brought to the table packed inside the original fruit, enveloped in a veil of finely spun sugar. I selected Henri Maire wines for the fish and the cheese that would allow the special bottling of rosé every chance to be the star.

The dish, transported expeditiously by Air France from restaurant door to restaurant door, was something of an anticlimax: I can only describe it as minced wild-boar patties in a brown sauce. Unfortunately, the wine offered neither compensation nor distraction. Henri Maire had decided, at the last minute, that there was barely enough Vin Retour des Iles for the swelling number of guests at the Grand Véfour and therefore none—not a single bottle—was sent to London. I was asked to serve the standard Arbois rosé instead. I have to say, it was a perfectly satisfactory wine. But it was not, as Dr. Johnson once said of a perfectly satisfactory dinner, what you would ask a man to. Least of all at Prunier's.

Who knows what vinous perspectives the actual Vin Retour des Iles might have opened up for us? In a brief but charming new book, *La Légende du Vin,* subtitled (in French, of course) *A Short Essay of Sentimental Enophilia,* Jean-Baptiste Baronian, French novelist, essayist, critic, and editor, says that those who appreciate wine find in every glass traces of a history, of a civilization, and of a gesture that bind together a time and a place.

A few years ago I tasted, on an exceptional occasion in California, the 1771 and 1791 vintages of Château Margaux. Both wines were a vibrant strawberry color and astonishingly fresh; their bouquets were extravagantly scented. In the eighteenth century, wine, like fruit, was bottled for preservation, not aging, and it was common practice to perk the aroma of red Bordeaux with powdered orrisroot, the rhizome of iris.

It was used then, as it still is (but in perfume, not in wine), to contribute a scent of violets. In any case, both wines were made before Cabernet Sauvignon, with its distinctive pungency and dense garnet color, had replaced Malbec as the principal grape of the Médoc.

With Fragonard, Couperin, and Beaumarchais as touchstones, anyone speculating on how an eighteenth-century French wine tasted back then would imagine something with very much the delicacy, the luminosity, and the perfumed intensity of those wines. I confess, though, that foremost in my own mind as they slipped down my throat was the thought that I was drinking—in Los Angeles, the quintessential twentieth-century city—wines made by men alive in Bordeaux at the time of the American and French revolutions. Just to look at Chardin's painting of a bowl of raspberries can be an eighteenth-century experience. But, in absorbing alcohol converted from fruit-sugar two centuries earlier, I was actually sharing calories transmitted in the solar energy that had also warmed the faces of Thomas Jefferson and Marie-Antoinette.

~ ~ ~

What, then, has so far been the *most* memorable wine of my life? Were it not that people casually met might assume I was making fun of them, I would in fact explain to those who ask that it was, and remains, unidentified. I drank it at a mountain inn near the Simplon Pass in the early summer of either 1962 or 1963. From 1955 until 1970 I spent weeks on end visiting suppliers all over Europe to taste and select the wines we brought to London. For much of that time, there were neither *autoroutes* nor *autostrade,* and I drove a Triumph TR4 (which I'd had refinished in deep Burgundy red instead of its original British racing green) to get myself quickly from place to place. Well, that was the rational explanation at any rate.

I'd spent the night at Sion, in the Swiss Valais, after an evening of *raclette*—molten slivers of the local cheese draped over hot potatoes— and the cooperative's Fendant, a flowery white wine with which we were having a modest success in England. I was on my way to Verona and had set off early to be sure of reaching Milan by evening.

There was little traffic on the road—the Simplon is more often used as a rail route—and by noon I was high in the Alps with the Swiss-Italian border behind me. It was early June, and for most of the way wild flowers were scattered along the roadside. At the higher altitudes drifts of snow still lay dazzlingly white in the midday sun. The exhilaration of the climb—the TR4 would respond with its distinctive soft roar as I changed gears on those steep turns—the crisp air, the brilliant light, and the grandeur of the mountains made me feel I was on top of the world. And I almost was, literally. But I was also hungry and had many curving miles ahead of me to Domodossola, where I planned to stop for a late lunch.

Then an inn appeared. It was small but comfortably appealing. The deliciously simple set lunch of sautéed veal scallops and buttered noodles with a salad of green beans was typical of what one finds in the mountains. My glass was filled with a light red wine poured from a pitcher, left on the table. I was relaxed, carefree, and happy. Oh, how ruby bright that wine was; it gleamed in the sunlight. I remember clearly its enticing aroma—youthful but with a refinement I'd hardly expected. The wine was sweetly exotic: lively on my tongue, perfectly balanced, and with a long, glossy finish. It was the sort of wine that Omar Khayyam might have had in mind for his desert tryst. The young woman who had poured it for me was amused when I asked what it was. It was, she said, *vino rosso*.

It was exquisitely graceful. I have never learned what it might have been. But the pleasure in any wine is subjective: We each bring something to what is there in the glass and interpret the result differently. Perhaps, on that June day more than thirty years ago, I had contributed an extra-large dose of well-being.

Originally published as "A Memorable Wine" in *Gourmet*, September 1995.

MISSOURI

Return of the Native

I'd arrived in Hermann, Missouri, two days too late for the annual Great Stone Hill Beast Feast, so I'd missed the possum teriyaki, the raccoon pie, and the beaver jambalaya. Every year local hunters and trappers provide for the charity benefit a selection of fauna worthy of Daniel Boone. Along with the possum, raccoon, and beaver, Gary Buckler, proprietor of Hermann's Vintage 1847 restaurant, had been able to prepare other old-time frontier favorites like bobcat *bourguignonne,* marinated Montana mule deer rounds, coyote and fox salami, and stuffed water buffalo Florentine.

The wines, donated by Stone Hill Winery, were all Missouri-grown—the best of them a red made from Norton, an indigenous American grape that might yet do for Missouri what Cabernet Sauvignon has done for California. Norton is unusual, a native wine grape with no hint of the grape-jelly aroma and flavor we associate with Concord and other *labrusca* hybrids. But then Norton is not *labrusca*; it's a "summer grape," known to botanists as *Vitis aestivalis.*

More than a century ago, Missouri Norton was described as one of America's finest red wines— "full-bodied, deep-coloured, aromatic, and somewhat astringent... only needing *finesse* to equal a first-rate Burgundy"—by no less a wine judge than Henry Vizetelly, one of the great names of nineteenth-century wine commentary. Vizetelly, an Englishman, had tasted a Missouri Norton from Hermann at the 1873 Vienna World Exhibition, where it had taken a gold medal. In a report to the British government, Vizetelly described the town of Hermann as the hub of Missouri's vineyards, "which promise to become," he wrote, "not merely the most prolific vineyards of the [United] States, but also those yielding the best wines."

That promise, alas, has yet to be fulfilled. A combination of problems had already begun to undermine Missouri's viticulture even as Vizetelly wrote of the state's imminent triumph, and Prohibition delivered the *coup de grâce*. From then on, the changed use of grapes from wine to juice and jelly meant that almost all the Norton vines of the Missouri River valley, and with them the expectations they had raised, were ripped out. Acres of Concord were planted instead on the Ozark highlands farther southwest, a site more convenient for the Welch's Grape Juice plant in Arkansas.

It was probably just as well that the dinner I shared at Vintage 1847 with Gary Buckler, Jon Held, and Patricia Held-Uthlaut (the latter two are the son and daughter of Stone Hill's owners) was less eclectic than the Great Beast Feast. I was raised on *The Wind in the Willows* rather than *Huckleberry Finn,* and I'm not sure how sharp my appetite would have been for badger pâté. But we did have venison steaks with an appropriate—considering the company—Norton red-wine sauce. (In fact, the sauce was doubly appropriate: The deer had been shot by Gary Buckler, from his kitchen door, as it was munching its way through some choice Norton grapes on a row of vines planted in 1868, part of the sole quarter acre of Missouri's Norton to have survived Prohibition.) The Helds had placed on the table four vintages of Stone Hill Norton—1989, 1988, 1985, and 1984—so that I'd have an idea of how Norton tasted both young and with a little age.

Even after reading Vizetelly, and others, I was astonished to find the wines so remarkably good. They were more meaty than fruity, with something of the Rhône about them. The 1985, in particular, rounded out by its time in wood and fully developed by several years in the bottle, was quite delicious. I finally understood, as I never really had before, why Vizetelly had been so confident of Missouri's wine future.

We have lost the habit of seeing Missouri as a wine state, but in Vizetelly's day few Americans could have been surprised at Norton's success at the Vienna exhibition. Missouri's vineyards were important, and the state's wines enjoyed high regard. According to U.S. census figures from 1869, Missouri contributed 42 percent of the total United States wine production, compared with California's 27 percent and New York's 13 percent.

In that third quarter of the nineteenth century, almost all who led in viticultural innovation and research in the United States were in, of, or associated with Missouri. They included Frederick Muench of Augusta, Missouri, whose book, *School for American Grape Culture*, is as clear a guide to grape growing as anyone might want even today; George Husmann of Hermann, whose *American Grape Growing and Wine Making* remained the standard viticultural textbook for American growers until well into this century; and Isidor Bush, a Missouri nurseryman whose catalogue gave such detailed information on laying out and maintaining a vineyard and on the advantages, disadvantages, and correct cultivation of each grape variety named that it was translated and published internationally for use as a growers' manual. A Swiss-trained Missouri viticulturalist named Hermann Jaeger was responsible, with Husmann, Bush, and Thomas Volney Munson of Denison, Texas, for finding and supplying by the million most of the appropriate root-stocks (both resistant to phylloxera and adaptable to French growing conditions) that saved French viticulture from the root louse inadvertently introduced into France from America in the 1860s. The idea of permanently grafting European *vinifera* onto resistant native American rootstocks, the method of protection still used today, had been first proposed by Missouri's state entomologist, Charles Riley, who was honored by the French government for his timely intervention. Both Jaeger and Munson were also decorated handsomely in recognition of their exertions on behalf of French winegrowers.

~ ~ ~

If Missouri's place in the history of American viticulture has been neglected, so has the role of the Midwest in general, although American winemaking can be said to have begun there. Every earlier attempt to grow grapes for wine on the Eastern Seaboard had failed. In his *History of Wine in America,* Thomas Pinney tells us that Midwest viticulture started with a vineyard planted at the end of the eighteenth century by Francis Menissier, a Frenchman, at what is now Main and Third in Cincinnati. Menissier succeeded in an attempt to grow *vinifera* but failed in his 1806 petition to Congress for a grant of land on which to plant more vines. His achievement nevertheless impressed Nicholas Longworth, then recently arrived in Cincinnati from New Jersey.

According to Pinney, Longworth soon made a fortune in property speculation—at one time he and John Jacob Astor were the two largest contributors of taxes to the United States Treasury—and was devoting it to his passion for horticulture. Along with helping to develop the cultivation of strawberries, he turned his attention to viticulture and began, in the 1820s, to plant Catawba on the banks of the Ohio River. His first cuttings came from John Adlum, a Washington, D.C., grower who had discovered Catawba in a garden in Clarksburg, Maryland, in 1819.

Adlum claimed that he had rendered greater service to his country by this chance discovery than had he "paid off the National Debt." But there was little profit for Longworth in Catawba until the 1840s, when he first used the Champagne method of bottle fermentation—perfected in France not long before—to produce a sparkling version of the wine. It was an immediate and enormous success. Henry Wadsworth Longfellow, perhaps under its influence, wrote the now notorious lines in which sparkling Catawba is described as "more divine,/More dulcet, delicious, and dreamy." A London journalist visiting Cincinnati in the 1850s on behalf of the *Illustrated London News* praised the wine in equally mawkish verse as "The pure and the true,/As radiant as sunlight,/As soft as the dew." But no matter how fatuous the endorsements, demand was overwhelming, and there were soon thousands of acres of Catawba around Cincinnati.

Disaster loomed almost at once, however, as mildew and rot, conditions to which Catawba is particularly vulnerable, took hold in the vineyards, encouraged by the warm and humid summers of the Ohio River valley. "By the end of the [1850s]," Pinney says, "it was clear that the very existence of the industry was . . . problematical."

~ ~ ~

While Longworth was busy in Cincinnati, German immigrants were settling the Missouri River valley west of Saint Louis. They had been drawn there by romantic descriptions of its idyllic landscape published by Gottfried Duden, a German social reformer who had lived in and explored the valley in the 1820s. According to Peter Poletti, assistant professor in the department of economics and geography at the University of Missouri, Saint Louis, thousands of Germans bought copies of Duden's report of his travels in Missouri and used them as guidebooks when fleeing to America from the harsh repression that followed Europe's revolutionary disturbances of 1830. Many had been members of what we would call the intelligentsia rather than craftsmen or farmers, but they settled into the simple life of America's then-frontier. Pinney tells us that earlier arrivals from Germany called the Duden-inspired immigrants *lateinische Bauern,* Latin peasants, a snide reference to their classical learning and intellectual pursuits.

Philadelphia's German Settlement Society, founded to establish in North America a specifically German colony where all that had been best in the Old World could be preserved in the New, was enough encouraged by Missouri's distinctly German flavor to send an emissary. He bought eleven thousand acres on bluffs above the south bank of the Missouri River, about eighty miles west of Saint Louis and just downstream from the confluence of the Missouri and its tributary the Gasconade. The first settlers arrived in the winter of 1837 and, in character with their *lateinische* education, named their new home Hermann in honor of an ancient German hero revered for defeating a Roman army. The newcomers made their aspirations clear from the start by building houses of brick instead of wood. They laid them out on straight, broad streets and planted shade trees. The town's main street was wider than Market Street in Philadelphia because Hermann was intended to be an important city, a beacon of German thought and culture. A German-language newspaper began publication almost immediately. (Most—indeed, almost all—of the houses built in Hermann in those years are now on the National Register of Historic Places.)

～ ～ ～

Wine had not been a priority at Hermann, despite the urgings of George Husmann's father, Johann, a native of Bremen. (Bremen is far from any wine-producing region but was, and is, a port much involved with the international wine trade.) Most of the other settlers were from northern Germany, too, and had brought neither the skills nor a wine culture with them. But in 1845 a good first crop of Catawba on a few vineyards "only three years old" seems to have caused considerable interest, which was intensified by the sight of newly bearing, bunch-laden Isabella vines trained over an arbor at Hermann's Main and Schiller streets. A report in the *Hermanner Wochenblatt,* the town's newspaper, concluded that the quantity of grapes on the vines gave hope for Hermann and its region. The town's trustees, thinking Hermann's rocky bluffs could be put to good economic use only as vineyards, had already begun to offer special lots at the low price of fifty dollars each, with five years to pay and no interest asked—provided the buyers agreed to plant vines. Six hundred lots were sold. In 1847 Michael Poeschel founded the town's first winery (eventually to be known as Stone Hill), doubtless in expectation of the considerable harvests to come.

Though both varieties were brought into Hermann at that time, Catawba was favored over Norton. Norton's red wine needs to be aged, as do most potentially great red wines, and that would have been difficult for newly established growers with meager capital and pressing cash needs. In any case, Hermann's growers were at first influenced by Longworth—the first Catawba vines had come from Cincinnati—and by the time the first sizable crops were appearing in the early 1850s, demand for the variety was running high, thanks to the success of Longworth's sparkling wine.

John Zimmermann, Nicholas Longworth's partner, wrote to the

Wochenblatt offering Hermann's growers the price paid in Cincinnati provided they would sell him juice rather than wine. ("Winemaking is different from grape growing and the Hermann growers do not understand the work. The problem can be avoided if we are allowed to purchase the juice as soon as the grapes are pressed.") He urged Hermann growers not to plant Norton, though it was increasingly in favor, because the grape was "not suitable for mass produced wine. . . . The Catawba grape is the best grape," he said, doubtless thinking of his company's needs.

The *Wochenblatt* reported a few weeks later, on October 15, 1852, that Hermann's grape crush for the year had yielded only six thousand gallons, less than half the volume of previous harvests and barely a quarter of what was to be expected from the town's maturing vineyards. The vines, mostly Catawba, had been badly affected by the maladies to which the variety is prone, and to which Norton is largely resistant.

Norton had been "discovered" in more than one place at more than one time, causing confusion later when two differently named varieties appeared to be one and the same. The accepted origin, as given in Thomas Volney Munson's book *Foundations of American Grape Culture,* is Cedar Island in Virginia's James River, where it was found growing wild in 1835. It was named for, and cultivated and introduced by, Dr. Daniel Norton of Richmond (though it was not he who had found it). After that Catawba disaster of 1852, Missouri's growers turned to Norton increasingly. Frederick Muench, who thought the grape a gift to the state "worth millions," wrote that it was much in demand for the excellence of its dark red wine—"When three or four years old it is hardly to be surpassed." But what probably appealed to Hermann's growers was the vine's resistance to summer diseases and its tolerance of winter cold.

Norton grapes ripen evenly and resist rot. ("[Their] thin, tough [skin] never cracks," Munson wrote.) It was for similar reasons and at about the same time that Cabernet Sauvignon became the preferred grape of Bordeaux's Médoc. Norton's spread in Missouri was slower than Cabernet Sauvignon's in France because Norton is not easily reproduced from cuttings. With an alternative process, layering—the technique of burying a shoot and separating it from the parent plant when it has thrown out its own roots—years can pass before there are enough vines to set even a small vineyard. Muench hoped that Missouri's growers would persevere. "This one State," he claimed, "could [then] supply the whole Union with red wine, cheaper than any good foreign wine can now be had."

The "other" Norton, Cynthiana, is said to have been found in Arkansas. Husmann obtained samples of it from the Prince nursery in Flushing, New York, in 1858 and urged its adoption. He thought it superior to Norton and said it would produce "the best red wine we yet have, resembling but surpassing Burgundy." Isidor Bush's catalogue called Cynthiana "OUR BEST AND MOST VALUABLE grape for red wine."

Even though these men and many others thought Cynthiana better than Norton, everyone agreed that the two varieties—both *Vitis aestivalis*—were remarkably similar. Researchers at Cornell University's Agricultural Experiment Station at Geneva, New York, just published their finding that Norton and Cynthiana, at least as presently grown, are indeed indistinguishable. This conclusion suggests that either the two always were one, or, if once different, then all present plantings, under whichever name—including the 1868 plot of Norton at Hermann, which provided some material for the study—must have been propagated from just one version of the two.

Like the growers of the Ohio River valley, Missouri growers had had to contend with mildew and rot from the start. They also had to bear constantly increasing costs as wages rose in response to the manpower demands of Missouri's new industries. For these reasons a pound of grapes grown in Missouri in 1899 cost twice as much to produce as a pound of grapes grown in California. The result was inevitable: From having produced 42 percent of the nation's wine in 1869, Missouri contributed a bare 3 percent thirty years later.

The woes of Missouri's winegrowers were aggravated by local Prohibitionists, whose tactics had been weakening and eroding the wine market even before the Volstead Act destroyed it altogether. In today's not dissimilar climate, it is ironic, and sad, to read of George Husmann attempting to point out, in 1870, the medical benefits of drinking red wine. America waited (and wasted) 120 years to see it on *60 Minutes* before paying attention. In Missouri, Prohibitionists, no doubt believing that their end justified any means, struck the lowest blow at their vintner neighbors toward the end of World War I by appealing to nationalist sentiment of the worst kind. The Citizen's Dry Alliance, having made much of the connection between German Americans and Missouri's breweries and vineyards, fought for ratification of the amendment outlawing the sale of alcoholic beverages by advertising in Missouri newspapers that a "dry vote is a vote against the Kaiser." "This patriotic appeal," says Poletti, "was to prove decisive in the passing of the Eighteenth Amendment."

With the onset of Prohibition, the Missouri wine industry died. At Stone Hill, the second largest winery in the country at the turn of the century and possibly the third largest in the world, the huge carved casks—known as the Twelve Apostles—were carted away and the underground cellars were stacked with trays for the cultivation of mushrooms.

~ ~ ~

Perhaps it's excessive to suggest that this vision of mushrooms sprouting in the dark under a hill that had once been covered with vines is vaguely reminiscent of those Greek myths of Dionysus dying, like all the nature gods, only to be reborn. But Dionysus *was* reborn, in Hermann anyway, and in just the sort of tell-me-a-story circumstances the ancient Greeks would have loved.

In 1965 Bill Harrison, then owner of Stone Hill, invited Jim and Betty Ann Held to use a small part of his underground cellars to make some wine. The Helds had very little land, very little money, and four small children, but they were cultivating an acre or two of Catawba on their small farm near Hermann and selling the grapes to a winery out of state. Jim Held, descended from a family that had arrived in Hermann at its founding in 1837, says he tried his best to remember what he had seen his grandfather do, and did it—with whatever primitive utensils could be found in a winery that had been dormant for fifty-odd years. The family (even seven-year-old Jon helped mangle the crush) made 1,500 gallons of wine, the first commercially significant quantity of wine to be made in Hermann since Prohibition. Harrison, having allowed the Helds to see for themselves what they could do, then insisted that they buy Stone Hill and bring the winery back to life. In 1992 Stone Hill produced 136,208 gallons of wine.

There had been about sixty-five wineries, large and small, producing three million gallons of wine a year in Hermann when Prohibition closed it all down. Wine had been the town's lifeblood. Since then, Hermann had been in fast fade: Two of its three banks had been forced to close, the population had dwindled, and buildings had been abandoned. That first creaking turn of the grape crusher at Stone Hill brought back to life more than a winery. Hermann itself has flourished, thriving along with its wineries (the town now has four) and the restaurants their revival has encouraged. Small hotels and bed-and-breakfasts bring business to art galleries, antiques shops, and local craftspeople. And, thanks to owners and employees who need families fed, clothes cleaned, cars serviced, and plumbing repaired, Hermann, a grim statistic less than thirty years ago, has a growing tax base. It's now a daily stop for Amtrak trains running between Saint Louis and Kansas City. Tens of thousands of visitors come to the town every year, and, although they arrive expecting little more than a jolly picnic, a hop to a polka band, and a few bottles to take home, most leave with a greater appreciation of the state of Missouri; possibly with a broader feel for its history; and, especially at the time of the fall grape harvest festivals, with indelible memories of the Missouri River valley's beauty.

Stone Hill is the largest winery in Missouri, but there are roughly thirty others that followed its lead. They range from Lucian Dressel's elegantly restored Mount Pleasant Vineyards in Augusta—once the property of Frederick Muench's family—and Jim and Pat Hofherr's St. James Winery—an emporium as much as a winery—on busy Route 44 that produce every year, in the simplest facilities, a thousand or so cases of more than creditable wine. All these vintners, whatever their size, depend on direct sales for most of their revenues. The volume of Missouri wine distributed through stores within the state is growing, but it still represents less than 20 percent of the wine produced.

So Missouri wineries, like Muhammad's mountain, must encourage potential customers to come to them, occasionally resorting to tricking out staff in lederhosen and dirndls as attractions that would have horrified the original *lateinische Bauern.* Their tasting rooms and shaded decks, however, are not unlike nineteenth-century *guinguettes,* those simple garden taverns by the Seine preserved for us forever on the Impressionists' canvases. They offer a relaxed and convivial atmosphere, with tours of the winery for those who want them. Most provide at the least a selection of sausages, cheeses, and bread, and a few are even more ambitious, offering full meals or lodging. If some—such as Montelle, on Osage Ridge near Augusta—have magnificent views of the Missouri River valley that draw crowds of tourists, others—such as Heinrichshaus or Adam Puchta, both hidden away on back roads— are destinations known only to the initiated. Every winery has its own personality.

Much of what the Missouri wineries sell, it must be said, is still slightly sweet, slightly pink, and slightly fizzy, because that's a wine formula that has never been known to fail. The state's viticultural renaissance began with Catawba, after all, because Catawba was already planted—as in the Helds's vineyard. (Advances in methods of protecting Catawba vines from mildew and rot give more consistent crops than were possible a hundred years ago.) Using what was available in the state also meant accepting Concord occasionally. And some wineries still blend fruit juices with their wine—producing a local version of the "cooler"—to give it a broader appeal. Some of these practices might raise eyebrows, but if the vintners must depend on those who come to the winery for their sales, then they have to be sure that those who do come will find something they like, whatever their taste.

At the same time, the winemakers understand that if there is to be more than just folklore in their future they have to produce wines with more than popular appeal. They have to restore if not the glory then at least the former good standing of Missouri's viticulture. The movement to upgrade the vineyards began in the mid-seventies. A concerted effort was made by the state's Wine and Grape Advisory Board, by the state department of agriculture, and by Southwest Missouri State University to fund research at the State Fruit Experiment Station into the varieties best adapted to Missouri's climate and growing conditions. The station also provides hands-on, practical counseling for the state's growers and winemakers.

~ ~ ~

The results are already impressive. French hybrids (crossings of French and American varieties that are tolerant of Missouri's winters and largely resistant to the region's vine maladies) rather than Catawba and Concord now predominate in Missouri vineyards. Winemaking techniques have been adapted to suit them. Seyval, for example, produces an excellent wine when barrel-fermented, as happens at Stone Hill and Heinrichshaus among others. Vidal makes a delicious Champagne-method sparkling wine, as anyone can judge at Stone Hill or at Hermannhof, where it is winemaker Al Marks's specialty. Vignoles, an unusual white hybrid genetically based in part on Pinot Noir, gives wines the rich texture and fragrance of Pinot Gris. Some producers—in particular Blumenhof, Hermannhof, Heinrichshaus, and Stone Hill— make this wine in a mellow, slightly sweet style, but it is stunningly good when dry. A mellow 1991 Vignoles from Hermannhof was declared Best White Wine of the New World at the International New World Wine Competition in California last year; it was given stiff competition from a dry 1991 Vignoles, an exceptional wine from Montelle, which took a gold medal. I understand that even the judges were surprised when their blind choice was revealed to them.

When I was in Missouri last December I tasted some good wines from red hybrids, too—most notably a 1992 Chambourcin made by Blumenhof in a "nouveau" style, and a sprightly 1991 Chambourcin at Heinrichshaus. To extend the choice of black grapes available to Missouri growers, Bob Goodman, a plant pathologist and professor emeritus of the University of Missouri, now working as an adjunct professor at the State Fruit Experiment Station, has been combing the vineyards of Eastern Europe (especially those in Hungary and Moravia) for cuttings of varieties tolerant of severely cold winters. "Our summer diseases we can hope to deal with," he told me. "But no one can change this state's weather." In Missouri, evidently, even Dionysus has to wear earflaps.

Norton (or Cynthiana—some growers insist on using the other name) already offers everything they need, of course, and has a history of success in Missouri. It has the obvious commercial disadvantage of needing to be aged, and its complicated acidity can set traps for winemakers. (I can't explain that without going into pH, something I vowed long ago never to do.) But it is well adapted to Missouri's climate and maladies and gives superb wine if handled right. That much is clear not only from the wines I tasted at Stone Hill, but from others produced by Hermannhof, Adam Puchta, Blumenhof, Heinrichshaus, and the Augusta Winery. The acreage of Norton has been increasing discreetly in the last year or two, showing that Missouri wineries believe in this grape. (They all seem to sell out of one Norton vintage before the next is ready for release.) We should cheer them on. It could be that Henry Vizetelly will be vindicated at last.

Originally published as "The Return of the Native: Missouri's Vintage Grape" in *Gourmet,* April 1993.

SPREADING THE WORD

Books on Wine

B ooks for those who buy rather than make wine tend to be compendiums of maps and facts: They define appellations, list growers, measure vineyards, and quantify wine production. Lively, readable commentary, experiences of wine, or just personal reflections on wine in general, are much rarer, even—perhaps I should say especially— in France. Pierre-Marie Doutrelant's *Les bons vins... et les autres* (*Good Wines... and the Rest*), published in Paris in 1976, is a sparkling exception.

Perhaps it is because the English didn't produce wine until quite recently, and so were never able to take it for granted, that they have been more willing than others to share their experiences and opinions of it between hard covers. Needless to say, their stance has always been essentially consumerist. Neither Andrew Boorde (*The Breviarie of Health*, 1547) nor William Turner (*A Book of Wines*, 1568), physician-authors of the first texts on wine in English, had much to say on the water-holding properties of soils or on the advantages of alternative pruning methods. Both approached the subject in terms of wine's contribution to good health—nourishing the brain and scouring the liver, that sort of thing—finding their justifications in the ancient wisdom of Galen, Aristotle, and Pliny.

Firsthand accounts of wine regions and winemaking, of differences in taste and style, and of the fluctuations of quality and price from one vintage to another began to appear in English toward the close of the eighteenth century. The letters and travel diaries of Thomas Jefferson, one of wine's earliest and most acute English-speaking observers, are richer sources of information about late-eighteenth-century Bordeaux, for example, than the journals and ledgers written by local vintners themselves. They took their craft and business for granted and saw no reason to describe, let alone record, much about them.

By the nineteenth century, however, such reports had blossomed into wine travelogues and consumer guides. Physician Alexander Henderson's *History of Ancient and Modern Wines,* published in London in 1824, was obviously inspired more by André Jullien's tersely instructive *Topographie de Tous les Vignobles Connus* (from which Henderson borrows freely), first published in Paris in 1816, than by the obscure accounts of intestinal hygiene presented by Boorde and Turner. Henderson had first intended to revise and reissue the *Observations* of his fellow physician Sir Edward Barry, published some fifty years before. But fortunately for us he abandoned that plan in favor of researching a book of his own, the earliest in English to use assumptions we share in discussing wines still familiar to us.

Henderson, a joy to read and a model for writers on any subject, provides insight as relevant today as it was 150 years ago. His book is distinguished especially for its accurate reporting and intelligent discussion. Among the book's many minor benefits, Henderson helps shed light on why published tasting notes are so boringly repetitive. "The English language," he says, "is particularly limited in this department: and when we have gone through about half a dozen phrases, we find that our stock is exhausted." His thesis that tastes and smells reside not in objects themselves but in the unreliably fluctuating senses by which they are perceived should be taken to heart by those inclined to accept the numerical rating of wines by critics as something other than fallibly human.

Henderson makes no mention of American wine. But then in 1824 there was hardly any to be found, even though John Adlum's book, *A Memoir on the Cultivation of the Vine in America, and the Best Mode of Making Wine,* had been published in Washington the year before. Apart from its importance in the history of wine on this continent, Adlum's book has significance as the first book written in English to instruct farmers in vineyard practices and in the art of winemaking. His approach to the subject was as unassuming as it was practical: "I would advise every person having a farm or garden, to plant some Vines, of the best he can procure in his own vicinity, and others, where hardy kinds may be had. A garden may produce enough for the table and some to make Wine. There ought to be one Vine planted for every pannel of fence he has round his garden."

As Americans took Adlum's advice, vineyards spread west to Missouri and north to New York's Finger Lakes, thereby encouraging a succession of books on growing grapes for wine. John Dufour's *American Vine-Dresser's Guide* appeared in Cincinnati in 1826; Alphonse Loubat's, similarly titled, in New York in 1827; and Alden Spooner's story of success with native American vines after repeated failures with European varieties was published in Brooklyn in 1846. More followed, the most important of which were Friedrich Muench's *School for American Grape Culture* (Saint Louis, 1865), George Husmann's *American Grape Growing and Wine Making* (New York, 1880), and Thomas Munson's *Foundations of American Grape Culture* (New York, 1909).

Munson, whose experimental vineyard of hybrids was located near Austin, Texas, made a valuable contribution to salvaging the vineyards of France from phylloxera through the grafting of European *vinifera* varieties onto the rootstocks of native American vines. It is today the standard mode of protection from phylloxera all over the world. In recognition of his work he was decorated with the Mérite Agricole by the French government.

Perhaps the best known of all nineteenth-century American wine books—and, despite its forbidding title, the one with most appeal for the layperson—was Agoston Haraszthy's *Grape Culture, Wines, and Wine-Making with Notes upon Agriculture and Horticulture.* Haraszthy's book, published in 1862 as a report to the Senate and Assembly of California on the state of viticulture in Europe, together with an account of current practices in California, contains vivid descriptions of all Haraszthy saw and experienced in 1861 during a European tour of investigation, on which he was accompanied by his son Arpad. Along with detailed information on vineyards and cellars, almond orchards, silkmaking, the drying of figs and prunes, and the production of sugar beets and other crops that he felt could be profitable in California, Haraszthy gives insight into subjects as diverse as the social conventions of matchmaking in a German spa and the most comfortable seats to procure when traveling in a Spanish public conveyance.

Haraszthy's flamboyant reporting was exceptional, however, among nineteenth-century American wine books. Most were severely technical, written to provide novice vintners with practical instruction. Little was published in the United States specifically to inform, let alone beguile, the consumer. That is largely because the role of wine in an expanded English-speaking world had shifted.

But even in England, the perception and use of wine had changed in the centuries between Boorde and Henderson. Though still recommended for its nutritional value, wine in England was unabashedly accepted by an enriched gentry as one of life's pleasures: Its geography, its history, even its chemistry were subjects for agreeable intellectual curiosity. Henderson's book had been followed, in 1833, by the first edition of British journalist Cyrus Redding's *History and Description of Modern Wines,* the most detailed viticultural world tour that had until then been published. From France and Spain, Redding's account led eventually to Greece, Persia, and India—where he found Australian wines "made so successfully as to sell in the market at Calcutta for thirty-two shillings per dozen." Though with no opportunity to have tasted them, Redding mentions favorably wines produced in Pennsylvania, as well as in Ohio and Indiana, where "the crop in 1811," he says approvingly, "was as much as twenty-seven hundred gallons."

Of a piece with the prevailing interest in antiquity, eighteenth- and early-nineteenth-century authors in England, like Barry, Henderson, and Redding, drew on the works of Columella, Hippocrates, and Athenaeus to discuss wine. They assumed in their readers a more than passing acquaintance with the classical world (Henderson's text is strewn with footnotes in Latin and Greek), which implied a fairly restricted market for wine—and for wine books.

That was indeed the case. Almost two centuries of using wine duties as a means of waging economic warfare with the French had made a luxury of table wine in England, leaving those of modest means to wallow on gin lane. But in the early 1860s, William Ewart Gladstone, the new Chancellor of the Exchequer, made sharp, successive cuts in wine duties while extending wine licenses to village grocery stores. Moved to help change social behavior by easing table wine onto the family dinner table at the expense of spirits taken in the freer atmosphere of the tavern, Gladstone helped create a vast new market for wine among those who would not have known Athenaeus from Charley's Aunt. Imports of French wine into England more than tripled from 1859 to 1861.

In this booming but inexperienced new market there was both a need and an opportunity for books on wine. Charles Tovey, with his *Wine and Wine Countries: A Record and Manual for Wine Merchants and Wine Consumers,* published in 1862, sought to use his own experience as a wine merchant to educate both the new consumer and the untutored grocer who served him. To set the High Victorian tone of admonition then conventionally used for instruction, Tovey, in the preface to his book, quotes a member of the Board of Trade who spoke before a select committee hearing of the House of Commons in 1852: "The wine trade itself is much altered from the respectable character it used to bear; persons of inferior moral temperament have entered into it, and tricks are played, which in former times would not have been countenanced." (Tovey conveniently ignored contradictory court records that showed the wine trade to have had its share of "persons of inferior moral temperament" at least as far back as the thirteenth century.)

A reader looked in vain to *Wine and Wine Countries* for elegant phrasing and classical references. He found instead the excessive drinking of the doubtless jolly but uncouth Saxons pointedly compared with the more moderate and refined habits of their Norman conquerors—seen by the English upper classes as their own forebears. Where Henderson was careful and showed respect for his reader ("The description of the mode of conducting the fermentation of the grapes in Burgundy is partly copied from notes made on the spot, in the autumn of 1822: but as I unfortunately did not arrive there in time to witness the vintage, my information is less satisfactory than I could wish, and possibly, in some respects, erroneous"), Tovey is authoritarian and patronizing ("As it is next to impossible for a stranger to judge with precision and accuracy of the promising qualities of Bordeaux Wine in wood, or even in bottle, when young . . . and as deception is always easily practised, we should advise the trade to apply only and exclusively to firms known in the country as being of *high respectability* . . . .").

He puts in a depressing plug for Champagne ("We know of remarkable instances of persons who having been prostrated by illness to almost the last extremity, were resuscitated by taking Champagne"), repeats with relish every tale ever circulated to the detriment of Port, and dispatches American wine with brief ambiguity: "Before proceeding to notice the wines of our own colonies, we will just mention that North America is cultivating the vine to a considerable extent; and that, in the United States, the native wines, especially the sparkling kinds, are fast supplanting the foreign. . . . They are even said to exceed in purity and delicacy any other known wine, whilst it is their peculiar property that no spurious compound can be made to resemble them."

It is a relief to turn to Robert Druitt, in his time a well-known London physician, whose *Report on Cheap Wines . . . Their Use in Diet and Medicine*, first published in book form in 1865, is both encouraging and entertaining. It was based on articles Druitt had been prompted to write for the *Medical Times and Gazette* in 1863 and 1864, because, as he says in his introduction to a later edition, "rivers of strange wines were coming in from all parts of the world [thanks to Gladstone's reduction of the wine duty], and both the medical profession and the public wanted to know what they were good for."

Druitt's tone is cheerfully good-natured, even when he exhorts his fellow physicians to prescribe wine as a tonic for their patients instead of the "filthy mixtures" prepared in hospital dispensaries. "We must take people as we find them," he says, reasonably enough. "Man, as a social animal, requires something which he can sip as he sits and talks, and which pleases his palate whilst it gives some aliment to the stomach, and stimulates the flow of genial thoughts in the brain."

Elsewhere, in a passage that should be printed as a government warning on every page of every edition of every newsletter that picks apart wines, he says: "Wine should have an absolute *unity*, it should taste as one whole." It is only in bad wine, he went on, that "here a something sweet meets one part of our gustatory organs, there something sour, there something fruity, or bitter, or hot, or harsh, just as if half-a-dozen ill-blended liquids came out of one bottle, with perhaps a perfume atop . . . ."

His asides are as delightful as they are pungent. For instance, in describing the effect on wine of even a trace of some substances, he points out how small a quantity of garlic will give "a rich, full, savory fragrance to a leg of mutton" and then adds gratuitously: "The same in excess would be pronounced detestable by any one who had not got over his Anglican prejudices."

And, though fervent in the cause of table wine, he was ready to throw in all but the kitchen sink to condemn Port, then probably the most popular fortified wine in England: "The reign of Port coincides with the growth of the national debt, the isolation of the English from continental society, the decay of architecture. . . . "

Though with more humor than Tovey, Druitt could hector his readers when necessary. Apart from castigating them for drinking Port, he complains rather sternly that they are apt to keep their Burgundies and red Bordeaux beyond the time when they have arrived at their prime. He therefore recommends a cellar weeding from time to time and suggests that the surplus bottles be sent to "widows of limited income, girls at cheap boarding-schools." He presses his fellow physicians to encourage their patients to drink red Bordeaux. "You will add ten years to your patient's life and to your own fees."

Just as Gladstone's tinkering with duties and licensing had expanded the market for table wine (and for wine primers), so pressure from London importers on their suppliers in France to ship dry rather than sweet *cuvées* doubled the annual shipments of Champagne between 1860 and 1865. Champagne had been a sweet, sparkling dessert wine, therefore competing, in England, with Port and sweet Sherry. Several houses, including Veuve Clicquot, had shipped dry versions of the 1857 vintage in 1860. By the late 1870s almost all the producers were shipping dry *cuvées* to London, and the heyday of Champagne had begun.

Henry Vizetelly, engraver, writer, and publisher (he was sued for obscenity for publishing translations of Emile Zola's work in London), had launched his *Wines of the World* in 1875 and followed it with the first specialized consumer book on wine: *Facts about Sherry.* The success of the Sherry book must have helped him see the potential for just such another specialized book, one more extravagantly produced, dedicated to the prestige of Champagne. He first published the abundantly engraved *Facts about Champagne and other Sparkling Wines* in 1879, but by 1882 he had revised and expanded it into his *History of Champagne,* still one of the most remarkable, most beautifully produced, and most sought-after wine books in English.

Inevitably, after such bravura, other new wine books seemed anticlimactic for a while. But at the same time that a stream of technical books in English was being published for the growing number of wineries in Australia and South Africa, let alone the United States, Silas Mitchell, a Philadelphia physician (it is to be noted how many lay writers on wine have been medical men), produced his classic *Madeira Party* in 1895. The book is a fictional re-creation of the conversation of a group of men at a Madeira-tasting party, supposedly taking place in

Philadelphia in the earlier part of the century. Of social historical value, apart from its interest for those researching the use of Madeira wine in the early 1800s, the book contains rather self-conscious and high-minded exchanges (somewhere in it one of the group observes: "I have noticed that the acquisition of a taste for Madeira in middle life is quite fatal to common people") that nevertheless suggest that wine pretentiousness has never been an exclusively English vice.

In the first years of the new century, before World War I, the then very young André Simon, later to found the International Wine and Food Society, produced both his *History of the Champagne Trade in England* and his *History of the Wine Trade in England,* thereby beginning a flow of books on wine (and on food) that continued until his death in 1970 at the age of ninety-three.

Usually both instructive and diverting, Simon's published work ranges from slim reprints of his straightforward lectures to students of the London Wine Trade Club (which he also helped found) to learned papers as diverse as descriptions of the dinners of the powerful six-teenth-century Star Chamber, based on an investigation of its wine and food accounts, and an analysis and discussion of the private cellar book of J. Pierpont Morgan; and from books of erudite gastronomic connoisseurship to pamphlets encouraging higher standards of everyday eating and drinking. Simon's personal charm comes through in all his books, but in nowhere more than in the brief comments he attaches to each of the menus and lists of wines served at lunches and dinners with friends, compiled and published in 1933 as *Tables of Content.*

One of the most successful of Simon's works, in terms of the number of repeat editions, has been *Vintagewise,* a book first published in 1945 as an informative postscript to George Saintsbury's *Notes on a Cellar Book.*

It is ironic that Saintsbury's entire, voluminous, and distinguished body of work, published both before and during his tenure as professor of rhetoric and English literature at the University of Edinburgh (it includes important histories of French and English literature, as well as innumerable articles for the *Encyclopaedia Britannica*) is overshadowed by one small, anecdotal volume written in his retirement. Though no more than a collection of thoughts provoked by a review of the cellar book he had kept for most of his life, *Notes on a Cellar Book* is nevertheless the work for which he is remembered and is probably the book in which he stands most revealed. In table talk of the greatest urbanity, it fuses, in fact and commentary, opinion and reminiscence, Saintsbury's twin loves of wine and literature.

Perhaps, in those frenzied years of the twenties, nostalgia for the prewar pace and the amenities Saintsbury had taken for granted gave the book added attraction. In any case, it was an enormous success, ran to three editions within a year, and has been repeatedly reprinted in new editions ever since.

~ ~ ~

Along with André Simon's works, *Notes on a Cellar Book* set a high standard. Whether by way of inspiration or challenge, both men have encouraged more than one generation of writers on wine. Outstanding among them are Morton Shand, dazzlingly well informed and entertainingly opinionated; Cyril Ray, who, apart from the books he himself wrote, was responsible for compiling the twelve annually issued volumes of *The Compleat Imbiber,* each an enticing anthology of stories, essays, and poems on wine (and sometimes food), now hard to find and dear to collectors everywhere; Edmund Penning-Rowsell, whose regular revisions of his *Wines of Bordeaux* are accepted as the first and last word on the subject; William Younger, whose extraordinary review of wine history in *Gods, Men, and Wine* has been, until now, an unequaled accomplishment; Hugh Johnson, André Simon's successor as editor of the Wine and Food Society's journal, whose work has changed the way we think about wine books, let alone wine, and whose latest offering, *Vintage: The Story of Wine,* makes him a fit contender for Younger's crown; and Jancis Robinson, whose *Vines, Grapes and Wines,* one of the best and most original wine books of the last decade, has appealed alike to professional and amateur, grower and consumer, because of its seductive combination of unobtrusive scholarship and literary grace.

Happily, on this side of the Atlantic, too, the useful thicket of technical books and encyclopedias for which we have long provided fertile ground is now blossoming with reflective commentary, the sharing of experience and opinion, and the kind of anecdotal ornament that both enhances and is enhanced by the pleasures of a glass of wine.

A few that spring to mind are *Notes on a California Cellarbook: Reflections on Memorable Wines,* by Bob Thompson, a not-unworthy borrower of Saintsbury's plumage; *Thinking About Wine,* by Elin McCoy and John Frederick Walker, a wide-ranging collection of essays and stories; and *Making Sense of Wine,* a book in which the Oregonian Matt Kramer, musing under chapter headings taken from Bossuet and T. E. Lawrence, at first suggests expectations of his readers as daunting as those implicit in Alexander Henderson's quotations from Martial and scattered allusions to Timarchides of Rhodes and Philoxenus of Cythera. But suddenly, apropos of the drinking of great Sauternes and *Beerenauslese* Rhine wines, Kramer makes the brilliant play of offering a recipe for bread pudding. The reader, from then on, is eating out of his hand.

Originally published as "Between Hard Covers: Wine Books in English" in *Gourmet,* April 1990.

Although Adlum's book on viticulture was the first published in English for the encouragement of commercial grape growing, it was in fact preceded by William Speechly's *Treatise on the Culture of the Vine,* published in England in 1790.

Also, a propos of the reference to the "journals and ledgers" of Bordeaux vintners at the time of Thomas Jefferson, an exception should be made for the extensive archives of Château Latour. They provided much of the material for *La Seigneurie et le Vignoble de Château Latour* published in 1974 in two volumes by the *Fédération Historique du Sud-Ouest.*

SIMPLE PLEASURES

Warm Bread and Hot Chocolate

It was a Saturday in June. The sun was flooding into the apartment. A mass of flowering privet that had caught my eye on one of the stands in the market that morning was making the living room smell green and woodsy.

I had a lazy-day feeling, but I made a pot of *ratatouille* anyway and ate some at midday with quartered eggs that had been simmered in the shell just to the point where they were no longer soft but were not quite hard, either. I ate alone in the dining room, looking through the open window into the studio of the painter across the street. The air was warm and still, and I could faintly hear the rumble of traffic on the Boulevard Clichy.

I was drinking a 1995 red Burgundy—a Mercurey—and the second glass, even better than the first, was just right with a slice of Charollais, a soft goat's milk cheese from the hills above the Mâconnais. I hadn't tried it before. I picked out a few small ripe apricots—they were sweet and had an intense flavor. It was a simple lunch, but I took my time and there were roses on the table so it seemed quite luxurious. I made some coffee, helped myself to a square of chocolate, and, back in the living room, put on a CD of Carlos Gardel singing tangos he'd composed and recorded in the 1930s.

I like simple food. Keep it simple—*faites simple*—was the constant admonition of Auguste Escoffier, the great French chef who transformed nineteenth-century cooking into twentieth-century food. Escoffier was exhorting us, the late British food writer Elizabeth David suggests in the introduction to her book *French Provincial Cooking,* to avoid "unnecessary complication and elaboration." But *faites simple,* as the novelist Sybille Bedford once remarked, "doesn't mean *faites* slapdash."

It doesn't mean ascetic austerity either, for that matter. The notion of simplicity applies just as well to the uncluttered but cosseted lunch of caviar, *blini,* and bottle of Bollinger that I share from time to time with a son and daughter-in-law in a tiny *salon,* hung in green damask, above Kaspia on the Place de la Madeleine, as it does to the *pan y tomate* with which every meal began at a small hotel in Catalonia I once stayed in for several days.

As soon as I sat down at the table, at lunch as at dinner, I would be served a carafe of robust red wine, some warm grilled bread, a peeled clove of garlic, half a ripe tomato, salt, and a flacon of olive oil. I'd rub the grilled bread with the garlic and then, quite hard, with the cut tomato. I'd drizzle it with oil, sprinkle it with salt, and then munch on it with a glass of wine while deciding what to order. Spanish white bread is bland, but the grill gave it flavor and the applied regimen of garlic, tomato, oil, and salt transformed it into such a savory treat that sometimes, especially at lunch, I half thought of calling for another carafe of wine and more grilled bread and waving the menu away altogether.

The longstanding affinity between bread and wine, with or without tomato and garlic, needs no emphasis. I remember arriving one evening some years ago at an informal dinner hosted by one of Oregon's pioneer vintners to find him offering bread to his guests along with a welcoming glass of wine. It was unself-conscious—he happened to be slicing bread at the time—but perhaps more instinctive than he knew.

The gesture of offering bread and wine is an ancient and hallowed prelude to hospitality, one we've transmuted into a glass of Champagne and a canapé. A friend who has a reputation as a cook, and an enviable cellar, gets the most pleasure from his best bottles (he mumbled something recently about a Château Margaux '61) when he opens them for friends to enjoy with nothing to distract them. Just good plain bread.

Bread, one of the simplest as well as one of the most satisfying of pleasures, can't be taken for granted, however. Even Paris has for some time been in the throes of a quiet revolution over the quality of its bread. Most blame the deterioration of the standard baguette on flour from new high-yielding, over-fertilized strains of wheat. Many Paris bakers now offer, for a small premium, bread made from flour milled from the old-fashioned kind of wheat. "Bread as it was in the thirties," claims the baker at the corner of my street (in a recent survey his baguette was justifiably ranked among the city's best).

In an attempt to meet the demand for better bread, yet another *boulangerie artisanale* with a wood-fired, stone-built oven opens in the neighborhood every few months, and in no time at all there are lines as people stop to buy a loaf on their way home from work. Recently I noticed one baker announcing that bread warm from the oven is available at his shop every evening at five, a subtle reminder that it is freshly baked, on the premises, not only for breakfast and again for lunch but also for dinner. "What is that supposed to mean?" my neighbor said with a sniff when I pointed the sign out to her. "Every Paris baker offers oven-warm bread at five o'clock. They always have."

But that baker is shrewd: He knows that even the *promise* of warm, freshly baked bread goes straight to the heart. Writing of the harvest in Sicily in her book *On Persephone's Island,* Mary Taylor Simeti describes her husband wrapping his sweater around a loaf just out of the oven while they race home to dip the warm bread in their newly pressed olive oil and enjoy it with a glass of their own, barely fermented, red wine.

~ ~ ~

In my previous life as a wine merchant, one of the occasional rewards of the annual dash along leafless French roads in bleak January weather to get first pick of the latest vintage was to find a young wine already in bloom—a Beaujolais-Villages, perhaps, or an aromatic young Chinon— and taste it with a crust of warm bread. A white Sancerre I used to select in good years had an irresistible aroma of white peaches when taken straight from the vat. The grower I bought it from in Verdigny would join me, once the deal had been struck, in drinking a glass from whichever lot I'd chosen. As if on cue, his wife would appear with bread hot from the oven and a tray of *crottins,* the local Chavignol goat cheeses—nutty, firm, and fresh.

Simple pleasures make us content, and that's when happiness creeps up on us. An occasional evening in a gastronomic temple is something I look forward to and remember long afterward, but my day can be made just as easily by a lunch of beer and a baguette sandwich (*rosette* sausage with Beaufort cheese is my favorite) with a friend at a neighborhood café near the Buci market, by coming to terms with a well-stuffed burrito at *the* Taqueria on Mission at 25th Street in San Francisco (please note: not just *any* taqueria); or by eating pizza almost anywhere with my grandchildren.

Along my road to personal contentment are the dense ham from the village of Jabugo in the remote wooded hills of northern Andalusia, where native Ibérico pigs forage for their diet of acorns and truffles; a glass of aged Tawny Port and a dried Smyrna fig after dinner; See's chocolate-covered ginger—one of the least-publicized treasures of California; and the thick white asparagus that dominate restaurant menus in Germany from early May until late June. In the evening I am comforted by Jerusalem-artichoke soup spiked with a dollop of Fino Sherry, and on gray winter mornings in San Francisco by a mug of rich hot chocolate and a brioche from the Noe Valley Bakery. (I discovered in Italy, long ago, that a little cornstarch thickens drinking chocolate so voluptuously that with every sip I get a better grip on how the world must have looked to a seventeenth-century cardinal, propped up in his Roman bed under a scarlet silk baldachin.)

Satisfactions less precise than these are the subject of *La Première Gorgée de Bière—et Autres Plaisirs Minuscules (The First Mouthful of Beer—and Other Insignificant Pleasures),* the slim collection of reminiscences published in Paris a year or so ago by the writer Philippe Delerm. It sold in huge numbers despite having been condemned by the French literary critics, who could smell a popular success—horrors!—from the title alone. Delerm articulates pleasures we hardly ever acknowledge: driving alone on a clear night on a deserted freeway with a favorite music program on the radio; the invitation to stay for potluck lunch that suddenly signals tacit acceptance into another family; pulling on a favorite sweater and realizing, with a sense of anticipation, that the season has changed; having the luxury of time to read the morning paper at breakfast, the world's woes kept at bay by the coffee cups and marmalade jar.

Mildly surprising, however, even to me (a man who sometimes has difficulty remembering what game it is the 49ers actually play), Delerm includes no discussion, either as participant or observer, of sporting activity among his accounts of minor pleasures. Other than obscure references to bicycles, the only physical exertion he describes is walking home with the family breakfast on a cold morning and eating one of the warm croissants straight from the brown paper bag. Has he never sat in a boat, I wonder? Or skied on new snow?

I learned to ski in the Vorarlberg, the western tip of Austria, so long ago that our varnished wooden skis were fixed to laced leather boots— an inner boot and an outer boot, in fact—with straps as well as "safety" bindings. We were taught to keep our knees tightly together as we moved, something virtually impossible today with those man-on-the-moon ski boots. "*Zusammen! Zusammen!*" Herr Schilli, our instructor, would yell if we cheated with just a little snowplow to slow our progress as we made our way gingerly down the mountain. For me, skiing was a pleasure like no other.

I began skiing again when I moved to San Francisco and could drive up to Lake Tahoe. I discovered, though, that the point of skiing in California, back in the early seventies at any rate, was to get up the mountain and down again as many times as possible in the day. So there were always lines for the ski lift. There were lines, too, for the rather wretched, cafeteria-style food. In Europe, skiing had been a social activity. There was usually a modest restaurant with stews and soups at the top of the lift and often a cabin or two somewhere on the mountain where one could stop for coffee and cake or a glass of mulled wine and hot sausages. Everyone liked to ski fast, but no one was in a hurry. In Austria, in the postwar years, the food was simple—mostly veal, veal, and mystery veal—but it was good, and we would linger over our meal. There was no choice in any case: Everything stopped for lunch. And in the late afternoon, as we drifted in from the slopes, the bars had music and we would clump about on the dance floor in our leather boots before changing for dinner.

Having once again slipped on ski pants and parka, I soon moved on from Tahoe to Taos Ski Valley in New Mexico—difficult skiing, but delicious, homey French food from chef Claude Gohard at the Hotel St. Bernard (where he has been cooking for nearly thirty years). And then to Deer Valley, Utah, which opened with impeccably manicured ski slopes, no lift lines, and food orchestrated by Bill Nassikas, son of Jim Nassikas, at the time still president of the Stanford Court Hotel in San Francisco.

But my most vivid memory of skiing has nothing to do with food or wine. It's of a day spent on a remote slope in the Sawtooth Range of Idaho, north of Sun Valley. Three of us (I was in the company of a *Gourmet* photographer and a guide) were set down by helicopter on the flat spur of an isolated ridge. Once the engines were out of hearing range we stood there in absolute silence with nothing around us but snow-covered mountaintops. The photographer did his work, and then we all set off for our distant rendezvous, gliding quickly over the fresh snow with hardly a sound except for the occasional light swish from a tight turn. I noticed among the trees the bright eyes of small animals watching us go by.

~ ~ ~

My clearest recollections of food and wine usually involve the surprising or the unexpected: drinking new—still fizzy—Brunello with hot roasted chestnuts on a damp November day in Montalcino; the burst of flavor in a glass of Joseph Phelps Napa Valley Délice du Sémillon dessert wine; and the texture of tender young fava beans eaten raw, straight from the pod, with an apéritif of cool white Tuscan wine. A surprisingly fine *blanquette de veau* served with a well-aged Vouvray at an otherwise ordinary roadside restaurant outside Tours has become the standard by which I judge all others. A delicious salad of chickpeas in a village café on the way to Draguignan, and an exquisite dish of *cèpes,* just in season, that I had with a carafe of red Côtes de Bourg at what was little more than a bar off the *place* in Bourg itself have also taught me that good food needs no *Michelin* star.

A sauté of rabbit eaten in the mountains of Crete on a day when the sun had finally emerged after a week of depressingly continuous rain was particularly unforgettable. The restaurant was really not much more than a ramshackle kitchen; its yard was populated by a troop of cats and filled with flowers growing in old, massed, multicolored cans. It held half a dozen tables, and we chose one in the shade of an arbor.

I was traveling with a friend from Athens, and we knew it would be a while before the meal would be ready. "You should have let me know you were coming," the elderly proprietor had said, with a clear implication that her preparation would now have to start from ground zero with a visit to the hutches.

We ate bread and hummus and black olives and poured a sweetish, amber-pink wine for ourselves from a plastic jug. She had filled it by dipping it directly into a large terra-cotta pot. We talked and time passed. Eventually, a salad of cucumber, tomato, onion, and feta appeared, and I knew we were getting close.

And so did the cats. Long and thin, and with small, sleek heads, they quickly gathered around us in a circle, sitting upright on their haunches. They made me uneasy: Many of them had white in their eyes, which gave them a strange stare. When the woman came with more wine I asked about them. "Many of the cats on Crete are albino," she replied, adding patiently, as if explaining the riddle of the sphinx, "They came from Egypt long ago."

There could hardly have been time for her to marinate the rabbit, but it was deliciously tender, and aromatic with garlic, lemon, and the generous quantity of herbs she must have used. The "sauce," I guessed, was just a reduction of wine with the juices in the pan. We sopped it up with more of the bread. She brought us melon, and offered us coffee. We sat there, quietly content. Through a gap in the clutter around us we could see the slope of the mountain falling away toward the shore where that morning we'd visited an all-but-deserted monastery, at one time a way station for escaping British servicemen after Crete had fallen to the Germans in World War II.

Perhaps it was the warmth of the sun after a week's deprivation, or the effect of the wine and our modest but perfect lunch, or just the spirit of the place—of Crete itself—that brought to mind a particular scene in Nikos Kazantzakis's novel *Zorba the Greek*. Zorba and the narrator are sitting on a beach late at night—drinking wine, talking, and warming themselves by a brazier on which they're roasting chestnuts. The narrator is marveling at how uncomplicated happiness really is. A glass of wine, he thinks to himself, the warmth of the coals, the sound of the sea. That's all. But enough to make a man happy, if his heart is simple enough to recognize what he has.

Originally published as "Serendipity: Warm Bread and Hot Chocolate" in *Gourmet*, February 1999.

INDEX

abbey viticulture and winemaking, 5–
 6, 17–18, 66, 101–102
acidity, 60–61, 114
Adams, Leon, 149–150
Adlum, John, 232, 243–244, 252
age and aging, 200; Armagnac, 61;
 Cabernet Sauvignon, 129, 130, 133;
 Champagne, 17; food with old
 wines, 182, 254; Franconian wines,
 119–120; sea-journey aging, 225. *See
 also* barrels and barrel aging
Alba, 90–91, 92
Albania, 130
alcohol levels: California Cabernets,
 134–135; Zinfandel, 167
Alexander Valley, 134, 166; Robert
 Young Vineyards, 196–197
Alfonso II of Aragón, 101
Alix, 53
Almaden, 189
Alsace, 28
Alvarez, Salus, 102–103
Amador Zinfandels, 166, 167
Ambonnay, 20
Ambrosi, Hans, 111

*American Grape Growing and Wine
 Making* (Husmann), 231, 244
American grape varieties: Catawba,
 232–233, 234–235, 237–238, 239; Con-
 cord, 229, 230, 239; Cynthiana, 236,
 241; Isabella, 234; Norton, 229–
 230, 234–236, 241. *See also* French-
 American hybrids
American oak: at Beaulieu, 154–155, 156;
 California Cabernets and, 129, 130,
 139, 150, 151, 155
American rootstocks, 8–9, 231, 244
American Vine-Dresser's Guide (Dufour),
 244
American Viticultural Areas, 166. See
 also *specific AVAs*
American Wine (Quimme), 138
American wines and viticulture: early
 manuals and guides, 231, 243–245,
 247; nineteenth-century midwest,
 231–233. *See also* California wines
 and viticulture; Missouri wines
 and viticulture
American Wines (Schoonmaker), 128, 165
Amerine, Maynard, 135

261

Text	10.75 Janson
Display	Janson
Compositor	BookMatters, Berkeley
Indexer	Thérèse Shere
Cartographer	Lohnes + Wright
Printer and binder	Thomson-Shore, Inc.